Praise for William F. Buckley Jr.'s

NEARER, MY GOD

"Read it and wince, read it and weep, read it and smile, but read it."
—*National Catholic Reporter*

"Breathtakingly powerful . . . A rollicking adventure story of the spirit, an elaborate trek around and about the lofty peaks of belief and conviction . . . Buckley's book is wonderfully exciting—whether you are a believer or a skeptic."
—*The Baltimore Sun*

"A splendid story about a modern pilgrim's progress . . . erudite, engaging, poignant, and inspiring."
—William J. Bennett, author of *The Book of Virtues*

"It is one of his best, and Buckley at his best is as good as you are likely to find. Rich in anecdote, witty, and animated by what Buckley refers to as his 'polemical inclinations' . . . Buckley's faith [is] at once complex and many-sided and as simple and trusting as a child."
—*Christianity Today*

"A book that celebrates and propounds Buckley's Christian faith and the Roman Catholic Church to which he has belonged all his life . . . It is certain to provide many insights into the mind of a polished writer, passionate logophile, and dean of controversy, and it will do much to explain how the hopefully changeless faith of a Catholic jibes with the politics of a late 20th century American political conservative."
—*The New York Times Book Review*

"This is the most respectful and serious treatment of the sweep of Catholic theology coming from a lay person—and published by a mainstream house—that I have seen in many years."

—Fr. Robert Sirico, *The Detroit News*

"Who would have thought that debating Christian dogma could be, well, so much fun? Makes difficult theological concepts accessible and relevant . . . Buckley shows us what it's like to struggle to find faith and to keep it."

—*The Atlanta Journal-Constitution*

"The story of the abiding, sustaining faith of a true believer . . . As always, his thoughts are invigorating. His doctrinal investigations reveal a religious temperament that is respectfully questioning but not doubtful. In this Mr. Buckley, despite his formidable intellect, is probably not so different from the average American churchgoer."

—*The Wall Street Journal*

"Refreshing, original, and illuminating. I suspect many people, both cradle Catholics and converts, and indeed those with other faiths or none at all, will find reading this sincere and straightforward book a fruitful experience."

—Paul Johnson, *The American Spectator*

"Informative and entertaining . . . This is a book by a man who eschews the merely trendy and speaks his own mind."

—*Publishers Weekly*

NEARER, MY GOD

ALSO BY WILLIAM F. BUCKLEY JR.

God and Man at Yale

McCarthy and His Enemies (WITH L. BRENT BOZELL)

Up From Liberalism

Rumbles Left and Right

The Unmaking of a Mayor

The Jeweler's Eye

The Governor Listeth

Cruising Speed

Inveighing We Will Go

Four Reforms

United Nations Journal: A Delegate's Odyssey

Execution Eve

Saving the Queen

Airborne

Stained Glass

A Hymnal: The Controversial Arts

Who's On First

Marco Polo, If You Can

Atlantic High: A Celebration

Overdrive: A Personal Documentary

The Story of Henri Tod

See You Later Alligator

Right Reason

The Temptation of Wilfred Malachey

High Jinx

Mongoose, R.I.P.

Racing Through Paradise

*On the Firing Line:
The Public Life of Our Public Figures*

*Gratitude: Reflections on What We Owe
to Our Country*

Tucker's Last Stand

In Search of Anti-Semitism

WindFall

*Happy Days Were Here Again:
Reflections of a Libertarian Journalist*

A Very Private Plot

Brothers No More

The Blackford Oakes Reader

The Right Word

NEARER, MY GOD

An Autobiography
of Faith

―――――――

WILLIAM F. BUCKLEY JR.

A HARVEST BOOK
HARCOURT BRACE & COMPANY
San Diego   New York   London

First published by Doubleday in 1997

Library of Congress Cataloging-in-Publication Data
Buckley, William F. (William Frank), 1925–
Nearer, my God: an autobiography of faith / William F. Buckley, Jr.
p. cm.
Originally published: New York: Doubleday, 1997.
Includes index.
ISBN 0-15-600618-9
1. Buckley, William F. (William Frank), 1925– .
2. Buckley, William F. (William Frank), 1925– .—Religion.
3. Journalists—United States—Biography. I. Title.
PN4874.B796B83   1998
282'.092—dc21   98-16194
[B]

Printed in the United States of America
First Harvest edition 1998
E

In memory of
Aloïse Steiner Buckley
1895–1985

ACKNOWLEDGMENTS

Nearer, My God

In the text, I acknowledge persons to whom I am indebted for material I have used, some of it previously published, some of it written privately, some in letters to me. I acknowledge also the one-page cartoon from *Punch* magazine, with thanks.

Fr. Kevin Fitzpatrick, to whom I owe so very much, was with me at every point during the five years since I began this book. He gave me guidance and help. Fr. Fitzpatrick is a doctor of moral theology (Pontifical Lateran University, 1996). He is, at this writing, a parish priest in Stamford, Connecticut. If anywhere in this volume heterodoxy lurks, the fault is in my transcriptions, not in his learning, or recommendations.

Faithful readers will expect my customary prostration at the feet of Samuel S. Vaughan. But the pains he went to, and the devotion he paid to this enterprise, require me to acknowledge, yet again, with ever-lasting gratitude, his contributions.

Several friends read the manuscript. Lance Morrow, as the narrative will reveal, permitted me to quote from an essay he had written for *Time* magazine and from a correspondence that ensued. I opportunized on his interest by sending him the manuscript. I was astonished by the generosity of his response, a twenty-page letter of suggestions and commentary. I am deeply indebted to one of America's finest writers.

I am indebted, also, for careful readings by (Professor) Chester Wolford of the State University of Pennsylvania, and (Fr.) Richard John Neuhaus of *First Things*. My brother (Judge) James, and sisters Patricia Bozell, Jane Smith, and Priscilla Buckley read it, as also my wife Pat, with great profit to me.

Doubleday's Eric Major came a little late to the project, succeeding as he did Tom Cahill as Director of Religious Books for Doubleday. My thanks to him for his fine and useful work.

And my thanks to Dorothy McCartney and John Virtes of *National Review* for great help with research, and to Joseph Marcello for his enterprising work on religion in private schools.

I am as always grateful, yet again, to Joseph Isola for copyediting, as also to Bill Betts.

As ever, Frances Bronson of *National Review* was indispensable; with thanks also to Tony Savage for his work on the computer, and for his counsel.

Wm. F. Buckley Jr.
Stamford, Connecticut
April 1997

CONTENTS

INTRODUCTION

It was over ten years ago that I was asked to write a book whose title would be "Why I Am Still a Catholic." I demurred, using as an excuse that I had books charted for two book-writing seasons ahead. But after a month or so, I thought to accept the commission, provided I could put off work on the book until 1992.

When I sat down in Switzerland (which is where I write my books) to begin the project, one thing occurred to me quickly, something else later. The first was that the proposed title had in it an unnecessary word; moreover, a word that implied something I would not have been honest in implying, namely that to continue as a Catholic is in some way remarkable, as in "Why I Am Still a Whig." That reservation didn't turn out to be important. The publisher was vaguely un-happy (he had conceived a series, Why I Am Still a Protestant, etc.), but he understood my problem, whereupon the working title became simply "Why I Am a Catholic." But the truncation of the title rein-forced the second reservation, which was that for me to write a book about my faith would be to put my faith at a fearful disadvantage.

I say this without any thought to promote a titter of appreciation—WFB acknowledges his Faith is Greater than his Powers to Describe It. Because, of course, "inadequate resources" are in some sense a dis-ability of everyone who has written about Christianity: no one can do "it" full justice. But it is also true that for two thousand years books about the faith have been written that can be said to have enhanced the faith for many readers, books that widen the eyesight of the reader, or quicken his heartbeat. There are, in fact, a great many of these, but one's mere knowledge of their existence—of those one has read and even of those one *hasn't* read—induces a painful assessment of one's own limitations.

Well, enough on that point. What then happened, and why did I proceed?

What happened was that in midsummer 1992 I came disconsolately to a decision to abandon the project I had begun in January, despairing over the reading and studying I wished to do and had no time to schedule. I returned to the publisher his advance payment, put aside the copious notes I had taken, filed away the only chapter I had actually written (it survives, slightly altered, as the opening chapter of this book), and then proceeded to feel lousy about my capitulation. The reason for this you can probably guess: I felt I owed something to God.

In my book *Gratitude* (which I wrote during the hiatus) I pleaded the case for a volunteer service by young men and women in their late teens and early twenties. In that book I recalled Anatole France's story of the juggler. It is the familiar tale of the monk who sought to express his devotion to Our Lady, having disconsolately witnessed, during his first week as a postulant, the prodigies of his fellow monks, among whom there were those who sang like nightingales, played their instruments as finished artists, rhapsodized with the tongues of poets. All that this poor novice had learned to do before entering the monastery was to entertain in the streets as a juggler. And so on the chosen day, in the dead of night, he makes his furtive, ardent way through the dark dormitory, across the cloister, into the chapel, and up to the altar, with his sackful of wooden mallets and balls. He does his act for Our Lady.

I have thought the force of this act unrivaled in devotional literature. The ostensible grotesquerie—repaying the mother of the Maker of the universe with muscular gyrations designed to engross the six-year-old; it is inexpressibly beautiful in the mind's eye. But of course the special magic of the juggler's ache to express his gratitude and devotion was in the privacy of the devotion. Anatole France's story would not have worked if the juggler had proposed doing his act in Madison Square Garden.

I am not, with this book, entering Madison Square Garden, but of course books *are* public acts (even some privately published books: Did ever a book beckon for more public attention than *The Education of Henry Adams?*). I solved my personal problem effectively enough to proceed by conjecturing that probably no believing Christian who reads this book is likely to lose his faith after reading it. The arguments I frame are imperfectly done, have been used and said time and again in other quarters, by other postulants; I have only to contribute this, that the mix here is my own, for better or worse.

That mix is a result of several things, none of them flattering. The first is that I am not remotely qualified as a theologian or historian of Christianity. A second is that my mode tends to be argumentative. For this I have to offer as an excuse only that when I entered the public arena, everybody (it seemed) was on the other side, and for that reason my polemical inclinations have always been reactive. The liberal public square was obliged to hear the occasional complaints of the dissenter, but we were hardly expected to *initiate* a colloquy. This argumentative habit makes for poor exposition, and readers of this book are entitled to put it down in disgust if exposition alone is what they are looking for. It gets worse: so habitual is it for me to learn and perform by contention, I have been derivatively influenced by *others'* contentions.

Consider, for instance, the chapter here on Arnold Lunn and Ronald Knox. I explain in the text what their book *Difficulties* was all about, and here it is only appropriate to say that I am spellbound by the kind of thing they engaged in and for that reason have given it the attention I hope the reader will join with me in thinking it deserves. These two learned gentlemen argued sixty years ago about theological points, sometimes reached joint conclusions, sometimes didn't, but always illuminated the questions they touched on, doing so better than I'd have done attempting first-person exposition.

And then, too, certain things catch my eye. The painful, detailed "vision" of the Crucifixion by Maria Valtorta (chapter 8) did that when I first read it—so that I proceed simply to pass it along to you, justified only by the conviction that some of you will react as I did.

I thought also, when in 1995 I set out again to write such a book, to rely quite openly on the thinking of a few people for whom I have a special respect. In selecting those who would make up what I refer to as my Forum I asked only that they should be inherently interesting men (Clare Boothe Luce, as will be noted, was too ill to participate) and that they should have come to Catholicism as adults. I wanted the sense of their metamorphosis, the booster phases that I, as a born Catholic, could not describe. I am immensely obliged to these learned coadjutors.

Finally I make note of what is noted in practically every treatment of the religious question and is nevertheless widely ignored. It is that the Christian faith is a quite timeless affair. Its decisive moment was the Incarnation of Christ, but our inevitable concern with the here and now is very difficult to shake off. It is consequently hard to take in the idea of an eternal commitment by a Creator who, yes, knows when every sparrow falls to the ground.

I tried to shed a little light on this point, only to recognize that, my own warnings notwithstanding, the desirable perspective is by no means constantly even in my *own* mind, so easy, and tempting, it is to digress. I did by design give over a chapter to the dominant contentions of a half century ago, and another to current contentions; the larger perspective never changes.

But isn't that also so with secular questions?

There is this difference. I remember participating in a forum, twenty-odd years ago, in which the principal guest was the representative of *The Economist* (the London weekly). He had been designated its "futurist." The original idea was that of Walter Bagehot, the magazine's founder. He thought to devote an entire issue every ten years to the primary concerns of the ensuing ten years. To prepare himself for that assignment (said our guest), he had gone over the futurist issues of the past hundred years and learned that there was only this constant: the predicted concerns of the next decade turned out in no case—not ever—to be the actual concerns of the ensuing decade.

So is it in theology, with different questions of public moment. Martin Luther was terribly exercised over the granting of indulgences. It would be distracting to go on, listing concerns heatedly divisive at one time, only to make the point that, fifty years later, they seem remote.

But the Church is unique in that it is governed by a vision that has not changed in two thousand years. It tells us, in just about as many words, that we are not accidental biological accretions, we are creatures of a divine plan; that the God who made us undertook to demonstrate his devotion to us as individual human beings by submitting to the pain and humiliation of the Cross. Nothing in that vision has ever changed, nothing at all, and this is for all Christians a mind-shaking, for some a mind-altering certitude, with which Christians live, in our earnest if pitiable efforts to clear the way for a love that cannot be requited.

I didn't want to call this book *Why I Am a Catholic* for reasons already given. As I put it to bed I realize, also, that its tone is not what I'd have hoped for. There is the temperamental problem: I am not trained in the devotional mode, nor disposed to it. Moreover, this book is without the gratifying narrative one finds in many others, a narrative that generates excitement in the reader who believes in the faith *(the writer has come to share our table!)* and even for the nonbeliever *(interesting, how the writer moved from disbelief to faith—I can enjoy a narrative even if I decline to take the same journey).* I was baptized a Catholic and reared as one by devoted parents whose emotional and intellectual energies never cloyed. My faith has not wavered, though I permit myself to wonder whether, if it had, I'd advertise it: Would I encourage my dinner companions to know that I was blind in my left eye? I wish I could here give to my readers a sense of my own personal struggle, but there is no sufficient story there to tell. I leave it at this, that if I could juggle, I'd do so for Our Lady. I suppose I am required to say that, in fact, I have here endeavored to do my act for her.

So I thought to call my book, reaching for a piety I truly feel, "Nearer My God to Thee." But I had, once again, a second thought, that that might be a little impudent, co-opting the title of so famous a hymn. So I call it, merely, *Nearer, My God.* That is an incomplete phrase, but then my thoughts are incomplete, and I pray that my faith will always be whole.

CHAPTER ONE

St. John's, Beaumont

It was during the summer of 1938 that we were given the dreadful news. I forget from whose hands it came. Probably from "Mademoiselle," our governess. She was the authority in residence at Great Elm, given that my mother, father, and three of my older siblings were traveling in Europe. That left six children to romp happily through one more summer in my father's large house in Sharon, the small village designated by the Garden Club of America two years before as the most beautiful town in Connecticut after Litchfield. The six of us left behind ranged in age from Jim (fifteen) to Maureen (five). We were superintended by Mademoiselle Jeanne Bouchex and by three Mexican nurses; fed and looked after by a cook, a butler, and two maids; trained and entertained in equestrian sport by a groom and an assistant, making use of Father's eight horses; instructed in piano by a twenty-three-year-old New Yorker who came and stayed with us three days of every week, giving us each a lesson every day on one of the five pianos in the house; and in the guitar or banjo or mandolin (we were allowed our pick) by a Spanish-born violinist who traveled once a week from Poughkeepsie.

It might have been Mademoiselle who told us what Father had decided, or it might have been "Miss Hembdt," Father's secretary. She lived in Yorktown Heights, New York, and regularly relayed to us bulletins from Father, transcriptions of letters he would mail her, mostly to do with his business affairs but now and then something directed to one or more of his absent children, supplementing what we would learn from letters received from Mother or from one of our siblings traveling with them. With these notes came our monthly allowances, a directive or so touching on this or that subject, references to a book Father had just read which we should know about, or read ourselves . . . That dreadful day in August the directive, however transmitted, was as horrifying an edict—my two afflicted sisters and I agreed—as had ever been sent to three healthy and happy children from their father. The directive was to the effect that the next school year we would pass in boarding schools near London, the girls at St. Mary's in Ascot, I at St. John's, Beaumont, in Old Windsor.

The news fractured the arcadian spirit of our summer. We had got used to quite another routine, where summer vacations evolved almost seamlessly into a return to school where academic life required no radical departures from our way of life and none at all from our surroundings, because we were taught by tutors right there in the same rooms in which we played when indoors during the summer. When school began for us at the end of September, we continued to ride on horseback every afternoon, we swam two or three times every day until the water got too cold, our musical tutors continued to come to us just as they had done during the summer, some of us would rise early and hunt pheasant at our farm before school; our classes began at 8:30, ended at noon, and there would be study hall and music appreciation between 4:00 and 6:00. Three or four neighborhood children joined our school, and though we sorely regretted the summer's end, the academic regimen was light, and at our age—Jane had turned fourteen that summer, Trish was eleven—the schooling we got was as tolerable as schoolwork could be. Now, suddenly, we were to go to boarding schools in England.

Why?

We fled to Aunt Priscilla. She lived with her maiden sister in a house nearby, returning home to Austin, Texas, in the fall. We went to her: *Why? Why? Why?* Aunt Priscilla was infinitely affectionate, sublimely humorous, but also absolutely self-disciplined. After hearing out our outrage, she agreed to write to Father in Europe to put our case before him: What really was the point in going to England to school? We had all already *been* to England to school . . . only five years ago—it was there that Trish and I had first learned English. Jane, Trish, and I had gone to Catholic day schools in London, the oldest four to boarding schools, the two girls to that same St. Mary's, Ascot, where now Jane and Trish would go.

They hadn't liked St. Mary's, hadn't liked it one bit. Aloïse, the oldest, was fourteen, possibly the most spirited girl the dear nuns at St. Mary's had ever come across, with her singular, provocative independence. They had got on at Ascot because by nature Aloïse and Priscilla were irrepressible; but they had never pretended to "like" their school. John (thirteen) and Jim (ten) had gone to the Oratory Preparatory School in Reading. John had kept a diary at the school and was manifestly amused by his foreign experiences, which he depicted in words and in drawings. But the entire family had been shocked and infuriated to learn that not once but t-w-i-c-e, our brother Jim had been—caned! Called into the headmaster's study and told to lean over. The first time, he had received one "swipe." The second time, two swipes. Not quite the stuff of Nicholas Nickleby's Dotheboys Hall, but news of the punishment was received as such in the family corridors, and the rumor spread about the nursery in our house in London that Father and Mother even considered withdrawing the boys. It did not come to that, but Jim was for at least a year after the event regarded by his brothers and sisters as a mutilated object. He, being sunny by nature and serenely preoccupied with his interest in animals and with flora and fauna, actually hadn't thought very much about the episode. For the rest of us, it was the mark of Cain, discoloring our year of English schooling.

And now we were headed back for more of the same kind of thing? We needed to know—why? Surely Aunt Priscilla would set things right.

The Word came, about two weeks later. A letter from Father. She didn't read it to us, but she explained that Father "and your mother"—this was a blatant invention, we knew; it would never have occurred to Mother to impose any such ordeal on us—believed it would be a very fine educational experience for us. "Besides"—Aunt Priscilla winked—"as you know, your father has complained that five years have gone by since he understood *'a single word' "*—Aunt Priscilla did a light imitation of Father, elongating a word or phrase, to give it emphasis—"uttered by any one of his children." In England we would learn to *open our mouths* when we spoke. We moaned our dismay at one of Father's *typical* exaggerations. It is true that Father was a nut on elocution, and true that his nine children, on returning from five years in Europe, had quickly adapted to lazy vocalisms which Father, then sixty, had a progressively difficult time deciphering in the din of the three-tiered dining room, the main table for the older children and the adults, the middle table for those roughly nine to thirteen, the third little table for the incumbent baby(ies).

We felt certain that his objective wasn't merely to put us into Catholic schools. Such a thing, in our household, would have been supererogatory. Mother was a daily communicant. Father's faith was not extrovert, but if you happened on him just before he left his bedroom in the morning, you would find him on his knees, praying.

Our eldest brothers and sisters, here in the States, were not at Catholic schools. So we ruled that out as one of Father's objectives.

We dimly understood that Father had always stressed the value of cosmopolitan experience—we lived now in Connecticut, rather than in Mexico City, where, bilingual, he had gone to practice law after graduating from the University of Texas, intending to raise his family there. But he had been exiled from Mexico in 1921, pronounced by the President of Mexico an *extranjero pernicioso*—a pernicious foreigner. Which indeed he was, having backed a revolution against President Obregón which, among other things, sought to restore religious freedom to Mexican Catholics. He bought the house in Connecticut, but soon, pursuing business concerns, he moved the family to France, Switzerland, and England. We lived abroad for four years. It was in Paris that I first went to school, speaking only Spanish. Was Father simply seeking out further exposure to another culture?

It was much, much later, after World War II, that we learned the hidden reason Father thought it prudent to have three of his children of sensitive age away from home. It was why Aunt Priscilla hadn't read to us out loud the explanatory letter she had received from him: Mother had become pregnant again, against her doctor's advice. It was not known if she would survive the birth of her eleventh child (one baby had died at childbirth, ten years earlier). At the time, we knew only enough to be vaguely apprehensive about Mother. We did not know how dangerous the doctors thought the birth, due the following November, could be.

But whatever speculation we engaged in, however horrified at the very thought of the ordeal ahead, there was never any doubt, in my father's house, what his children would be doing at any given time, i.e., what Father said we would be doing at any given time. So that, on September 18, 1938, after an indulgent twenty-four hours in New York City shepherded about by our beloved young piano teacher to movies, a concert, and Horn & Hardart Automats, we—Mademoiselle, Jane, Trish, and I—boarded the S.S. *Europa* for Southampton.

. . .

5

There was much political tension. We couldn't fail to note it immediately on landing in Southampton. British sentiment was divided between those who favored standing up to Hitler, who had just occupied the Sudetenland in Czechoslovakia, and those who opposed any move that might threaten war. Prime Minister Neville Chamberlain was scheduled to return from his meeting with Adolf Hitler in Munich the next day. Before boarding the train for London we were fitted out with gas masks.

In London we were greeted with Mother's distinctive affection and Father's firm embraces. Little was said, that I can remember, about where we would be taken the next day, but Father did tell me that he had found Fr. Sharkey, the headmaster of St. John's, a "fine" person, and Jane and Trish were told that the mother superior at Ascot was someone other than the mother superior, so disliked by my older sisters, who had presided five years earlier.

Mother drove in one car with Jane and Trish and their bags to Ascot, Father and I in another car, to St. John's.

It was late on a cold English afternoon (Father instructed the driver to detour to the landing field and we saw Neville Chamberlain descend from the airplane that had flown him from Munich to announce that he was bringing "peace in our time"). An hour later, we turned into the long driveway that took us to the pillared entrance to the school, the whole of it contained in one large square brick three-story building.

We were taken by a maid to a primly decorated salon, and Fr. Sharkey, short, stubby, his hair gray-white, came in, took my hand, and chatted with Father for a few minutes about the international situation. Tearfully I bid good-bye to my father and was led up with my two bags to a cubicle, halfway along a line of identical cubicles on either side of a long hallway that held about thirty. To enter you needed to slide open a white curtain that hung down from a rod going across the cubicle's width, about eight feet up from the floor. The rooms had no ceiling of their own—looking straight up, you saw the ceiling of the large hallway, perhaps ten feet up. To your right and to your left were white wooden partitions. On the right, a dresser—two or three drawers and a hanging locker. To the left, your bed. A small table of sorts stood near the bed and on it I quickly placed pictures of my family. On the window ledge I could reach only by standing on my bed I placed one end of a huge Old Glory I had bought that last day in New York, holding it down with two weights I contrived from something or other so that the United States flag could hang down behind my bed, all five feet of it. The dormitory master, Fr. Ferguson, knocked on the wooden partition, drew the curtain to one side, introduced himself, and told me he would lead me to the refectory, as it was time for supper.

The dining hall was crowded with the eighty boys who boarded at St. John's. The youngest were aged nine, the oldest, fourteen. After supper, we went to the study hall. I was three weeks late in arriving for the fall term and so without any homework to do, pending my introduction the next day to my form master.

I don't remember how I passed the two hours. In due course we were summoned to evening prayers. We knelt along two of the quadrangular corridors in the building, a priest at the corner, boys to his left. He led us in prayers, to which we gave the responses. Fr. Sharkey then materialized, and the boys filed by him. He shook hands with each of us and said good night. When it was my turn, he said, "Good night, Billy. You are very welcome at St. John's." We walked up the circular staircase to our cubicles and were given fifteen minutes before Lights Out. Just before the light was switched off, the dormitory master read the Psalm (#130) "De Profundis," to which we gave the responses in Latin. These were thumbtacked behind one of the dresser doors. The first two verses exactly echoed my thoughts. "Out of the depths have I cried unto thee, O Lord. Lord, hear my voice: let thine ears be attentive to the voice of my supplications."

I don't remember very much about the period of acclimation. I do remember the quite awful homesickness (I had never before spent a night away from my family). It lasted about ten evenings during which, smothering my face with the collar of my pajamas so that I would not be heard by my neighbors, I wept.

I think I remember praying for war, confident that if war came, Father would take us home. Mother had warned us that we would be homesick, that this would go away after a while, and that until then we should offer up our pain to God in return for any private intentions. In a closed conference, back in London, Jane and Trish and I had decided we would offer up our forthcoming torment for the safe and happy birth of Mother's baby in November.

The routine was extremely severe, up against what I had been used to. Rising in the morning always came as a wrenchingly disagreeable surprise. I remember ten years later reading C. S. Lewis's *Surprised by Joy* in which he told that throughout his early school days in England he remembered primarily how tired he always was. I assume Mr. Lewis had a special problem because once awake I was all right, but getting up was for me—for some reason—more difficult than rising, six years later, at 5:30 in the infantry, or, a few years after that, at 4:00 A.M. to do watch duty racing my sailboats. Once or twice every month the school matron, as she was called, would ordain that this boy or that should have a "late sleep," which meant we would sleep an extra forty-five minutes, rejoining our classmates at breakfast, after Mass. In those preconciliar days Catholics could not take Communion unless they had fasted since midnight. For that reason alone, breakfast could not have preceded Mass.

The pews were stacked along the sides of the chapel. Twenty boys sat and kneeled on the top right pew, looking down on the heads of twenty boys a foot beneath them. Then across the little aisle, to the faces of twenty boys at the lower level, and another twenty above them. To view the altar one needed to turn one's head. There was no sermon, except a brief one on Sundays. The Mass lasted about twenty-five minutes. School announcements were given in the refectory.

I have always been impatient, and so it was I suppose surprising that I came so quickly to feel at ease with the daily Mass and then became gradually engrossed in the words and the ritual. We were

studying second-year Latin and I was dreadful at it, incapable of understanding why, while they were at it, the Romans hadn't simply settled
for Spanish. But I paid increasing attention to the Ordinary of the
Mass, which is to say that part of it that doesn't change from Sunday
to Sunday. It was easy to follow—the right-hand column of the missals
carried the English translation. The liturgy took hold of me and I
suppose that this means nothing more than that liturgy has theatrical
properties. Yes, but something more, I reasonably supposed, and suppose so now. Twenty-five years later I would write a scorching denun-
ciation of the changes authorized by Vatican II and of the heartbreak-
ingly awful English translations that accompanied the jettisoning of the
Latin. The Mass, in Latin, had got to me.

I had of course attended Mass every Sunday for as long as I could
remember and thought myself something of a pro in the business
inasmuch as I had been trained, in Sharon, to do duty as an altar boy. I
very nearly became a godfather—I remember the thrill, followed by
the humiliation. Our devout black butler, Ben Whittaker (he was a
first cousin of Fats Waller), became a special friend of mine at Great
Elm. After his wife gave birth to quadruplets, he told me excitedly
that he wished me to serve as godfather. It transpired that I could not
act as godfather, not having yet been confirmed. The honor fell to my
older brother John, though by the time the formal event took place,
only one of Ben's poor babies was still alive.

It was then that I was told about emergency baptisms, extemporaneously given to anyone in danger of dying. I had once improvised on
this privilege. Mother had a friend who visited often at Great Elm,
sometimes bringing along her two daughters, one in her late twenties,
a second a few years older. On overhearing a conversation between
Mother and Mademoiselle, I learned that the two ladies had never
been baptized. I thought this shocking, talked the matter over with my
sister Trish, we devised our strategy, and knocked at their guest room
door early one morning, after establishing that they had both been
brought breakfast, in bed, on trays. I knocked and told them that Trish
and I were looking for my dog. They welcomed us in to search the
room. I knelt down to see if he was under the first bed and, a drop of

water on my forefinger, touched it on Arlie's forehead as if reaching to maintain my balance, silently inducting her into the Christian community, while Trish, emerging from under the other bed in search of the dog, did as much for her older sister.

My mother was solemnly attentive when I whispered to her the happy consummation of our Christian evangelism. She did not betray her amusement: that was a part of her magic as a mother. She would never permit herself anything that might suggest belittlement—whatever her child's fancy. And then, too, she was as devoted a child of God as I have ever known and perhaps she permitted herself to believe that her friend's two grown-up daughters, neither one of them at death's door, had in fact been baptized. When in England I found myself going to Mass every day and offering every Mass for the health of my mother, I felt a closeness to her that helped diminish the pain of separation.

In those days I remember a special reverence for Our Lady, to whom I appealed as a mother herself. I hadn't the capacity (even now I am not comfortable with the abstraction) to imagine infinity. I accepted it as a gospel truth that the Mother of God was "infinitely" wonderful, which meant to me that she was many times as wonderful as my own mother, but this hypothesis I had difficulty with: How was it possible to be many times more wonderful than my mother? I never asked any of the priests for help with that one. After all, I reasoned, they did not know Mother, so they might find the question surprising, impudent even. I knew that would not be the case if they had *known* Mother. But Our Lady became in my mind an indispensable character of the heavenly cloister. A long time after that I learned that a thing called Mariolatry had been especially contemned by noisy iconoclasts like Charles Kingsley. My first instincts were not combative, but sad: that someone so much like my mother should be disdained was incomprehensible.

No doubt my religious ardor was stimulated by the circumstances we lived in. St. John's was run by Jesuit priests. They were, as members of the Society of Jesus tend to be, thoroughly educated. It required thirteen years to become a member of the Jesuit order and the training was exacting, the regimen spare. Fr. Manning was our form master. At the end of the hour, at every other school I would ever encounter, a fresh master moves in to teach the class his specialty. Fr. Manning did not teach us French, for which purpose a layman was brought in whose British accent, when speaking in French, I would ostentatiously mock, my own being so superior, as anyone's would be who learned French at age six in Paris. But excepting French, Fr. Manning taught every other subject in "Figures IIA"—the equivalent, roughly, of first year junior high. Geography, History, Math, Latin, Doctrine. Each of the six school years at St. John's (grades three to eight) had a single form master. Two of these were pre-ordination Jesuits, climbing up the long ladder to priesthood serving now, so to speak, as field instructors at a boys' boarding school. They were addressed as "Mr." But they met with the priests at faculty conferences, which were conducted in Latin, and I often wondered when did they sleep, since they were always up and around before we rose, and never appeared ready to retire when our lights went out.

I remember once being handed a corrected paper from Fr. Manning in his study. I leaned over to retrieve it and accidentally overturned the can of pipe tobacco. I heard the slightest whinny of alarm and then the majestic Fr. Manning was on his hands and knees, picking up each tobacco grain, one after another, replacing them in his can. "That is my month's allowance, Billy. I cannot afford to let any go unsmoked!" I thought this extraordinary. That this . . . seer should have less than all the tobacco he wanted.

On those rare afternoons when we did not do school sports, we would be taken for long walks in that historic countryside. We were within a few hundred meters of Runnymede, where King John had signed the Magna Carta. Striding alongside Fr. Paine, a tall, angular priest, about thirty-five years old, I'd guess—he was the administrative coordinator at the school and also its disciplinarian—I asked about Fr. Manning's tobacco and he told me that Jesuits took a vow of poverty and that therefore they were given a monthly allowance which had to suffice for all their needs. I asked whether it would be permitted for a friend to give tobacco to a Jesuit priest and he said no, this was only permitted in the case of food, when it was in short supply. (After the war, for several years, meat was very scarce, and Father sent meat every month to the fathers.) Ten years later, at the wedding of my sister Trish, the Jesuit priest who officiated, a lifetime friend of the groom, told my father not to make the mistake of offering him a stipend in return for his services "because under Jesuit rules, we cannot turn down a donation, which in any event goes to the order, not to the priest to whom it is offered." Fr. Paine told me that Jesuit priests needed frequently to check themselves, to guard against the sin of pride, because Jesuits were in fact very proud of the Jesuit order and very happy in it. One inevitably wonders whether that pride is quite whole after the strains of the 1960s.

Fr. Paine would regularly check individual cubicles at night to say good night to each of the boys. When November came, I confided to him that my mother was soon to bear a child, her eleventh, and that I was anxiously awaiting a telegram confirming that the baby had come and that my mother was well. He leaned over and embraced me warmly and did so again extemporaneously after the baby came, and once finally seven months later when my father wrote to say that because of the lowering clouds of war, my sisters and I would be withdrawn from our schools after the winter term.

Fr. Paine's warmth did not affect what I judged the extreme severity of the punishment I was twice sentenced to, for whatever social infraction. The first time it was a single ferule stroke, smacked down on my open hand, the second, two ferules, one on each hand, the cumulative experience with corporal punishment in my lifetime, if you leave out an unsuccessful fistfight with the strongest and biggest boy at St. John's, a rite of passage for any potential new-boy challenger (his name was Burns—I forget his first name, though first names were universally used, among the boys).

Many years later when as a magazine editor I contracted for the services of European Correspondent Erik von Kuehnelt-Leddihn, I learned from him that while I was a student at St. John's, he was teaching the senior boys down the hill at Beaumont College and that on learning, soon after arriving from Austria, that the ferule was the regular instrument of discipline, he had gone to the priest-executioner and demanded to receive six ferules, the conventional ration for grave infractions, exactly as they were inflicted on student miscreants. He made his demand even after being reassured that, at his age, with adult, callused hands, he would hardly feel any smart. But he persisted, and after receiving the blows reported clinically that far from negligible, six ferule strokes, even for a husky Austrian in his twenties, were a singularly painful experience. I heard that for extreme acts of misbehavior the birch rod was used on the buttocks, but I never knew any boy who received this punishment at St. John's.

Fr. Paine and I exchanged a half dozen letters in the ensuing thirty years, and we spoke once in London over the telephone in the seventies—he was retired and had difficulty in breathing. He told me among other things that the young rowdies in London who were disturbing the peace should be given a good beating.

When Lent came, we were given a retreat by the brother of Fr. Sharkey, also a Jesuit. He was short, like his older brother, irradiating a singular charm on this thirteen-year-old (I had had a birthday soon after my sister Carol was born, and Father had redeemed his promise to make me the godfather). I thought back to this retreat twenty years later when I went to Washington with my brother-in-law for a retreat conducted by the president emeritus of Fordham University, Jesuit Father Robert Gannon, whose short, electrifying sermons I begged him to put on tape, eliciting an assurance that one day he would certainly do this (R.I.P., he never did). They were cognate skills, Fr. Sharkey's and Fr. Gannon's: dramatic, but never melodramatic; persuasive; poignant; inspiriting. I recall only a single parable, if that is the right word for it, from that retreat at St. John's, six months before the world war. I put it in an essay I wrote on my boat during a transatlantic sail. *Esquire* had asked me to write about where, that I had never been, would I most wish to visit? I wrote, on that sunny, breezy day in the mid-Atlantic, that I would most like to visit Heaven because it was there I would be made most happy. I gave Fr. Sharkey's exegesis: He had been approached some weeks earlier, he told us, by a devout elderly woman who asked him whether dogs would be admitted into Heaven. No, he had replied, there was no scriptural authority for animals getting into Heaven. "In that case," the lady had said to him, "I can never be happy in Heaven. I can only be happy if Brownie is also there."

"I told her"—Fr. Sharkey spoke with mesmerizing authority—"that if that were the case—that she could not be happy without Brownie—why then Brownie would in fact go to Heaven. Because what is absolutely certain is that, in Heaven, you will be happy." That answer, I am sure, sophisticated readers of *Esquire* dismissed, however indulgently, as jesuitical. Yes. But I have never found the fault in the syllogism.

My sisters in nearby Ascot were in regular contact by mail. Trish, with whom I had been paired since infancy, wrote me twice every week, always—always—closing, "I hope you are well and that I will see you soon." We did in fact see each other every week. Father had rented an apartment (50 Portland Place, I still recall) where Mademoiselle would stay, looked after by James Cole, a New Orleans–born, black cook-butler, a man of enormous spirits, a devout Catholic, who normally looked after Father in New York. Mademoiselle, driven by a chauffeur—his name was McCormack—would come to see us every Saturday afternoon, beginning after the two-week embargo against visiting new boys and girls. My sisters would be picked up at Ascot and driven to pick me up at St. John's, where I could be found sitting, waiting, at the end of the long driveway. We would all go off to Windsor, which, of course, is where Windsor Castle and Eton College are located. I remember, breathless with pride and pleasure, recounting to my sisters the tale I had heard about when in 1855, five years after the founding of Beaumont, the headmaster had issued a challenge to the headmaster of Eton to a soccer match, and got back a note, "What *is* Beaumont?" to which the fabled answer had been, "Beaumont is what Eton used to be, a school for Catholic gentlemen." We would eat and talk and laugh and then—sadly—go back to our schools in time for supper. We were allowed, if I remember, two hours away.

The principal extracurricular enthusiasm in my childhood was horses. Accordingly, as we neared the great day in March at Aintree, I wrote to my father in London—he and Mother had come to London in January, bringing the baby and her immediately older sister and brother and their nurse. Maureen and Reid were now the same age Trish and I had been in 1932, when we attended the same day schools in London they now attended. I asked my father if I might be taken to the Grand National. We spent winters in Camden, South Carolina, which is the steeplechase center of the region, and I would hear nothing, during the first two weeks in March, from horse owners and their grooms but talk about who would win the Grand National, in which one or more Camden thoroughbreds competed. Father wrote back that I would need the permission of Fr. Sharkey. I sought it. He said no, such exceptions to school rules could not be made. I wrote back to my father with the sad news. He then wrote a letter to Fr. Sharkey, a copy of which he sent me. Dire signs were visible on the horizon, my father wrote, and if I did not get to see the Grand National now, I might never have the opportunity again. Would Fr. Sharkey, under the circumstances, bend the rule to permit an American boy this experience?

I was summoned to his study. He had changed his mind, he said. I might go to the steeplechase.

Three days later Father's chauffeur drove up. Fr. Sharkey led me to the car and stopped me just as I was about to enter it. He reached into his pocket and withdrew a florin, a two-shilling piece. He leaned over and whispered to me, "Billy, put this on a horse called Workman, to win."

I was driven to 50 Portland Place, where my father and his close friend, his lawyer George Montgomery, got into the car and together we went to the station at Euston and into a private compartment.

I spent the three hours poring over the tabloid coverage of the thirty-six horses that would compete, carefully apportioning the ten shillings my father had given me among the horses I thought likeliest to prevail. I was startled, on reaching Aintree, by the appearance of the famous track: it seemed as though all of Liverpool squatted on the infield. It was impossible to see the horses after the first turn. They would reappear, after a minute or two, on the left turn. I was in a frenzy of excitement. Finally they were off.

Of the thirty-six horses that competed, six finished. On none of them had I bet. The winner was Workman. He paid 18–1.

And I had neglected to place Fr. Sharkey's bet.

I didn't dare tell my father about this egregious, unspeakable delinquency. It passed through my mind to "borrow" the thirty-six shillings from him, but I was too ashamed. I was preternaturally silent on the train ride back and altogether silent in the car with McCormack, on the hour's drive to St. John's. It was nearly midnight when we reached the door. Fr. Sharkey opened it, exultant over the news he had got on the radio about the horse that won the Grand National.

"Father," I said, looking down on the stone steps, "I forgot. I didn't place your bet." His dismay was acute. Then, suddenly, he smiled. "Those things happen. Now get to bed." I fell quickly to sleep, but not before praying that God would forgive me, that God should find a devious means of transmitting thirty-six shillings to Fr. Sharkey, that God should suspend the vow of poverty for long enough to permit Fr. Sharkey full and indulgent use of those thirty-six shillings. But I awoke in panic, fearing the obloquy of my schoolmates, already jealous about the privilege I had been given.

The scandal was stillborn, aborted by Fr. Sharkey. All that I heard the next day was from Fr. Manning, who wished to know what it had been like at Aintree, and had I been told that Fr. Sharkey had picked the winner? Yes, I said, just that, "Yes." We had a secret, Fr. Sharkey and I, and I wondered whether, by his confessional vows, he was bound to silence about my sin.

. . .

When my boy, Christopher, was ten, I took him to see St. John's. I had no intention of sending him there but I was curious about what we now call his chemical reaction. My father was wonderful with children (up until they were adolescents, at which point he took to addressing them primarily by mail, until we were safe again at eighteen). He loved especially about them that they were incapable of deception. "You can always tell," he said to me one day in his wheelchair, after a stroke, his grandson on his lap, "whether they really like something or if they don't." Perhaps my son, who was much taken by what he saw, was reflecting my own irradiations. I had been, notwithstanding my distance from home, very happy there, and I knew absolutely—about this there simply was no doubt—that I had had a deep and permanent involvement in Catholic Christianity. They say about alcoholics that they are never "cured." But I am a senior citizen and my faith has never left me and I must suppose that Fr. Sharkey and Fr. Paine and Fr. Manning had something to do with it; they, and the closeness I felt, every morning, to the mystical things that were taking place at the altar.

CHAPTER TWO

Growing Up

My father maneuvered his family in the anxious months of 1939,
before the world war broke out. He did so by sending groups of us
here and there before the summer and during it. Before returning our
group of three to the United States in June, my father wished to open
our eyes to the big Italian scene. To this end he hired a chauffeur
(Valerian Bibikoff, a White Russian who became a lifelong family
friend) and an Italian guide (Count Rhigini, widower of soprano Ella
Russell). He brought from the United States our music teacher

(Marjorie Gifford), whom we worshiped. We had had five years' exposure to her, three days of lessons every week.

One week of our month in Italy was spent in Florence, mostly at the Uffizi Gallery. The visit to Rome featured a private audience with the freshly inducted Pope. Pius XII remains in the memory as a most imposing presence, asceticism and resignation written into his face. I must have been carrying thirty rosaries on my left arm for him to bless, one for every Catholic I knew, six of them for the Irish maids at St. John's. My sisters and I agreed that the cardinals who had selected Pius XII had done a good job.

Back in London for two months before finally returning home, our time was mostly given over to music. I had seen that Toscanini was in London to conduct a Beethoven cycle, for which tickets were quite simply unavailable. I spent long hours in the lobby of the Queens Hotel hoping to catch a glimpse of him entering or leaving—which I did, appeasing my worship of him.

Felix Weingartner was doing the *Ring* in Covent Garden. We caught most of it, and practiced our scales under the supervision of Mrs. Gifford at our house in Portland Place.

My father had located an Irish-English tutor, Celia Reilly, who would return with us to Sharon, Connecticut. The other faculty was "Mr. Lockhart," an American bachelor who would handle the spartan subjects, Latin and math. "Miss Reilly," as we would always know her, would tutor four Buckley children and three friends from the neighborhood. She was full of fun and devoutly Catholic. When I left her dominion I was almost fifteen. My father entered me in Millbrook School, ten miles away, as a boarder, the school from which my two older brothers had graduated. My sisters Jane and Trish were sent to Ethel Walker School as boarders. For the first time, we were in non-Catholic schools, taught other than at home.

I graduated from Millbrook six months before my eighteenth birthday. My father, who already had two sons in the service, both of them in war theaters, had no intention of dispatching me to the army fifteen minutes before the statutory age of eighteen. Instead, after leaving Millbrook, I was one of six Buckley children who went to Mexico

City, where four of us enrolled in the University of Mexico. Six months later I was eighteen, but en route to Camden to register for the draft, I found myself in a Dallas hospital (after my first airplane flight), too sick to join the family caravan bound for our winter home in South Carolina.

I had badly infected sinuses, and every other day, at a second hospital in South Carolina, submitted to a painful operation. I remember about it only that a very large instrument crackled its way through some bone in the upper nose, looking for the fetid sinus pool and draining it, every treatment lowering its level until the relevant nasal secretions resumed their good work, helped along by the drug sulfa, which had just been discovered.

All of this meant a six-month deferral from the draft board. I left the hospital under instructions to reside for at least three months in a dry climate. My father sent me to El Paso, to receive counsel in that dry part of the world from a dear old friend, a retired judge, who, the night I arrived, introduced me to a passing rancher, a robust, hunky man with withered sunburned face who wore a large sombrero and what looked like jade spurs on his Texas boots. With his family, I would have my first experience under another roof than my school's, or my mother's.

At dinner the judge described my plight and my search for a dry climate to Tom Doyle. He looked at me, pleasantly enough, but said nothing, until after he had finished his beer. At that point (addressing the judge), "Jimmy, you know I have that bungalow outside my house. Nothing drier than the climate of Nogales, you know." And then to me: "My wife doesn't drive. You know how to drive a car?"

Oh yes.

He drew back and, anticipating disappointment, said quickly, "In my house you got to know how, because my family, especially Marina, don't speak one word of English. Do you understand Spanish?"

Yes, I told him.

The next day we were off, five hundred miles to the border town,

Nogales. Marina was a handsome, voluptuous, expressive woman in her early thirties. She presided over the substantial, if rudimentary, house built by Tom Doyle for his second wife and four children. The oldest boy, about sixteen, I remember primarily because polishing shoes was his passion. He would spend an hour or two on my shoes. Nachita, the oldest girl, about fourteen, studied English with me. Every morning I would drive Marina into Nogales and help her with the groceries. Her goal was to put weight on me, and early on she urged me to drink, after Tom left on a cattle-buying tour, a creamy blend of eggs and milk and honey and—I saw it with my own eyes— two jiggers of whiskey. I told her, in accents laboriously designed not to sound reproachful about others who did so, that I did not drink, *aunque mis padres sí, mucho les gusta el vino* (though my parents do, they like wine a lot). So did Marina.

On Sundays the whole family went together to Mass (Tom would not reappear until seven weeks later, after I had left), all of us crammed into the single car, me at the wheel. The question I yearned to ask Marina, but of course didn't, was about theological rectitude, a bit of Savonarola in me. *(How is it, Marina, that you're a Catholic and you've gone to Communion but you're married to Tom, who was married before and his first wife is living?)* Marina would have understood the question: she had a street knowledge of life and churchly complications, and almost certainly, Tom had told her not to worry. She would not have undertaken to put any of this down on paper, as she was nearly illiterate. I thought her a grand woman and when I left, six weeks later, it was after a festive and weepy evening, with my virginal egg-nog and Marina's several beers. Thirty-five years later my wife and I, an afternoon idle in Tucson, drove down to 34 Perkins Street, a photograph taken of us by the street photographer at the restaurant in hand. No one was home, and I tucked it, with an affectionate inscrip-tion, under the door. One week later I received from her the next day's issue of the Nogales (Mexican) daily, the picture on the front page and her excited account of the visit by the American journalist. When I left, my health returned, I went to the army.

I was sent to Camp Wheeler, Georgia, for basic training in the infantry. I developed a friendship with Ed Coady, an eighteen-year-old Irish redhead from New Bedford, Massachusetts, of wizened brow, with whom, in our pup tent for a week's bivouac, I shared the quite awful rigors of the damp cold Georgia winter. On Sundays we went together to church, presided over by the Catholic chaplain. Ed and I, fifty-two years later, are still intermittently in touch. He went from Georgia to fight in the Battle of the Bulge. I went to Officers Candidate School at Fort Benning. Eighteen weeks later I was given a commission, a week after Franklin Delano Roosevelt died in Warm Springs, a dozen miles away; three weeks before Hitler died.

From there to train recruits in infantry arts I had not the least idea of ten months before. Some scanner in army personnel discovered that I was fluent in Spanish and one day in August I was ordered to report to intelligence at Fort Sam Houston in San Antonio. The collapsing Nazi regime had sent to sympathizers in Mexico the counterfeit money plates the Germans had succeeded (too late) in contriving, and millions of fake dollars were flowing north. The United States retaliated by denying transit across the Mexican border to any U.S. denomination other than the two-dollar bill, which the Germans had disdained to counterfeit. An army intelligence team was being mobilized to penetrate the border to unearth the sources of the phony bills; I had been briefed in Dallas and now drove off to report for duty in San Antonio. The car horns were honking as I approached Fort Sam Houston, and I learned that V-J Day had come.

I would have, in San Antonio, the first direct exposure to the workaday juxtaposition of the Christian moral code and secular practice. Young men were still being drafted, in August 1945, and Fort Sam had many Hispanic recruits, sworn in and absolutely illiterate in English. I was given a quick course in sexual hygiene, instructed to translate it all in my mind into Spanish, and to lecture to the Mexican recruits, one squad at a time, on how to avoid catching gonorrhea or syphilis. I do not know whether, at age nineteen, I succeeded in putting any poetry into my sex lectures, but I do remember that I gave some thought to what I was doing, viewed in the Christian perspective, namely teaching the prospective sinner how to avoid at least the worldly wages of sin. But paradoxes on the sex business were something one got used to in the army, during the war. When admitted to Fort Benning we were told, quite simply, that if we contracted a venereal disease while there, we would immediately be dismissed from Officers Candidate School. The army was making not a moral point, but a military one.

After two weeks I was relieved as Spanish sex-hygiene lecturer and sent to what was called the Casual Department, and in a couple of weeks was named officer in charge. It was a hilarious detachment of approximately one thousand veterans who were chronologically qualified for discharge but could not be let go for particular reasons, mostly health and discipline. In most situations the detained soldier had been court-martialed and his sentence undischarged, or he had been either arraigned for a court-martial that hadn't taken place; or else the soldier was pronounced unready for discharge owing to venereal disease—he would need to be treated at an army hospital. If suffering from advanced syphilis, a spinal tap was (in those days) necessary. Some soldiers under my charge had had a spinal tap after a preceding affliction, and several of them announced to me most firmly over the ten months that I administered the department that they would rather be executed than undergo the pain of another tap.

I came to know a good deal about army policy and venereal disease. A regulation had quietly been initiated, some time after the war had started. The traditional rule was that a soldier who contracted a venereal disease was automatically suspended from the duty rolls, his pay confiscated, from the day the disease was detected until he was cured and put back on active duty. In those days, before penicillin, that could mean months of no pay. His record would show that during his treatment he was serving off-duty.

This incremental burden—administrative leave-without-pay—the Pentagon evidently decided the 15 million drafted American men could not be expected to put up with. Accordingly, at our personnel center we listed venereal disease soldiers as "On Duty," and would have done so even if the soldier awaiting the doctor's final okay had spent full-time in a bawdy house. Routine business. It catches the moral imagination, the first time the teenager comes upon misbehavior treated quite routinely by a major institution of government: the only penalty for unlicensed sex is three penicillin shots. No other perspective than that of the need to effect medical cure was so much as thinkable. Two worlds. It would be later, after I began serious reading in college, that I would learn that the two worlds, as often as not, conflate into a single world, where all of us, excepting, one supposes, Mother Teresa, dwell.

CHAPTER THREE

Where Does One Learn About

the Christian God?

The school at Great Elm, before I went on to Millbrook, had in it, as noted, three Buckleys, I and my contiguous sisters, and three girls our age (twelve to fifteen), all three Protestant. Two were daughters of family friends, one the daughter of Sharon's Episcopal minister (ten years later she was widely known as the actress and comedienne Audrey Meadows, the celebrated television wife of Jackie Gleason, and younger sister of Jayne Meadows, the actress and wife of Steve Allen). The school had two tutors. Religion was, as ever, an ongoing experience, unspokenly accepted as such. Neither of the tutors undertook to give us formal religious instruction, though we attended Sunday school at the local church. We didn't know whether Susan and Adelaide got such instruction at home, and naturally supposed that Audrey was taught by the Episcopalian priest who was her father. When I went on to Millbrook, it was generally understood to be a Protestant school.

Millbrook School's founder was an imposing figure. Edward Pulling had immigrated to America from England after doing duty as a naval officer in World War I. He studied at Gilman School in Baltimore, took a degree from Princeton, taught at Avon and at Groton, married the wealthy daughter of Russell C. Leffingwell, a partner of J. P. Morgan, and founded the school for boys in 1931 to make room for his exuberant pedagogic and moral energies. Mr. Pulling was a Presbyterian, and Bible study was required of all students, though the accent, in Mr. Pulling's classes, was on the Bible as literature.

Mr. Pulling's school began formal exercises, on Monday through Saturday, with a prayer, spoken by the headmaster or his representative, and a hymn, sung by the whole of the student body (about ninety boys, in my day). I would much later learn that Mr. Pulling was just a little anti-Catholic, in the cultural sense, as so many of his generation were. I would experience this denominational hostility unzipped when I published my book on Yale ten years later. But no bias of any sort was evident at Millbrook and not much of it in quarters one would tend to frequent in a preparatory school or even in college. Where anti-Catholicism was detectable was in some journals of opinion, though these tended to be impartially agnostic, and, here and there, in high academic society, where it expressed itself as a patient, disdainful irritation with Americans who, by their profession of a more or less alien faith, were not fully assimilated in the American tradition.

And of course this was in part correct: at the margin, the priorities of Catholics could be said to be different from those of non-Catholics. That point was heavily made by polemicist Paul Blanshard (brother of

Brand, the chairman of the department of philosophy at Yale), whose popular book, *American Freedom and Catholic Power,* brought up the question of double loyalty, even as the same kind of thing is here and there said about Jewish Americans. But then of course all of this blew away with the election of John Kennedy as President. It was required of him only that he should persuade the most diligent critics that his religion did not in any way affect his behavior.

When my father negotiated with Mr. Pulling the education of his four sons, my father wrested (I cannot imagine it otherwise, in a session between the two sturdiest characters I have ever known) a dispensation from normal school-bound regulations. The Buckley boys would be permitted to spend Saturday afternoons (after football) and Sundays at home in Sharon (ten miles away), and when they did spend the full weekends at school (during the winter months, when my parents moved their household to Camden, South Carolina), his boys would attend Catholic Mass on Sundays at Amenia, New York, five miles from the school.

There was no objection from Mr. Pulling and on Sundays-in-residence I would be driven to Amenia by the school's caretaker, along with three or four other Catholic boys and the one Catholic master, Xavier Prum, a teacher of physics, born and raised in Luxembourg. He was a rotund, elderly, playfully sarcastic pedagogue ("Do I have zee answer to zhat question? Yess, Robinson, I have zee answer to *every* question"), and I would learn that it was not lost on those of his students impressed by his erudition that the cosmopolitan Mr. Prum should impose on himself, early on Sundays, the itchy burden of a ten-mile round-trip drive to Amenia, even in the bitter cold, to observe the demands of his faith.

But then religious observance at the Millbrook School was routine. Every boy was required to attend chapel services on Sunday afternoons (I pleaded exemption, and was granted it, on the grounds that I had already attended services). I remember explaining to the occasional inquirer among my classmates, who wondered how I had achieved permission to absent myself from chapel, that I had, after all, my own faith, which was in some respects different from theirs, and which I tended to in my own way, according to my own conventions or, rather, those of my Church.

That point—the dissenter's exclusion from an otherwise common religious convention—became relevant many years later when I undertook a monograph on anti-Semitism and quoted with vibrant satisfaction essays by Irving Kristol (in the *Wall Street Journal*) and Michael Kinsley (in *The New Republic*). Both were critical of the insistence of so many of their coreligionists, American Jews, who insist on secularist practices in the public schools. Critics of prayer at a public school cite the hurt done to the sensibilities of minority students who, if Christian prayer were recited, would need to stand up and hear intoned in reverential tones creeds to which they did not subscribe. Kristol and Kinsley simply deny the force of this objection. A Catholic at a Protestant school, granted, does not have problems of equivalent theological order. Christian interdenominational divisions don't get in the way of a common recitation of the Apostles' Creed.

But the objection survives, that the religious dissenter must not be thought to suffer from the practice of religious ritual common to the majority. I suppose it is relevant to note that in my theological arrogance, as a teenager of aggressive political and cultural disposition, far from experiencing any of the pains of ostracism, I probably managed to convey to those of my classmates who inquired that we Catholics were prepared to wait however long was required for Mr. Pulling to discover the One True Faith. Meanwhile, I was attending a school whose moral and indeed eschatological orientation was unambiguously Christian. I had yet to experience Yale.

In my senior year at Yale I had resolved to write a book that would focus on two anomalies in Yale's education.

Forty-three years after *God and Man at Yale* was published, the Calvinist scholar ("My point of view," he identifies himself in his Introduction, "is that of a fairly traditional Protestant of the Reformed theological heritage") Professor George Marsden published *The Soul of the American University: From Protestant Establishment to Established Nonbelief* (Oxford University Press, 1994).

The thesis of Professor Marsden—it is more than that, actually; it is a documented finding—is that the administrators of higher education in the United States, thoroughly Protestant in tradition, turned education over to their faculties in the early part of the century. They did so in the serene conviction that the fusion of academic inquiry and religious inclination would vitalize evangelical Christianity even beyond where it then was on the typical campus.

What happened would not surprise any faculty member in upscale American higher education: the abandonment of Christianity. Some trustees are of course aware of this, and one wonders whether, however concealed, this was so at Yale when my book came out in 1951. Yet even now there are those who would deny this trenchant historical march to secularism, on see-no-evil grounds. It was, for Protestant Christianity, as if a Pope, after a few years' reign, set out to abolish the practices associated with his station. Christianity has been excluded by the very instrument—academic freedom—that Protestantism had counted on to further its mission, and this evolution came as a near total surprise. *"God and Man at Yale* would have caused a sensation even without the religious issues [i.e., because of the book's identification of the economic bias at Yale]," Professor Marsden writes. "In retrospect, however, the religious dimensions of the controversy are the most remarkable, since they are the least remembered. A generation later it seems almost inconceivable that there could have been a national controversy involving the question of whether a major university was sufficiently Christian. Yet not only the responses of Yale but also those of the reviewers, make it clear that it would have been news to admit that Yale had drifted loose of its Christian moorings" (Marsden, p. 10).

In my book I had quoted a sentence from the inaugural address (1937) of historian Charles Seymour, who served as president throughout my own residence at Yale. "I call on all members of the faculty," he had said, "as members of a thinking body, freely to recognize the tremendous validity and power of the teachings of Christ in our life-and-death struggle against the forces of selfish materialism. If we lose that struggle, judging from present events abroad, scholarship as well as religion will disappear."

That was a Christian mouthful, and Mr. Marsden is correct in suggesting that such sentiments could not safely be uttered today by an incoming president of a nondenominational university of standing. In the opinion of Professor Marsden, my book (whose prescriptions he disagrees with) "presented a formidable case . . . that a Yale education was more likely to shatter a person's commitment to Christianity than to fortify it."

As Professor Marsden reports, expressions of true astonishment and outrage came from the heart of the Yale establishment.* The trustees appointed a committee to look into the charges I made (Yale never officially acknowledged that this was their committee's mandate, but its findings were everywhere received as an official rebuttal by Yale of the findings of my book). The committee's chairman was the Reverend Henry Sloane Coffin, sometime president of the Union Theological Seminary in New York, a revered alumnus who had been closely considered for president of Yale in the thirties. The finding of the committee was that the accusation "that Yale was encouraging irreligion or atheism" was "without foundation." ". . . there is today, more than ever, widespread realization that religion alone can give meaning and purpose to modern life." Students especially needed the wholeness and sense of direction that religion provides. "It is by faith that man sees all things working together in the light of God and gives himself to work with them. To supply such light and truth Yale

---

* Some of these were perceptibly hostile to what they deemed a Catholic-inspired attack. McGeorge Bundy, dean at Harvard at the time (1951), wrote in the *Atlantic,* "Most remarkable of all, Mr. Buckley, who urges a return to what he considers to be Yale's true religious tradition, at no point says one word of the fact that he himself is an ardent Roman Catholic. In view of the pronounced and well-recognized difference between Protestant and Catholic views on education in America, and in view of Yale's Protestant history, it seems strange for any Roman Catholic to undertake to speak for the Yale religious tradition." The Reverend Henry Sloane Coffin, Yale trustee, wrote to an alumnus, "Mr. Buckley's book is really a misrepresentation and [is] distorted by his Roman Catholic point of view. Yale is a Puritan and Protestant institution by its heritage and he should have attended Fordham or some similar institution." The critic Dwight Macdonald (himself a skeptic), writing in the *Reporter,* commented: "Buckley is indeed a Catholic, and an ardent one. But oddly enough, this fact is irrelevant, since his book defines Christianity in Protestant terms."

was at birth dedicated, and to this high aim the University continues." The learned committee concluded that "religious life at Yale is deeper and richer than it has been in many years." Yale's theologians (if ever they were heard from) would perhaps not have disputed the truth of the vision of the Coffin commission of 1951. Yale's historians would have laughed at its findings.

Mr. Marsden's formal findings, encapsulated in the subtitle to his book ("From Protestant Establishment to Established Nonbelief"), are, as I say, pretty much taken for granted by the observant community, which is to say those who notice the sociology of nonbelief. The sheer loneliness of the Christian undergraduate at Yale was caught in a mini-essay published in the *Yale Free Press,* a conservative student monthly. Mark Chenoweth, class of 1995, is, in his own words, a born-again Christian. In seeking learned Christian company in New Haven he turned to the college chaplain, only to discover that the student was speaking to a dispirited inhabitant of a catacomb, who saw his role in contemporary Yale as no better than "promoting a healthy tolerance of Christianity." Chenoweth summarizes:

> The modern university with its emphasis on the rationality of the sciences has launched a veritable assault on Christian doctrine. Unspoken faith is now the practice of ghettoized Christians. It took a friend's ignorance of my own quiet faith to make me aware of my complicity. Simply put, a life led [merely] by example does no good if people do not know of what it is an example. Being a Christian has brought me an equanimity and confidence of purpose which are irreplaceable. [But] it is not the kind of feeling that should be kept to oneself if one hopes, as I do, that many others will find it for themselves.*

---

* Some implications of the offhanded jettisoning of the Christian idea at Yale, as seen by one undergraduate, were poignantly examined. The writer is Joshua Hochschild, class of 1994, also appearing in the *Free Press.* "The properly acculturated historian of ideas will explain the 'evolution' of Yale by pointing out—quite believably—that the institution simply *had* to change when people stopped believing the old ideas and started believing new ones." But Hochschild does not see, in the ashes of the institution discarded, a fresh one crystallizing, one animated by fresh ideas, convictions, purpose. "Institutions require purpose, discipline, a source of authority." No substi-

.   .   .

It was a coincidence that a few months before seeing the issue of the *Yale Free Press* I met Drew Casertano, the current headmaster of the Millbrook School. The occasion was the fiftieth anniversary of the graduation of my class at Millbrook. We were thirteen in the class of 1943, and nine, in 1993, now foregathered. The young headmaster is an enthusiast for his mission as educator of young people and as headmaster of a distinguished school. A few weeks after we met, he came with his wife to dinner at our house in Stamford and, sharing an evening with Millbrook graduate Schuyler Chapin, sometime dean of the School of Arts at Columbia University, the subject of religion came up. I asked what were the regularly scheduled religious services nowadays at Millbrook. He replied that there weren't any, but that the students were "encouraged" to engage in spiritual activity according to their own lights. That rather caught my breath. I had studied at Millbrook School at a time when the headmaster, reflecting his own judgment in the matter, and presumably that of the trustees, undertook the responsibility of deciding which was the best line of spiritual training for American adolescents, aged thirteen to seventeen.

I dropped the subject. But then, a few months later, I read in an alumni letter of the "special" "Candlelight Service" held just before the Christmas holiday under the auspices of the "Spiritual Life Committee." I wrote to the master in charge of spiritual life and asked if he would let me have some idea of what went into the Candlelight Service. He was kind enough to reply, enclosing a copy of the printed program. There were two dozen features. I reproduce the program:

---

tute has emerged, to replace the eschatological amplitude of Judeo-Christian idealism. The substitute is no "institution at all, and cannot begin to educate its 'students' away from their [own] ignorance of institution. Others, their moral convictions beaten out of them, stand by acquiescently. In this devastated landscape, the individual student can only begin again and try to be a student. But for what could the student muster a student's enthusiasm? For God? We have been persuaded of His death. For country? But for our state it is difficult to pretend enthusiasm, and those few who manage, border on the excess of fascism. For Yale? She is destroyed, her spirit separated from her body. Those who remember her life are left to wonder whether her spirit can survive the separation, and if so, whether the body will admit to resurrection."

"A Solis Ortus Cardine" (Sarum chant)

Reading: Genesis 1:1–4

Reading: "Chofetz Chayim al Hatorah"

"It Came Upon a Midnight Clear"

Invocation: Excerpt from *The Shepards* (a medieval mystery play)

Patapan (Burgundian tune)

"Noël Nouvelet" (traditional French carol)

"Kwanza" "Whence Is This Goodly Fragrance?" (traditional French carol)

Reading: "Take Something Like a Star"

Reading: "Winter" (from *Pilgrim at Tinkers Creek* by Annie Dillard)

"Sure on the Shining Night" (James Agee, text; Samuel Barber, music)

Reading: "The Little Match Girl" (by Hans Christian Andersen)

"Coventry Carol" (traditional English carol)

Reading: "Boy at the Window" (by Richard Wilbur)

"In the Bleak Midwinter" (Christina Rossetti, text; Gustav Holst, music)

Reading: Aramaic Lord's Prayer

Stille Nacht: "Night of Silence"

Reading: "Hanukkah"

Reading: "The Peace of Wild Things"

"Here We Come A-Wassailing"

Reading: From *The Four Quartets*

[And, concluding:] "A Gaelic Blessing" (by John Rutter)

Brandon Adams wrote me, in his covering letter (May 2, 1995), "I wish I could send you a tape of the Candlelight ceremony. . . . On paper the performance looks eclectic, yet the performance's prime asset was its cohesive form—a seamless chain of well-rehearsed events." He continued:

> Woman and Man's relationship to "light" was the common touchstone from which the proceedings unfolded. Events included fairy tales, a dramatic passion play, choral rounds, and solo art songs. It was a tasteful celebration of music and dramatic art. Rather than try to recreate a preordained "service" then, we began a kind of ritual of our own, focusing on what rings true for our specific community. In my experience, the feeling of universality is manifest in the overall form of the "Holiday" service—for instance, the Episcopalian ritual of lessons and carols. Instead, the "connectedness" here came from individual performances of various genres, thus permitting the audience to search for his or her own "truth." The collective result was of a new form, allowing the freedom to reemphasize relevant traditional selections. The texts from various cultures and religious denominations crisscrossed and overlapped. I believe the result was communicated in a spiritual language relevant to every member of this community, a non-denominational environment with a strong moral center.

How to comment? Yes, the performance, being eclectic, looks eclectic; no surprise. What is it that makes Kwanza, followed by *The Four Quartets,* seamless? What made the mix "tasteful"? Is the case against a preordained service a case that would, e.g., exclude the *Christmas Oratorio?* It is baffling how such a mix can satisfy the myriad curiosities of any specific community. On the other hand, if it does satisfy every curiosity, what is the purpose in singling out the Millbrook School community to hear it? What should distinguish it from a program designed for the town of Millbrook? How do we aid the inquiring student in search of his own truth by making a case for a

program of composites? How is the freedom to "reemphasize traditional selections" reinforced when there is such insistent care to guard
against any intimation of hierarchy?

Here is a more extended analysis of the year-end non-Christmas
celebration at the Millbrook School.

The salient meaning of the Candlelight Service is: *Let Us Not
Celebrate Christmas.* Is there such a thing as a Christmas carol that
does not celebrate the birth of Christ, or mention the birth at
Bethlehem? Answer, Yes. It is called "It Came Upon a Midnight
Clear."

Robert Frost, in talking about his star, didn't have in mind the Star
of Bethlehem. He wrote about a—any—star. James Agee was not
talking about Christmas, nor was Hans Christian Andersen, though in
his tale of the Little Match Girl there is a reference to a Christmas
tree, and to her grandmother's having risen up "to God." The Coventry Carol does not refer to the Holy Family though it does make a
slighting reference to Herod. Richard Wilbur's boy at the window is
staring at a snowman outdoors. "In the Bleak Midwinter" was originally entitled "A Christmas Carol."

—The Lord's Prayer! Ah. But it comes to us in Aramaic. Its
meaning is readily available to Millbrook students who study Aramaic.
Stille Nacht is German for "silent night." What are we a-wassailing
about, given that news of the birth of the Christ child is more effectively concealed at Millbrook than in Judaea by Herod? How do *The
Four Quartets* bear on the situation, except that they do, indeed, bear
on every situation? Though it is perhaps more fruitful to ask, What
would *not* bear on Millbrook's Candlelight Service?

But then of course the commentary above can be made to sound
provincial, philistine, ungrateful, pettifogging. The songs, the chatter,
the poetry, the folk tunes are undoubtedly splendid, and the collage
everything its impresario said it was, even if we permit ourselves to
wonder about a ceremony heralded as at once universal in its impact
and individuated for its listeners. Whatever the ceremony spoke, to

whichever pilgrim in search of whatever spiritual soundings he/she ached for, the epiphany of the candlelit night, as unmistakable as the star that shone over the first Epiphany, was: Millbrook School will on this night, as the students prepare to leave on their Christmas vacation, stroke every discoverable religious/ethnic sensibility, treating Christianity as just one more Zip Code.

I devote a few paragraphs, in Appendix A, to further analysis of Millbrook School's non-Christmas service, and to the cultural implications of the relegation of Christianity to the level of subspecies, religion. And I wondered whether Millbrook School, among preparatory schools, was unique in its attitude toward Christianity.

When I left Yale in 1950, I had become convinced that it and, presumably, other colleges like it were engaged in discouraging intellectual and spiritual ties to Christianity. I didn't stop to wonder whether this also was happening in the secondary schools. Successive Supreme Court decisions in those days were ruling that religious ties of public schools profaned the First Amendment. The Warren Court's rulings on the point began with the *McCollum* decision in 1948 that forbade released time for religious studies in the public schools and went on, in short order, to forbid almost all uses of public money to aid children who attended religious schools. In due course the Court forbade use of common prayer, any display of the Ten Commandments on school walls, and, in 1992, the recital by a rabbi of an invocation at a public school commencement ceremony. It did not occur to me that, without any prodding from the Supreme Court, something of the same order—the exorcism of religion—was under way in private secondary schools. The experience with the Millbrook School triggered my curiosity.

Before World War II, about one-half of the students entering Ivy League schools came in from the private secondary schools. The ratio is much changed. At Yale, to give one example, the class that began freshman year in 1940 was 48 percent private-school trained, the matriculating class of 1990, 30 percent.

The reaction during the Supreme Court's war against religion in the public schools was depressing for those to whom it mattered greatly that religion was being ignored. The reassuring chorus that the students will get their religious training at home seemed a platonic hope—most students think important that which they are taught at school. During this period I had thought it taken for granted that what was now missing in the public schools was not missing in the private schools. They would know something about ritual, practiced at regular school exercises—morning prayer, hymn singing, Sunday chapel—and something, taught in classrooms, about Christian literature and history. My exposure to the religious vacuity of my own alma mater led me, as suggested, to look elsewhere.* I inquired into religious practices in a dozen schools: Brooks, Choate, Deerfield, Exeter, Groton, Hotchkiss, Kent, Lawrenceville, Milton, St. George's, St. Paul's, and Taft. I record brief descriptions of religious fare at these important private schools in Appendix B.

Although there are secondary schools that attempt to keep Christianity prominently in sight, this much is absolutely plain: there is today another God, and it is multiculturalism.

In all twelve of the secondary schools, there is a faculty member engaged full-time in fostering multicultural learning. The advertised purpose of such exercises is to expose students to the ways of other cultures. But something more merely than cultural cosmopolitanism seems to be happening. It is on the order of a substitute for religion.

A vital feature in the new religious order is the institutionalization of the birthday of Martin Luther King, Jr., in some schools the most prominent feast in the calendar. Some schools celebrate the Monday in January with something approaching liturgical devotion. What is widely ignored, in the focus on Dr. King, is, paradoxically, his Christian training and explicitly Christian commitment. Every student is familiar with the phrase "I have a dream." Not many are familiar with the closing words of his peroration: *". . . and the glory of the Lord shall be revealed, and all flesh shall see it together."* The sermon he

---

* I am indebted to Joseph Marcello, Jr., of Bridgeport, Connecticut, for his critical aid in assembling these data.

preached at the Ebenezer Baptist Church three months before he was killed was selected by friends and family as the sermon to be replayed at his funeral. It closed, "And that's all I want to say. If I can help somebody as I pass along, if I can cheer somebody with a word or song, if I can show somebody he's traveling wrong, then my living will not be in vain. If I can do my duty as a Christian ought, if I can bring salvation to a world once wrought, if I can spread the message as the master taught, then my living will not be in vain."

King's sanctification traces to four features of his life. (1) He was black. (2) He led the civil rights movement. (3) He was a man of great eloquence and great courage. And (4) he was a martyr.

Now those credentials, combined, merit admiration and even devotion. But what is striking, as one ruminates on the great volume of data collected on life in the private schools, is how casually the lights that motivated and inspired Martin Luther King (by his own avowals) are neglected or even ignored, as if he could be wholly detached from them. Thomas More was everything Martin Luther King was, except that his skin was white. He was eloquent, learned, inspiring, hugely courageous, and a martyr. Central to the mythogenic More was his Christian faith. What moved so many about what King had had to say was its ground, not in constitutional exegesis, but in Christian dogma. Equality under the law, in America, has been a focus of constitutional evolution—blacks, women, minors. The Constitution, as everybody knows, implicitly condoned slavery. The approach to equality continues to be progressive. The Thirteenth Amendment abolished slavery, *Plessy v. Ferguson* authorized a prolongation of inequality, *Brown v. Board of Education* reversed Plessy, the Civil Rights Acts parsed equality. The ground of this evolution has been a religiously transcendent view of human beings, in the absence of which the bell curve is king.

In my wanderings in the seventies I spent more than one hour, in more than one encounter, with William Shockley. He was an engaging human being, just a little cuckoo, which did not disqualify him from winning a Nobel Prize for his achievements in electronic science. He was my guest on a *Firing Line* program a dozen years before his death. At the studio, and at subsequent encounters, he plied with enthusiasm his "dysgenic" propositions, which boiled down to this: that Afro-Americans reproduce at a rate faster than Caucasians, but inasmuch as their intelligence is lower, a social objective materializes, namely to reduce their number either by persuading them to submit to sterilization after their second child or by persuading them, in substantial numbers, to leave the country. There were, of course, abundant humane arguments at the disposal of religious agnostics for opposing his line of reasoning, but the argument that struck me and, in my judgment, most Americans as unchallengeable was the postulated equality of all men in the eyes of God.

Young boys and girls, young men and women, crave idealistic engagement, and I thought again, on encountering the new Millbrook School, that the Judeo-Christian tradition—the great moral vehicle of Western idealism—attenuates, in our institutions of learning, for reasons unrelated to the advancement of knowledge. Science has not discredited religious faith. Christianity is as viable in the post-Einstein world as when it first caught fire in the West, the *stupor mundi* that transformed two millennia of men and women who acknowledged God as the generator of human activity at its noblest, from the earliest martyr to Martin Luther King.

The time had come to explore further some of the profundities, and mysteries, of my religion. Time to make an additional effort to understand my faith, and seek out the means to pass along whatever it is that sustains me to those, if any, who can be helped by my exertions.

CHAPTER FOUR

___

On the Evolution

of Christian Doctrine

T ime, then, to open heavy theological doors. Where to start?

When for whatever reason the weather was not right for sports, the boys at St. John's took long walks with one or more priests guiding them. On such excursions talk was encouraged that aimed at inquiring after Catholic practice and doctrine. That was the first time (and very nearly the last) that I heard the word "species" used to describe the bread that would, by the doctrine of concomitance, be transformed into the body of Christ. Up until Vatican II, the great

Council (1962–65) summoned by Pope John XXIII, the communicant was given only the one species—the host—the wine having been reserved since the thirteenth century (with a few, rare exceptions) for the priest. We were taught that the host was equally the body and the blood of Christ, so that when we took the Communion wafer, we were taking both essences, body and blood.

I asked why the change had come about, from bread and wine to just bread (and, now, since Vatican II, back to both, for those communicants who desire both). Fr. Ferguson told me, and I probably only half listened, that there had been many "developments" in Church practice and Church doctrine. I wondered idly how such changes came about. Why this practice today, a different one yesterday, closer to the time of Christ?

To explore these questions thoroughly you'd have to familiarize yourself with many definitions pronounced, one after another, during the first few hundred years after Christ. Almost always these definitions came about as a result of heuristic challenges to current orthodoxy. The Arian heresy, for example, held that Jesus was something other than God. "If God the Son was begotten of the Father, does that not imply that the Father existed before Him?" (The answer to that question, before we move on, is yes, it would seem to imply exactly that.) This contention was held to be mortally dangerous to a correct understanding of the Incarnation and so the Fathers convened for the first General Council, in Nicaea, in the year 325. The consensus was that Christ was consubstantial with the Father, of one substance; and to relay that conclusion the word "homoousian" (from the Greek *homoousios,* "of the same substance") was selected as applying to Christ. In so declaring, the Fathers were confident that no Christian who acknowledged the homoousian nature of Jesus could go on to err about his godhood.

Heresies were grave matters. M. L. Cozens, a historian, notes in her book *Handbook of Heresies* (p. 43) that when the Council met to accost the Nestorian heresy (that Mary was the Mother of Christ, yes, but not the Mother of God), the Council faced the question, deliberated it, made its pronouncement, and when their bishop returned to

Ephesus in Turkey, "the populace received the decision of the Council with the utmost joy. Crowds surged through the streets bearing lights and joyfully acclaiming the honour of the Theotokos: 'Thou, O mother of God, hast destroyed the heresy.'"

The Jews had themselves learned that divine deposits of desiccated Scripture and the practices deriving from them were simply insufficient guides to human conduct. Thou shalt not kill? But the Old Testament enjoins exactly that, ordering killing, here and there: when combating the enemy, executing the criminal, discouraging idolatry. So that just as the Ten Commandments could not comprehensively prescribe moral behavior, neither could the words spoken by Christ or His disciples. Continuing instruction was needed together with the authority to conduct such instruction—the relevant insight. This teaching authority is vested in the "magisterium," the teaching Church. By the term "evolution of Christian doctrine" Catholics understand themselves to be saying *that which is better understood with the passage of time and the crystallization of theological thought.* It is often pointed out, usually with glee by religious skeptics, that Paul adjured the slaves to be faithful to their master. And it is of course correct that Christianity and slavery coexisted for almost two millennia. But how do we account for the perspectives that now so adamantly renounce slavery?

Students have spent lifetimes exploring such questions. In my search for a persuasive crystallization of "How is Christian doctrine evolved?" I was given John Henry Newman to read. I do not pretend to know whether his portraiture is thought imperfect, though it is worth noting that although it was written in 1844–45, it has been formally adopted in a number of documents in the present pontificate. It confirmed what I had prescriptively believed—that revelation and providentially guided reason were responsible for the evolution of doctrine—but did so with a resourcefulness of imagery and analysis I could not match, nor think myself equipped to find fault with. It is as simple as this: Newman satisfies me.

John Henry Newman wrote on the evolution of doctrine *(Essay on the Development of Doctrine,* 1878). He likened the Church to a child and his mother. Early in life the child cannot distinguish intellectually even between his mother and himself. But he can "feel" the bond with her. As he grows he comes to discover his own and his mother's characteristics and later, as he develops his own verbal powers, he can articulate his feelings. Still later he has developed the skills to confute slanders against his mother. So is it with the Church, Newman said. However complete the endowments of Christ, they required development, and this was done in the mind and heart as the child-Church grew. It is Newman's opinion that that process substantially ended with the patristic age, some six hundred years after Christ.

And then Newman believed *(The Prophetical Office of the Church)* that the "great outlines" of the faith were detectable by the "Vincentian Canon" (St. Vincent of Lérins, c. 450), which held (Commonitorium II, 3) that what is true is good and vice versa. *Quod ubique, quod semper, quod ab omnibus creditum est*—what has been believed everywhere, always, and by all.

But there were Anglican theologians in the late eighteenth and early nineteenth centuries who wondered whether the Vincentian Canon was sufficient. Yes, the canon tells us that what is true is good, but it does not tell us everything that is good, or true.

In 1843 Newman wrote a sermon ("The Theory of Development in Religious Doctrine") in which he drew a distinction between "implicit" and "explicit" reason. Implicit reason is the spontaneous interpretation of experience. Explicit reason is the logical analysis of implicit reason. It's an exercise that often results in the elaboration of formal categories and statements. If we train the two forms of reason on the Resurrection, we know that man instinctively ("implicitly") grasps from it wonder and awe. But wonder and awe are different from—are less than—the explicit credal statements that flow from investigation, analysis, and articulation. Explicitly we know now that Christ *fulfilled* prophecies; that He *manifested* His power; that He gave to His disciples *dispositive proof* of His divinity.

The bounties of explicit reason go on. Newman was writing about the evolution of doctrine when he was still an Anglican. He had to face the problem in his own Church: What to do with the difficulty posed by different explications of implicit doctrine? Who is to decide which, within the Anglican Church, will govern? That of course is a hierarchical question, but by what criteria should the wise man be guided?

It was central to Newman's theory of the development of doctrine that one examine an "idea" in a number of aspects. An "idea" has to be examined from multiple perspectives. He calls these "aspects" and writes that an idea is "commensurate" with the sum total of its discernments, so that the idea of the Resurrection takes into account everything, from the view of it by those who most directly experienced it to the view of those who see in it the least and the greatest metaphorical meaning. These perspectives are continuing. Ideas "admit of being walked round and round, surveyed on opposite sides, and in different perspectives, and in contrary light, in evidence of their reality." Newman was a poet, and it is painful to paraphrase him when he has given us a sonnet. "All the aspects of an idea are capable of coalition and of resolution into the object to which it belongs: and the prima facie dissimilitude of its aspects becomes, when explained, an argument for its substantiveness and integrity, and their multiplicity for its originality and power." He is telling us that the thousand insights, trivial and majestic, experienced by peasants and theologians, sinners and saints, do not, in the hands of God's interpreters, result in contradiction. Rather, they fuse into progressively integrated thought.

And for Newman it isn't a sequence, chronological or logical. "First one truth then another is told, then another; but the whole truth or large portions of it [which] are told at once, yet only in rudiments, or in miniature, are expanded and finished in their parts, as the course of revelation proceeds."

What are the features of a "true" development as distinguished from mere accretions, which are finally discarded as heresy?

Newman compresses his considerations into seven categories. These are,

- "Preservation of type"
- "Continuity of principles"
- "Power [authority] to assimilate"

- "Logical sequence"
- "Anticipation of its [the idea's] future"
- "Conservative action upon its past"
- "Chronic vigor"

Consider the doctrine of papal infallibility. Here is what Vatican I affirmed (July 18, 1870, the Dogmatic Constitution on the Church):

> We . . . teach and explain that the dogma has been divinely revealed: that the Roman Pontiff, when he speaks ex cathedra, that is, when carrying out the duty of the pastor and teacher of all Christians in accord with his supreme apostolic authority, he explains a doctrine of the faith or morals to be held by the universal Church, through the divine assistance promised him in blessed Peter, operates with that infallibility with which the divine redeemer wished that His Church be instructed in defining doctrine on faith and morals and so such definitions of the Roman Pontiff from himself, but not from the consensus of the Church, are unalterable.

Let's run that through Newman's seven criteria.

1. *Preservation of type.* Newman is asking that the newly defined doctrine reflect the impact of the earlier form of that doctrine, the purpose of this being to affirm continuity of the whole. Newman leans heavily on the metaphor of physical growth—"the parts and proportions of the developed form, however altered, correspond to those which belong to its rudiments. Small are a baby's limbs, a youth's are larger, yet they are the same." The (finally matured) idea of papal supremacy and infallibility grew over centuries, but its final crystallization, in 1870, reflected—*preserved*—the original investment, the designation of Peter as pastor by Christ. ("Thou art Peter and on this rock I will build my church.") Peter was instructed to "feed my sheep." Successive understandings of the authority of Peter's successors do not alter. Tertullian (d. 225) speaks of the Church "which was built on [Peter]." St. Cyprian (d. 258) wrote that Christ "builds the Church on one person." St. Clement of Alexandria (d. 215) wrote that Peter was "the chosen one, the selected one, the first among the disciples."

And Pope (St.) Leo the Great (d. 461) wrote, "Only Peter was chosen out of the whole world to be head of all called peoples, of all the apostles and all the fathers of the Church." At the Council of Chalcedon (451) Leo's "Tome" was accepted as the classic expression of christological doctrine.

2. *Continuity of principles.* A mature doctrine needs to assert a link to the principle that gave it birth, in this case the principle of papal precedence. "Doctrines stand to principles," said Newman, "as the definition to the axioms and postulates of mathematics." The doctrine of papal infallibility must embody the final fruition of the postulate seeded by Christ.

3. *Power to assimilate.* The papacy, as it developed, assimilated a great deal from the secular sphere. The idea evolved, for instance, of the "Pontifex Maximus"—the maximum bridge builder—the old title of the Emperor, who bridged the gap between Heaven and earth. Experience bared the need for a central authority to rule on thorny ecclesiastical and theological issues. The assimilation, evaluation, and enunciation of the views and the learning and the exploration of fellow bishops, theologians, and even the faithful became more and more obviously something that was required.

It is not surprising that theological authority found itself extended beyond its necessary boundaries. The papacy, in its experimentation, extended itself to the point of exercising power in purely secular matters, hence the papal states and the warrior Popes. The nature of the Church's authority went to malformation, extending to the secular hubris of supposing that it could depose monarchs (Pius V informed Queen Elizabeth that she was no longer Queen of England). But it retreated, coalescing today in the Vatican city-state. So the "idea"—Newman's anchor word—of the papacy continued to assimilate, discarding this, incorporating that—from medieval concepts to modern ones—but doing no violence to principles and doctrine defined along the way.

4. *Logical sequence.* It is not here intended, said Newman, that a syllogistic extension is always in the offing. But related movements in thought must be logically executed, and the need soon transpired for a

doctrinal authority—indeed, this was so from the moment of the Ascension. The successors to Peter exercised their authority in virtue of the antecedent authority of Peter. When necessary they could, and did, expatiate on the deposit of the faith, and did so without error, leading, logically, to the perception and then articulation of infallibility.

5. *Anticipation of the idea's future.* Faith in papal infallibility in matters of doctrine was implicit in the obedience paid to him over the centuries by his bishops. His infallibility was an act of implicit reason made explicit with the enunciation of infallibility.

6. *Conservative action upon its past.* The enhanced understanding of doctrine necessarily rests on conserving the past that generated it. What exactly did Jesus mean when He spoke to Peter of the "rock"? What does the authority He conferred mean, exactly—that authority to "bind" and to "loose"? What is required to explain the mandate to "feed his sheep" and "tend his flock"? The answers—that the rock was Peter and his successors, and that they had authority to absolve from sin and to govern the Church—haven't substantially changed since they were reified by St. Leo (440–61) and Gregory the Great (590–604), even if there have been instances of exaggeration or abuse, as when Popes thought themselves empowered to discharge temporal rulers.

7. *Chronic vigor.* The emphasis placed on the papacy at Vatican I reflects a vigor in the institution that does not appear to wither. Thomas Macaulay died before Vatican I, but his line on the vigor of the Church would appear to apply alike to the papacy. He said of the Church, "She may still exist in undiminished vigor when some traveler from New Zealand shall, in the midst of a vast solitude, take his stand on a broken arch of London Bridge to sketch the ruins of St. Paul's."

Ultimately, Newman concluded, one needs to judge the question whether a doctrine has been developed by appeal to authority. "A revelation is not given, if there be no authority to decide what it is that is given." Without such authority one merely gets (whether in the Church of England or in the Catholic Church) "a comprehension of opinions," a "hollow uniformity."

In the travail of his struggle, Newman found the authority that forever after satisfied him. "There is but one Voice for whose decisions the people wait with trust, one Name and one See to which they look with hope, and that name Peter, and that See Rome."

CHAPTER FIVE

The Never-Ending Debate.

The ''Difficulties'' of Arnold Lunn

I had some satisfaction from Newman on the evolution of doctrine and hoped now to review some of the great controversies over Christianity, some of these continuously at war, some resting in the DMZ. I don't remember ever seeking out Catholic company at Yale, or after Yale, as a matter of fact, primarily for the sake of theological exchanges or religious camaraderie. The most influential professor at Yale—on me—was Willmoore Kendall. Although he was the son of a Methodist preacher, when I met him he was a religious agnostic. We became very close friends. And then a few years after I graduated he told me that he intended to convert to Catholicism and asked me to stand in as his godfather.

But although we spent many hours together (he moonlighted for two years as a senior editor of *National Review*) and corresponded regularly up until he precipitated an estrangement in 1961 ("Willmoore makes it a point not to have more than one friend at a time," was the commonly heard wisecrack about him), there was little grist in our exchanges to fuel religious curiosity or to bring on talk about religious questions. He taught me a great deal by his discursive reflections (Willmoore thought out loud and was a very great teacher) on how to view Catholicism from the eyes of an outsider.

In a vague kind of way I always thought of myself as surrounded by Catholics, though, as related, I went to other than Catholic schools after my year in England. I wooed and married an Episcopalian. In later years, Mrs. Kathleen "Babe" Taylor—my wife Pat's mother— became an intimate friend. She had been civil and attentive on learning that her popular, beauteous daughter (who was Miss Vancouver back then) had become engaged to me. It hurt her pride that Pat would be marrying a Catholic. Babe Taylor was born in Manitoba of parents who were Irish Protestants from Kilkenny, in the Irish Republic. Her parents were dead when I became engaged but they had left with their daughter a heavy deposit of Protestant pride. Babe now faced the second of her two daughters marrying a Catholic. Before World War II, Pat's older sister had married a Catholic Californian. That had been the first religious affront to Mrs. Taylor, who was in those days perhaps the premier hostess in British Columbia. I would learn that the first wedding, in Vancouver, had been performed by a Protestant minister. The bride and groom then traveled to Los Angeles (his home) on a Pullman sleeper and did not consummate their marriage until after a priest had performed a second ceremony. It is worth noting that a "priest" does not marry a bride and groom: he witnesses their exchange of vows.

The negotiations between Babe and me were pretty strenuous, as I thought it wrong to be even ostensibly married by a minister not of my own faith. The negotiations, in hindsight, were amusing. Vancouver's Catholics were presided over by a crusty old bishop who devoted much of his energy to alienating non-Catholics, and in doing so managed to alienate a great many Catholics. The bishop had decreed that any Catholic marrying outside the faith could do so only in the sacristy of a Catholic church, not in the church itself. The idea of excluding from the ceremony Babe and Pat's one thousand best friends was simply inconceivable, and for a little while, owing to these complications, our wedding date was in abeyance. My father came up with an impish plan, which was to import from Camden, South Carolina, the parish priest there, a beloved and humorous man. Ask *him,* unbound by the Vancouver bishop's jurisdiction, to do the wedding. Fr. Burke looked into that possibility and of course learned that it was a violation of diocesan rules for *any* priest to perform a marriage without the consent of the bishop.

"What would happen if you went ahead and performed the marriage?" Father asked him.

"Well, I guess I'd be reprimanded."

"Well," said my resourceful father, "couldn't you just tell the bishop that you're sorry—and will never again perform a marriage in Vancouver without permission?"

It was too neat, of course; and subjectively deceitful, and so the stratagem was abandoned. At about then, thanks to the good offices of someone—I can't remember who—the Vancouver bishop relented, authorizing a full-scale church wedding. After it, at the wedding reception at Babe's splendid mansion, the Protestant minister pronounced a blessing on the bride and groom, an intercredal civility entirely in order and welcome.

We raised our son as a Catholic, but I never exerted pressure on my wife to join the Church, which she has not done. Perhaps it was owing to my background that I never felt religious loneliness. Perhaps, too, I have been sustained over the years by steadfast temperamental inclinations, in matters religious and ideological. When I wrote *God and Man at Yale,* among other things singling out the antireligious bias there, I had been careful, as suggested above, to define Christianity in language used by an undeniable Protestant theologian, addressing an organization at Yale only months before I wrote. Reinhold Niebuhr had said, "Christian faith stands or falls on the proposition that a character named Jesus, in a particular place at a particular time in history, is more than a man in history but is a revelation of the mystery of self and of the ultimate mystery of existence." Niebuhr had not gone on, in that paper/sermon, to engage in apologetics, i.e., in a formal defense of Christian dogma. I did not hear this done, while at Yale, other than at my own church, in Sunday homilies.

It wasn't until I met Arnold Lunn that the world of Christian apologetics caught my eye. When in 1960 I was preparing an agenda for the celebration of *National Review*'s fifth birthday, I found myself talking over the telephone with a very British-voiced man who told me he was in New York, though he lived in Switzerland, where he received *National Review* enthusiastically. If I wished him to do so, he said, he would happily pronounce a five-minute benediction at our fifth-anniversary party given from a European perspective. He went on to do this, with captivating wit.

In 1959 I initiated what became a habit, to spend two winter months in Switzerland to write books and ski. My wife and I have lived ever since then in the area of Gstaad, one hour and a half by car and funicular from Mürren, where Arnold Lunn and his wife, Phyllis, lived. We visited with them every year until his death in 1974.

When we first went to Mürren, Lunn was working on his fiftieth book, if memory serves (his last book, his fifty-fourth, he dedicated to Pat and me). About a third of his books dealt with mountaineering, one-third with skiing (Lunn invented the slalom, indeed the whole idea of skiing holidays), an exciting one-third with religion.

Lunn stood about five feet ten inches. His hair was thick, unruly, and white. His face was a totally weather-beaten red, his eyeglasses slightly obscuring brown, drowsy eyes. He spoke with animation and laughed a cackly laugh after every sentence or two, almost always provoking in his listeners similar laughter. He had been an agnostic into early middle age, but a religious curiosity induced him to do extensive reading. It reached high tide in 1932, when he persuaded the renowned and scholarly British Catholic convert Ronald Knox to explore with him what Lunn designated as the "difficulties" that stood between him and Catholicism; indeed, in some areas, between him and Christianity.

By then Lunn was a fellow-traveling Christian, as I think he'd have agreed to be called, not a practicing Christian or an avowed Christian. He was anxious to level specific objections to Christian dogma, and especially to Catholic presumption.

Ronald Knox was then a Catholic priest. He had joined the Church while serving as Anglican chaplain at Oxford, becoming now chaplain to Catholic students. The itinerary of Knox was startlingly similar to that in the mid-nineteenth century of John Henry Newman. Both were star undergraduate scholars. Both received holy orders in the Anglican Church, resided in Oxford, and taught and preached to students; both wrote deep philosophical tracts, converted to Catholicism, and did further duty at Oxford.

Knox, like Newman, was an intellectual luminary. After he "poped,"* as the English when in a hurry call conversion to the Catholic Church, he increased the volume of his publications, and now consented to engage Arnold Lunn.

Arnold was the first person I ever knew who brought up theological questions in conversation, managing always to make them every bit as interesting as whatever else he had been discussing—most often, world affairs. I cannot say that our friendship caused me to turn to a serious examination of theology—that I have never done. But Lunn stirred in me a sense of the liveliness of the exploration of dogma. I remember hearing from Vladimir Nabokov his enthusiasm for the game of Scrabble, which he played using the Russian alphabet. In somewhat the same spirit, Lunn exercised his analytical skills, giving them over to the construction of great religious ideas. From the exercise itself he drew a measure of satisfaction, but he did not lose sight

---

* *OED:* "1608 H. Clapham *Errour Left Hand:* "Are you now ready to go apoping? . . . I had thought there had bin many grounds that would have kept you from poping."

of the purpose of it all and during his lifetime he had such satisfaction as the Scrabble player would have had on learning that the answer to the conundrum was God.

It was when I agreed to write about my religion that I took what, by my measure, was a formal step. I pulled out and very carefully read *Difficulties: A Correspondence About the Catholic Religion Between Msgr. Ronald Knox & Sir Arnold Lunn,* published in 1934 by Sheed and Ward. It has served for me an exhilarating purpose, namely to observe two heavyweight polemicists contend on Catholic Christianity. And then, too, the editorial formula was fine for me: Objection, Reply. The volume has slipped from regular use, and even from the memory of younger people, but it is not anachronized, though it takes on some questions that no longer vex the religiously curious.

Lunn would state his difficulty in anything from four to eight pages and argue strenuously its cogency. Weeks later Knox, learned, sinuous, tethered by his formal commitment (gladly tendered) to the Church, would reply. Lunn would go on to another difficulty. There were some breathtaking analytic highlights in the exchange, and the contenders were well matched. Even granting the singular firepower of Lunn/Knox, one wonders why exchanges in that mode are so infrequent.

I am aware that it is not essential to dissect religious faith, no more than patriotism or love. The illiterate who believes and is sustained by his faith is as airborne as Thomas Aquinas after completing his Questions. But after a session or two with Lunn/Knox I could understand why the town of Ephesus, as noted, went mad with joy seventeen hundred years ago when Mary was declared by the Council of Ephesus (431) to have been the Mother of God, not merely the Mother of Jesus. You would have thought Ephesus had won the Super Bowl.

. . .

It wasn't that long ago, 1934. Even so, that's far enough away to demonstrate that some of the objections Lunn had (and some of the answers Knox came up with) reveal shifting theological emphases. There would be no arguments today over "indulgences" (reprieves from penance). Alleged traffic in indulgences incensed Martin Luther. They are mentioned below in order to recapture an animating subject just one-half century ago.

What *were* Lunn's difficulties?

They do not surprise the contemporary reader who ponders the Christian proposition. I'll be staring the Crucifixion in the face later on. It is after all the heartbeat of Christianity. But even for Christians, who accept the risen Christ, there are residual itches. It was less than an eternity ago that I was a student at college and every now and again, even in banter, would run into such questions as Lunn posed to Knox.

In those days, immediately after World War II, skeptics and atheists were a pretty energetic breed, feeling the need to evangelize their skepticisms every bit as keenly as Christian evangelists felt a need to propagate the faith. Here and there one still hears, or more often, hears about, objections put to Christian doctrine. Most of this is gone, leaving mostly arguments about birth control and abortion to trigger religious dispute. Mostly one hears nothing. Expressed disbelief is preferable to the lacerating disdain of utter disregard. When nobody took the pains to demonstrate that the earth was in fact round, the flat-earthers knew they had lost the argument.

What keeps Christians afloat is the buoyant knowledge that no devastating damage has in fact been done to Christian doctrine. Contemporary disregard isn't dialectical confirmation that nothing more need be said to establish the emptiness of the Christian creed. The problem, I think, is the quite general ignorance of Christian thought and an absence of curiosity about it. If the Big Bang theory of the origin of the universe were only one of competing postulates, hotly defended, hotly denied—on the order of the division over the divine right of kings in the eighteenth century—apostles of the Big Bang would not think it safe to ignore the contrarians.

Although the "women's issues"—birth control, abortion, the ordination of women—take up most of the time in contemporary religious discussion, they do not figure in the Lunn-Knox exchanges for the obvious reason that the questions were not then preoccupying. What did enter into the argument, and still does, is the question of hierarchy, and of doctrinal authority. So, finally, we draw the curtains. Lunn wants some answers on—

1 . *The Question of Imperfect Leaders*

The first difficulty raised by Lunn was, Just where do Catholics get off claiming theirs to be the one true Church, founded by Christ and presumably guided by Him, given the awful history of the Church? Consider only the monstrous people who have at one time or another headed it. Murderers, fornicators, torturers . . .

The indictment isn't hard to make. One has only to describe the life of Pope Alexander VI. But then of course the question becomes: Christ was responsible, yes, for the selection of Peter. Is He responsible for the selection of Peter's successors?

Knox answers pretty much as one would expect. He can't find any responsible Catholic source that claims any special immunities for cardinals or Popes. They are simply people who pursued a religious calling and were elevated in the hierarchy. They were not, for that reason, spared workaday temptations. If Judas Iscariot could have been accepted as one of Christ's twelve Disciples, then Alexander VI could serve as Pope. What the Church does indeed aver is that the man who is elected Pope will not, in matters that have to do with defining as a part of the deposit of faith a matter of doctrine or morals, *mistake the will of God*. The sinfulness of an Alexander VI did not disqualify him from the exercise of priestly or even ministerial authority. Popes and bishops are to be formally obeyed when they exercise their offices.*

Knox never suggested that a divine trip wire disables a sinful priest—or Pope. But, he coached Lunn, whatever the prelate's personal failings, when he consecrates the Host, or when he absolves from sin, that Host is consecrated, the sin forgiven.

Protestants tend to think in terms of a community of the elect who stand together to protect their churches, protected from infirm policies by their peers. That position appears less vulnerable than the Catholic acceptance of a single leader, infallible in matters of faith and morals. Yet a company of men and women is subject to fits of passion, vulnerable to demands of fashion. What the Protestant churches cannot claim, Knox argues, is any direct, historical link to Christ, who through Peter founded not many churches, but a single Church. And although the Church's Popes were sometimes wayward, the assumption that they were regularly venal, let alone consistently venal, is high exaggeration. ("How many bad Popes have there been since the Council of Trent?" Knox asks.)

Lunn drew attention to what he deemed the greater sensitivity of Protestants to venal or sinful leaders of their own churches. They are quicker, he insisted, to be scandalized by scandalous behavior; whereas when *their* spokesmen are exposed as sinful, Catholics tend to shrug the matter off as just one more pedestrian experience in a sinful world.

I lingered, from recent American experience, on the point. There was the public scandal of the Protestant television preacher who built himself castles from offerings sent in by devout viewers. For sundry sins he was exposed and sent to prison. By contrast, Catholic bishops, in the early nineties, kept silent the terrible scandals in the United States involving priests and pedophilia. The sluggish reaction of the

---

* I recall that Cardinal Segura of Seville grew pottier as he grew older and toward the end, in the early 1950s, threatened excommunication for anyone who engaged in dancing. Visiting Seville, I asked a pious Spanish guide what life was like now that the cardinal had died. She replied in lyrical Castilian, "When Cardinal Segura died, he, and we, passed on to a better world." Evelyn Waugh, in an article on what he wished for from Vatican II, discussed in chapter 6, singled out as overdue a more exact prescription of the authority of bishops. He might have had Cardinal Segura in mind.

bishops had the effect not only of magnifying the scandal when finally it broke but of keeping one or more of the priests in question in a parsonage rather than in jail or in a psychiatric hospital.

But the record would seem to confirm that perversion is inter-credal. And the contempt trained on the Protestant television preacher wasn't exactly a discipline imposed by his colleagues. The preacher in question lived in the public eye and died by the sword. The perverted priests practiced away from the cameras.

Surely it is the case that a sin of the flesh is less terrifying than a sin of doctrine by which we hope to be guided. If ever a Pope were to pronounce something as true that contradicted the *depositum fidei*—the deposit of the faith—then the inconceivable would indeed have happened, and the very believability of the Church would collapse even as it would collapse if an ancient Zapruder came up with a film of Christ stage-managing His resurrection.

Knox leaves it this way: the confidence of the Catholic is reinforced by the knowledge that such a thing will not happen, even as it has not happened—neither a Pope denying God nor credible evidence that Christ did not rise again. The Protestants are hostage to the schisms and heresies from which, the Catholic necessarily concludes, they have suffered.

The "difficulty" that most arrested me, pondering Arnold Lunn's list, was—is—the doctrine of divine omniscience alongside the doctrine of free will. Christians have to believe in free will, else eternal life cannot be earned, or forfeited. The theologian John Wesley dismissed the problem—the irreconcilability of God's knowing what will happen, and your and my free will to act—as quite simply insoluble. "If anyone asks, 'How is God's foreknowledge consistent with freedom?' I must plainly answer, 'I cannot tell.' " Nor, said Lunn, tossing the matter in the lap of Ronald Knox, "can anyone else."

Fr. Knox impressed me with three insights. They are unrelated and yet I view all three as primal, especially appealing. The first teases out of all of us who have pondered this mystery of Christianity something we'd almost certainly not have volunteered. I certainly would not have thought of it save for the searchlight of Ronald Knox into the secrets of our minds: namely, our inner conviction that if we had been given the job of creating the world, we'd have done the whole thing better. Knox borrows the formulation of Protestant Bishop Joseph B. Butler (1692–1752) in his *Analogy (The Analogy of Religion, Natural and Revealed, to the Constitution and Course of Nature,* 1736, p. 52). *"I do not think there is any getting over the force of Butler's argument in the* Analogy, *that if we had been set down to build this world according to our own specifications, it would not have been the world as we know it."*

It is amazing to me what the Butler Escape, as I'll refer to it, does. This singular invitation to imagine the world as reordered by *you*. (No rock music, say.) But to disport with Butler at any length is to experience the awful thinness of the air at the summit of Hubris. We climb down from that mountain and find ourselves face-to-face with only two alternatives: reject the Christianity that asserts the unwelcome doctrine; or accept Christianity, irrespective of our incapacity to understand, or our disinclination to approve of, this or that doctrine.

A second insight is that while many thinkers prefer vagueness to mystery, he, Knox, does not; and neither does the Church. Knox would prefer to believe in the infallibility of the Pope than to wonder whether he is infallible. When he accepted the Catholic faith, his principal reservation was the existence of Hell. He came to believe in Hell not because he suddenly, or gradually, discovered its inevitability in the Christian cosmology, but because he deferred—without reservation—to the ''wisdom'' of the Church.

The third is the insight that demands that we accept the implications of infinity. ''Unless you are prepared to admit that God's omnipotence is drastically limited by the nature of things, there is no escape from the old dilemma: 'If God is all-good He will not tolerate the existence of evil, and if God is all-powerful He will not permit the existence of evil.' '' On this point Lunn was unwilling to give ground: these are irreconcilable attributes, to be at once omnipotent and all-good, in a world in which evil is pandemic.

So what does the inquirer do?

MENU

Grapefruit au Port

Whiting

Egg Sauce   Crèmed potatoes

Pork Chops

Chips   Greens   Diced Roots

Cabinet Puddings

Jam   Custard

Savoury Biscuits

Pears   Tea   Coffee

"... I do not think there is any getting over the force of
Butler's argument, that if we had been set down to build this world
according to our own specifications, it would not have been the
world as we know it."

Cocktailetto

"Cote d'Azur" apéritif substitute. Pharma-
ceutically bottled. Officially classified as non-
poisonous.

Château Malsain-les-Odeurs, 1940

Dernier Cru. From the cellars of the Station
Hotel, Burslem

MacStingus' Tawny Wine (Port Flavour)

What I do is accept—or try to—the burden of a finite mind incapable of comprehending an apparent paradox, which I accept as other than the forbidden exercise in formal contradiction (something cannot *be* and *not be*). The challenge remains to discover a perch from which the perspectives permit an understanding of a God that cannot (will not?) heed His own impulses to discreate evil.

The dispute on this point provoked Fr. Knox to his most severe polemical ultimatum. As a polemicist, Knox was suave but also granitic. By reputation he was the soul of courtesy. I found his handling of Lunn, on this point, abrupt. Knox formulated his position and then called an end to the exchange: "I think the point of our difference may be expressed thus. You will not go with me to worship a God who is limited by nothing outside Himself, because you do not think that He exists. And I will not go with you to worship a God who is limited by anything outside Himself, because I do not care a rap whether He exists or not." Knox, in one way of looking at it, was not going to let God off (e.g., for permitting pain). What he declined to do was to reconcile, or attempt to, that which, on the plane of human perspectives, can't be done; or, at least, has not been done.

On studying Knox, whose voice in the matter is that of all his thinking colleagues, I began to understand. Pain has got to be looked at as something tolerated by God and *for that reason alone* understandable.

Even if reasonable men agree that the Christian can legitimately abandon to divine perspectives the problem of paradoxes impenetrable on earth, the burden on Christian reason is not eliminated. Even if we agree that philosophical analysis can proceed on another plane than that within which the human mind is immured, there are nevertheless rules to be observed. One of these is the law of contradiction, already noticed. God cannot make a circle square. He cannot decree that an object identical to another object is also different from it.

If we acknowledge another plane of thought than the plane within which we are confined, does it follow that the Christian is denying reason? Is the assumption of a second plane of thought a reasonable retreat when we ask, How can it be that God knows what we will do tomorrow even as we are genuinely free to make up our own minds what to do tomorrow and wait until then to decide? Is this duality an act against reason? Christian theology holds that the believer is never required to believe anything that contradicts reason *within the postulates of Christian faith*. (A miracle is certainly not a reasonable event, let alone the Resurrection, or the Virgin Birth, or the trinitarian unity of God.) How, then, does reason countenance the God who is at once omnipotent and all-good, and yet the licensor of evil?

We need to postulate the coexistence of the two by asserting that there is no nexus between them, but I do not see that we can go further. We assert the different perspectives, but we do not provide scaffolding for them in human reason. We are left with a God the infinity of whose attributes permits Him what in more modest circumstances we would classify as this "liberty"—to ordain for Himself freedom from the iron consequences of paradox. Yet in agreeing that such a God can do such things I am engaged in an act of faith but not in an act of unreason. If Christ was that Son of God which explicitly He told His disciples He was, making their faith in His believability relatively easy by performing miracles in their presence, then they could "reason" to the apparent irreconcilabilities. Christ not only knew that Peter would disavow Him, He *told* Peter that he would disavow Him. Did Christ's foreknowledge deprive Peter of his power to tell the truth to the bystanders in Jerusalem—that indeed Peter was an apostle? Peter knew even as he made his disavowal that he was not being propelled by fate, but by cowardice. An early encounter with the two planes of thought.

Intervals between the two correspondents went for as long as several months. In 1931 Ronald Knox was serving as chaplain to Catholic students at Oxford, which he would continue to do until 1939, when he resigned, took a deep breath, and began to retranslate the Bible. Arnold Lunn had fewer preoccupations and, as we see, was much excited by his search for the Achilles' heel of Catholic Christianity. The subject turned now to familiar anti-Catholic territory.

2. What About the Inquisition, and Slavery?

The Inquisition, said Lunn, was a *Catholic* phenomenon and there is no excuse for its longevity or for the severity of its practices. How is it that the resulting shame doesn't bring Knox to question whether the Church that tolerated the Inquisition and the practice of slavery (to be sure, near universal) over such a lengthy period can have been the Church Christ intended?

Lunn proceeded with gusto. His detailing of inquisitorial practices was done in the manner of a prosecuting attorney making a closing statement to the jury. He describes in (fair) detail the practices of the inquisitors. The torture, the trials, the secret testimony. All the machinery of the Inquisition, he says, was geared around the proposition that it was preferable that ninety-nine believing Catholics should be put to death than that a single heretic should escape death. In due course, granted, the Inquisition itself died. And it is not an unimportant historical point that the Inquisition was a state policy (1479–1820), done, to be sure, with ecclesial collusion. But when it was abandoned, this came about not so much at the prompting of a Church set on reform as at the prompting of a civilized world progressively indignant, even revolted by, practices which, finally, the Catholic Church abandoned.

As much is true, Lunn said, of other indefensible human practices, most conspicuously slavery. What does one say about a Church that was not in the social vanguard in condemning slavery? Lunn said he hadn't been able to come up with a single Church document that threatened excommunication of any official who was instrumental in persecuting a citizen for the crime of manumitting his slaves. In brief, said Lunn, everyone acknowledges—including, for instance, Henry Cardinal Manning, who lived during the period—that the great agents of emancipation were non-Catholics. "Baccaria, the Italian disciple of Rousseau, in his attack on torture inspired the Empress of Russia and Frederick of Prussia to banish torture from their dominions. The lash

of Voltaire's invective broke down the crumbling defences of the Inquisition, and it was largely as the result of his campaign that the rack
and stake vanished from Europe." There isn't one prominent Catholic
name in all the literature of emancipation, summarizes Lunn, and he
asks, How can one account for this moral blindness?

Knox begins his answer by repeating in a most philosophical mode
that we have here two more instances of the world behaving in ways
other than we'd like the world to have behaved. He scores heavily with
me by recalling that when St. Thomas Aquinas was finished proving
the existence of God, he proceeded to list in some detail objections to
a belief in the existence of God (human suffering, etc.). He listed
these objections without any attempt to confute them. Why?

Because he had *already* established the existence of God. He was
finished with that task. If God is a given, then other data are arranged
around that given. However disorderly they may appear, however dis-
ruptive, they cannot subvert the animating axiom of philosophical
exploration, in this case that: *God is*. Thomas had undertaken to make
that proof. His arguments were, in his judgment and that of distinguished thinkers living and dead, dispositive. So that any further work
on the subject would be supererogation, disrespectful, so to speak, of
work already done, which work could not be undone. So that all else
became ancillary.

Yes, the fact of it is: The Inquisition *was*. Slavery *was*. And the
Church *is* divine. Struggle then with the Inquisition, struggle to understand why something more was not done about slavery: but do not
let your curiosity about such moral sluggishness subvert the postulate,
which is that God is, and that His Church is the Church of Christ,
divine.

I find myself thinking about Marxism as an analogue. There were
bitter-enders who, even after the Stalin purges—even after the Gulag
archipelago—used such reasoning: Marxism is historically and philo-
sophically correct. Accordingly, one cannot permit the disagreeable,
even offensive detritus of an evolving historical cosmology to interfere
with the initial postulate. It is that historical determinism and the class
struggle are the determining forces of history: Marxism.

It is here of course that the Christian can rely on singular data, historical and philosophical, that Marxism could never adduce. Karl Marx never wrought miracles, and the furious tensions and countertensions of his exegetes foundered over empirical data. To the extent that loyalists to Marx, Engels, Lenin, and Stalin were guided by faith in the founders, they were engaged in heliocentrism without an enduring sun. The incidence of slavery did not invalidate Christ's love of all men, nor the commandment to love one's neighbor as oneself. Surviving criteria of right reason and right conduct reinforce biblical injunctions, but leave Marx dispossessed.

Even so I wondered whether Fr. Knox was having a real problem. In a sense I still do wonder, however admirable the philosophical tightness of his argument. I try to understand. *Whatever my son does, he is in fact my son.* (This is me talking, not Knox.) *He was taught not to do A, B, and C. Even so, he went on to do A, B, and C.* From this, however (Knox is saying), you cannot glibly conclude that therefore he cannot have been my son. He continues to be my son, and our curiosity is therefore confined to wondering *why* he did what he did, not to questioning whether, having done so, he can still claim to be my son.

On slavery, Knox finds himself saying that though William Wilber-force was an Anglican, it can hardly be said that Anglicanism outlawed slavery, no more than that because Louis Pasteur was a Catholic, it could be said that the Vatican conquered hydrophobia. But on the larger matter I close by asking to what extent were the Popes morally responsible for inquisitorial practices and for the toleration of slavery? The answer: the Popes in question were responsible for their failure to apply right reason in condemning these practices. Their apparent indifference to slavery was a sign of moral torpor one would have hoped not to see in men elevated to the highest moral post in Christendom.

What should be resisted is the planted axiom of many devoted children of God, namely that mere exposure to Christian teaching automatically translates to Christian practice. On this point G. K. Chesterton is illuminating. In several of his works he defends dogma by asking where might we have been but for such lapidary postulates as dogma gives us concerning the uniqueness of the individual human being and his obligations under God to his fellowman. Imagine the fate of slavery and of the Inquisition in a moral vacuum in which the magnetic reach of Christianity was unfelt. Mightn't it be said that, but for Christianity, there is reason to wonder whether slavery would even *now* be extinct in the Christian world? And that whatever the historical slowness of its reflexes, the stability of Catholic-dominated Christianity continues to be central to the moral health and prospects of the human race?

3. Can We Believe in Eternal Punishment?

Lunn was on no subject more exercised than on the matter of eternal punishment, though here he was quarreling not so specifically with Rome: Christians in general, if guided by Scripture, believe in "eternal punishment."

Lunn makes the case that responsible Catholic scholars have insisted that "Hell" is exactly that, perpetuity in torment, most frequently described as eternal fire.

What this amounts to, he insisted, is everlasting torture. How can such a concept be assimilated by minds attuned to civilized contexts? We can excuse torture as routinely inflicted by our ancestors only on the grounds that they were living in an unenlightened age. Yet Christianity asks us to believe that God created men and women who He knew at the time He created them will die in a state of mortal sin and will therefore suffer pain everlasting. Lunn quotes John Stuart Mill: "Compared with the doctrine of endless torment, every objection to Christianity sinks into insignificance." Lunn believed in punishment; believed, even, in Purgatory. But he wanted to know about the Scriptures by which the Church is guided on the matter of Hell.*

---

* I once quoted the author Ralph de Toledano, whose editor lowercased the word "Hell" in a novel, which the author recapitalized on reviewing the editor's draft. "Why do you want to

There are two kinds of confession, he recalls from his reading in Catholic doctrine. "Perfect contrition" is defined as "sorrow for sin arising wholly from one's love of God." Perfect contrition was once believed to absolve the sinner even without the sanctifying medium of the sacrament of confession. "Imperfect contrition" is something less. It is defined as "sorrow for our sins because by them we have lost Heaven and deserved Hell." Imperfect contrition, Lunn accosted Knox, "according to the Penny Catechism is sufficient when we go to confession" to receive absolution. But the Council of Trent (1545–63) declared that perfect contrition cannot suffice to justify the sinner. He must experience the salvific sacrament of penance.

Lunn planted several hypothetical cases, which I boil down:

Case 1. A Roman Catholic, living in Africa, falls into mortal sin. He contracts a terminal disease. He performs an act of contrition, but it is imperfect because there is no priest around who can hear his confession. He goes to Hell.

Case 2. Situation identical, but at the last minute an airplane drops down with a priest in it who hears his confession—and now the man goes to Heaven. The future of two souls is determined by an accident, not by any scale of justice or of merit.

Case 3. A young R.C., a harmless man of amiable disposition, decides to play golf on Sunday, instead of going to church. On the way home he is run down by a bus and killed: he goes to Hell.

Case 4. Bluebeard tortured and then murdered small children. He is apprehended, makes a full confession, indeed goes so far as to keep a priest by his side until he is safely hanged. He will suffer Purgatory, but he will end in Heaven, while the golfer and the poor man in the African wilds will not.

Arnold Lunn's summary: (1) I object to God being represented as a torturer. (2) I object to any form of punishment which is eternal. (3) I object to the fact that a man's eternal destiny depends less on "striking a due balance between his virtues and his sins than on the pure accident of what takes place during the last moments of his life."

---

capitalize hell?" the editor asked. "Because," Toledano replied, "it's a place. You know, like Scarsdale." The Scriptures make the point.

Knox acknowledges that when he was himself received into the Church, the problem of eternal punishment was the single difficulty still on his conscience; i.e., he was uneasy about accepting it as doctrine.

It is natural, Knox observes, that Lunn should worry on the point. But to have submitted to authority, as Knox has done, consolidates his thought, and much then becomes thinkable which wasn't thinkable before.

Knox then argues on the basis of what is and what isn't generally accepted in civilized society. The very idea of eternal punishment is not rejected by the moral instincts of most people. Life imprisonment is human eternity, and is today increasingly popular. Many think eternal punishment is logically implied: the Church is expected to be unforgiving about a violation, unrepented, of its codes of behavior. Knox undertakes to establish that whatever Lunn's own instincts in the matter, eternal punishment is not contrary to reason.

Begin, Knox "suggests" (he is—mostly—courteous in manner), with objective perspectives. For instance, we see in the world around us pain inflicted by nature on human beings that we would not ourselves willingly inflict. This fact alone should serve to remind us that there are different scales at work in our examination of human and divine phenomenology.

We are dealing with a world in which infinities are present, one of them the majesty of God. It ought not to surprise us that an offense against that majesty should be infinite in its consequences.

The Bible tells us, Knox reminded Lunn, that "the fires of Hell are not merely a metaphor." Knox is telling us that there is *reason* to believe in eternal punishment, never mind that it is something that (availing ourselves of the Butler Escape) we ourselves would not have prescribed.

But having now discharged his formal responsibilities, Knox offers a few "suasions."

In his own case, he feels this: that what God has given him is so manifestly prodigious, Knox can't think of any punishment that would be excessive "if I were to turn my back on Him and live in defiance of His laws."

And then, too, eternal punishment provides a kind of symmetry to the Christian edifice, which deals, after all, with eternal life and with atonement. Oughtn't eternal punishment also to be there? Granted, the Church might have taught that what befalls the unrepentant sinner is simply the annihilation of the soul: that accommodation would have given us a dimension satisfactory to eschatological thought, yet finite in rejecting eternal life with enduring pain.*

But the Church did not do so, and that it did not do so is, for Knox, conclusive. Moreover, the prospect of eternal punishment is important in that it serves also to remind us that Heaven is not had for the asking, which is the way we would tend to go if we assumed that God's mercy would always intervene between the sinner and eternal punishment.

And as to intervention and such hypothetical episodes as Lunn had listed, there is simply no way of knowing why or when God will exercise that power of intervention. For instance: St. Paul might well have been killed by a stone meant for St. Stephen. God decided otherwise. But if one assumes that God must be guided only by the kind of reason known to us, then mercy "ceases to be gratuitous," becomes instead a "fresh kind of justice." You would replace a supreme Personality by a kind "supernatural checking machine."

Moreover, we can't know that the golfer, e.g., would in fact have repented; and then isn't it possible that the sheer triviality of the obligation he was forswearing by playing golf rather than spending the hour in church makes his offense more painful to God and therefore more grave than a sin to which he was driven by a temptation that overwhelmed him?

As ever, Lunn fought back vigorously. He began by saying that his rejection of eternal punishment had nothing to do with his difficulties

---

* I am informed that Hans Urs von Balthasar, much revered by John Paul II, who made him a cardinal, opines that there are good biblical grounds for *hoping* that Hell is empty.

about Catholic authority. He, Lunn, had no intrinsic problem with the idea of authority. Indeed he would be willing to accept doctrines to which he is not naturally drawn (e.g., the Immaculate Conception or transubstantiation) purely on the authority of the Church to decide such questions. But it is different with the question of eternal punishment in Hell. His rejection of it represents a deep-seated fundamental conviction—"My disbelief in eternal torture is stronger than my belief in God."

He asked Knox to look about him at the world (in the early thirties). Consider, for instance, the question of cohabitation. The religious prejudices against this are all but atrophied. And the very idea that the average man, on his deathbed, is going to repent to God for having violated this law, whether throughout his lifetime or in his youth with amorous adventures, is simply not believable. Are we really to believe, then, that countless millions of such people are going to Hell?

And what about the countless millions who have never been baptized? Are they really destined for Limbo? Lunn finds it difficult to suppose that God should have created a world with the foreknowledge that the majority of its inhabitants would spend eternity in everlasting torture.

Lunn rejects the idea that we should simply defer intellectually—simply by granting His supremacy—to God's disposition to inflict eternal pain. To inflict temporary pain has a purpose, namely to bring someone around to a recognition of the wrong that he has done. But to inflict eternal pain without any hope that any lesson can be learned, given that no relief is ever in prospect, would appear to have no design that is rational. Lunn has no use for the idea that because God is infinite in His majesty, therefore offenses against God must be correspondingly infinite. To begin with, the creature created by God is finite in his capacity to resist temptation. God therefore imposes, through the use of eternal punishment, infinite burdens on creatures only finitely capable of bearing those burdens. Lunn has no objection to the notion that the population of Heaven should be small, reserved for those who deserve it. But the difference between eternal punishment and soul annihilation is the difference between "an operation under chloroform and an operation without anaesthetics."

On the matter of contrition, Lunn makes the tormenting point that man was not born to love God, and therefore God cannot hold out the love of Him to be essential to redemption. He quotes Fr. Tyrrell* that a love of God "is the luxury of a few happy and imaginative temperaments. In the lump, man was not created nor designed for the love of God in that mystical sense, but for the love of man." God, says Lunn, has the right to demand obedience, but not love. He closes by saying that his opposition to the doctrine of Hell is not a moral *prejudice,* it is a rationally immovable *conclusion.*

I find Lunn on this point unanswerable by reason alone.

But Knox has an ace up his sleeve.

Look, he says, what you are really asking boils down to this: Does this particular person, guilty of that particular sin, deserve Hell? Knox has a knock-him-dead answer:

"Well, if he doesn't, he won't get it; that is certain."

I'd say that here (a) Knox abandoned reason altogether, and (b) he might not have objected to our reaching just that conclusion. Reason doesn't require an exact calibration of God's mercy or any measure of the incidence of His interventions. But reason calls for an understanding of the limitations that have to be put on an interrogatory that cannot proceed without some knowledge of the critical point. Unless we can know what it is that marginally causes someone to "deserve" Hell, we reach an impasse which does not, however, invalidate the inquiry. Knox relies, ultimately, on that mystery he later goes on to celebrate. He attempts to ease his way by insisting that questions of value must not be confused with questions of fact. It may be impossible for us to know whether this individual deserves eternal punishment, but it is entirely possible for us to know about him, and about

* George Tyrrell (1861–1909), onetime Jesuit priest, excommunicated for "modernism," a movement which, at the turn of the century, attempted to reconcile Christian faith with science and humanism.

all mankind, that which we would not know, save through the Book of Revelation: namely, that eternal punishment is a part of the divine order and that it is the end that awaits some sinners. And if Lunn is arguing that Hell should await not a *single* sinner, then he is pitting his insufficient reserves against those of Revelation, which is not ambiguous on the point.

Knox refuses to give up. It is one thing to say that you, Lunn, find no rational grounds for eternal punishment. But that position is not "rational." All you have accomplished is to bring to rational arguments what are really subjective judgments that have to do with value judgment, i.e., *Ought* so many people—or, for that matter, anybody—suffer that acutely, that endlessly?

And that, says Knox, is not the way into a theological argument, reminding Lunn what it is they are engaged in. The arguments against Hell would impress Knox if Hell were simply a theological corollary, i.e., a human conclusion about what it is that happens to sinful people when they die. But don't you see, dear boy, it isn't that: it is what we know through Revelation *does* happen. The only responsibility of the theologian, therefore, is to prove that the existence of Hell is not contrary to reason; and this they (I) have done.

Knox questions Lunn's invocation of the finite character of man, on whom responsibility has been placed that is infinite in character.

Nonsense. Man is not infinitely weak. If he were, then we would proceed on the assumption that man could never resist temptation; in which event we would all be Calvinist. But look! Look how many of us have resisted the temptation of Calvinism!

Knox ends by relying on formal logic. "The main point resolves itself into a hypothetical syllogism. 'If Catholic doctrine is true, then there is eternal punishment' is the major premise, and you must proceed by asserting the antecedent and therefore the consequent, or by denying the consequent and therefore the antecedent." Syllogism: Premise A: Sin demands punishment. B: John sins. Therefore, C: John is punished. If you deny the consequent—John is not punished—then the antecedent A-B dies an eternal death.

I am fascinated by the exchange. Yet Ronald Knox appears, in the end, to have done nothing more than to cause Lunn's difficulty with the idea of eternal punishment, so strenuously argued (he *disbelieves* in eternal punishment more than he *believes* in God), simply to . . . recede. It was in a later book that Lunn disclosed that if he had been required to believe in the fiery Hell described by certain theologians, he could not have accepted membership in the Church.*

Finally, his nose rubbed in the entrails of Revelation, Lunn could not refuse to acknowledge what was there. But if Knox thought himself engaged in plausible advocacy, he was wrong. Human resistance to such violations in their sense of values can't compliantly yield to the force of derivative reasoning from Revelation, not even in Knox's hands. Where Knox is transcendently convincing is in his appeal to that which all Christians or fellow-traveling Christians are prepared to concede, namely that God is as infinitely merciful as is congruent with being a God of justice. Knox ensnares by catching Lunn up (and me) by that one interjection, worth repeating: *if a man does not deserve eternal punishment, he will not get it.* That leaves us perpetually ignorant of what it takes to "deserve" that which we cannot bring ourselves to accept as *ever* deserved. Wouldn't a thousand years in flames take care of Caligula and Hitler? That difficulty we wouldn't have if Revelation had spoken of the annihilation of the soul as Eternal Punishment, rather than Eternal Hell. Butler Escape time!—Go ahead, play God! *You* make up the rules . . . Those of us who are awed by the authority of Revelation but cannot by the use of our own reason move our minds to make peace with all of its disclosures have no alternative than to conclude that our reason is not refined enough to take in divine perspectives.

---

* *And Yet So New* (Sheed and Ward, 1958). ". . . I certainly could not have become a Catholic if I'd been forced to accept as de fide the highly colored and to my mind repulsive views of the torments of Hell" (p. 130).

4. *The Fourth Difficulty—Indulgences*

Knox takes a refuge which, while intellectually defensible, leaves in the mind a sour, unsatisfactory taste. Consider—

Lunn is appalled by the place of indulgences—"the remission of temporal punishment still due for a sin that has been sacramentally absolved" *(American Heritage Dictionary)*—in Catholic history, indulgences granted, denied, promised, sold, ransomed, threatened.

What Knox said in effect—and this is different from what he wrote—was that human beings *cannot deceive God.*

Now, that is not a position that surprises anyone willing to concede the omniscience of God. But we see that Knox, when in trouble, retreats to his two primary redoubts.

The first is that if we find ourselves swimming about in problematic seas, writhing to stay afloat, snatch up a line that lands you in the lap of Revelation. It is required that you subordinate your own values, which are subjective, to Revelation, which is objective.

His second redoubt reduces to this: God cannot be fooled; and God's mercy, while enormous—as one would expect of a God whose love is infinite—is not to be trifled with. That being so, any worldly accretion (e.g., indulgences) must be creditable in the eyes of God, else that which the Catholic may think is being won (relief from time served in Purgatory) isn't in fact being won.

Knox makes his point strikingly in a single passage. "It is the story that one of the Saints—St. Philip Neri, I think—was preaching the jubilee indulgence once in a crowded church when a revelation was given to him that only two people in the church were actually getting it [i.e., the indulgence], one old charwoman and the Saint himself."

The traffic in indulgences, a sordid phenomenon that contributed to the disaffection of Martin Luther, is pretty much gone, though there is its equivalent in the (moderating) traffic in marriage annulments, about which some comment later on. Fr. Knox was taking retroactive satisfaction from the assurance that all those who did not deserve genuine indulgence never in fact got one.

5. The Difficulty with Biblical Inspiration: Jonah and the Whale

Lunn battled hard over this one. Coincidentally, years ago I was drawn to that chapter in the Bible by Whittaker Chambers.* But en route to reminiscence, I yield to Arnold Lunn, who began by reminding Father Knox that, manifestly, the Bible is replete with internal contradictions, historical and moral. The Catholic Church has special problems here, shared with many fundamentalist Protestants, because of the documented and seemingly implacable opposition of the Church to picking and choosing what it is in the Bible one accepts as inspired by the Holy Spirit. Lunn quotes from Pope Leo XIII's† adamant *Providentissimus Deus* (November 18, 1893):

> . . . it is absolutely wrong and forbidden, either to narrow inspiration to certain parts only of Holy Scripture, or to admit that the sacred writer has erred. . . . For all the books which the Church receives as sacred and canonical are written wholly and entirely, with all their parts, at the dictation of the Holy Ghost; and so far is it from being possible that any error can coexist with inspiration, that inspiration not only is essentially incompatible with error, but excludes and rejects it as absolutely and necessarily, as it is impossible that God Himself, the supreme truth, can utter that which is not true.

Lunn proceeds to quote from Benedict XV, writing in 1920, and then back to St. Jerome (fourth century) on Scripture passages equally assertive about biblical inerrancy.

* Whittaker Chambers (1901–61) was the writer who joined the Communists and, in 1935–37, engaged in espionage. He is best known for having identified State Department official Alger Hiss as a coconspirator.

† This is the same liberal-minded Pope who a few years later issued his famous encyclical *Rerum Novarum,* in which he appeared to be criticizing the capitalist system (he was indicting materialism). He was (still is) widely applauded for these sentiments by the same people, roughly, who would wince on reading *Providentissimus Deus.*

Knox acknowledges it is obvious that some biblical passages are parabolic. That is self-evident in those passages introduced by Christ as that, as parables. But when Christ did not frank a story as such, only the Church, we are to gather, can exercise the liberty of interpretation.

Okay, says Lunn. How, then, do you account for contemporary Catholic writers who are today precisely taking those liberties you deny are theirs, interpreting parts of the Bible to their own satisfaction? Lunn quotes Hilaire Belloc, who came close to a semi-disavowal of the entire Old Testament but was never disowned by Catholic authority. Belloc wrote, ". . . the decision of the Church to stand by the Jewish scriptures was not maintained without difficulty. The documents were alien to that glorious civilization of the Mediterranean which the Church generated and transformed. Their diction was, in its ears, uncouth and irrational. The deeds they recounted (with approval) sounded barbaric and often absurd; taken as moral examples, some were found repulsive, others puerile; and the whole was of another and (to Greek and Roman) lesser and more degraded world."

The perspectives have broadened. In April 1993 the Pontifical Biblical Commission published "The Interpretation of the Bible in the Church." Especially pertinent is the following (from its 3rd Section), "Characteristics of Catholic Interpretation." The commission points out, "Granted that tensions can exist in the relationship between various texts of Sacred Scripture, interpretation must necessarily show a certain pluralism. No single interpretation can exhaust the meaning of the whole, which is a symphony of many voices. Thus the interpretation of one particular text has to avoid seeking to dominate at the expense of others."

The Church's position appears to be that different interpretations of Scripture are not inconsistent with fidelity to the faith. What must not happen is one exegete claiming to have excluded alternative means of interpreting Scripture by his own methodology, for instance by restricting the approach to scripture to historical exegesis. ". . . it is [only] the Magisterium of the Church . . . that exercises authority in the name of Jesus Christ" *(Dei Verbum,* 10—from Vatican II).

The best that Knox could do was try to cope with Lunn's specifically cited objections.

There was the question of Jonah. Lunn's demand had been unequivocal: the Church must absolve its communicants of any requirement to take literally the story of Jonah and the whale. (And can't we do without the Garden of Eden? To say nothing of Balaam's Ass?)

Knox dug in.

Just to begin with, Christ himself made several references to Jonah. He answered the Pharisees (Matthew 12:39–40): "A wicked and adulterous generation asks for a miraculous sign! But none will be given it except the sign of the prophet Jonah. For as Jonah was three days and three nights in the belly of a huge fish, so the Son of Man will be three days and three nights in the heart of the earth."

No doubt, then, that the New Testament specifically franks the Old Testament story of Jonah. Knox remarks, more or less in passing, recent scientific findings, one of them an anthropological discovery that in days gone by there did exist a species of whale with a belly large enough to hold a human being. But Knox interrupts himself to point out that the use by Christ of the Jonah story does not necessarily mean that Christ certified it as history. He quotes a priest, "Why shouldn't Christ have used Jonah? As an accepted legend?" Even as someone might use Romulus and Remus without actually underwriting them as the founders of Rome.

Lunn was dissatisfied. In the first place, the book of Jonah is not a *prophetical* book. Moreover, it isn't only Jonah's having allegedly been swallowed by a whale that overwhelms the reader's credulity, it is his subsequent career. ". . . a series, if not of impossibilities, certainly of improbabilities. The whole scene on board ship reads like a story from the Arabian Nights; Jonah's prayer in the fish's belly is made up of phrases from the Psalter, and they seem more like a prayer of thanksgiving for deliverance from his trip than a petition; the scene in Nineveh itself is dramatic, while Jonah's disgust at the turn events have taken seems to remove him from the category of the prophets. There is not a vestige of prophecy in it. . . . But if Jonah is neither history nor prophecy, then what is it?"

Knox tries again. Is there any reason why we should not read Jonah as a divinely inspired parable, giving us, through the medium of fanciful happenings, a wonderful statement on the mercy of God?—"so that the whole becomes a commentary on the words addressed to God by Moses and here put into the mouth of Jonah: 'I know that Thou art a gracious and merciful God, patient and of much compassion, and easy to forgive evil.' "

I found it useful to look back at the critical role the book of Jonah played on the thinking and career of Whittaker Chambers. Chambers was the most important American defector from Communism. In his renowned autobiography, *Witness,* he wrote of the torments he experienced after consenting to act as a witness for the prosecution. These pursued him past the conviction of Alger Hiss, on which Chambers' reliability officially hung. They dogged him up until his death and pursued his memory thirty-five years later, though with diminished effect. In his last years (1954–61) we were close friends, and more than once he wrote to tell me of the special impact the book of Jonah continued to have on him.

It struck me then, and does so with greater force after dwelling on the exchanges between Lunn and Knox, that the Bible is forever doing this sort of thing. Although a deeply thoughtful man, Lunn is here disposed to expunge Jonah as quite simply irrelevant to the great missions of the Bible; and yet it was Jonah that singularly intrigued a mind (or man) like Chambers. Not because he thought it an Arabian night, but because he found in it mysterious and compelling insights into the God with whom he, Chambers, had once had an insuperable problem.

Chambers tried to reconcile himself with the God of Jonah, the God with whom Jonah himself could not be reconciled. Why? Because of God's final decision *not* to visit His wrath on Nineveh, notwithstanding that He had called on Jonah to travel to Nineveh precisely in order to bring God's apocalyptic tidings to the people there.

Jonah at first had refused to go, refused to be the bearer of such awful tidings. He concealed himself in the fishing boat bound for Tarshish. But the boat encountered the great storm that caused the crew, in desperation, to jettison Jonah as benighted cargo, an act that brought calm to the troubled ocean and Jonah into the stomach of the whale. There, the Bible continues the very short, four-page story: he prayed for three days in language Lunn finds inexplicably irrelevant. (When one finds oneself inside a whale, appropriate prayers should come instantly to mind.) But God heard the prayer and commanded the whale to vomit Jonah out on dry land. This was done on the shore of Nineveh, whence Jonah proceeded to do his duty, only to be frustrated by God's unpredicted and (of high importance) unpredictable compassion.

It was the failure of Jonah to understand the reach of God's compassion that caused him to be angry, yea, even unto death. And it was Chambers' refusal (incapacity?) to understand why God had not redeemed whatever pledge Chambers thought Him to have made to Chambers that tormented him.

I reproduce, as an irreplaceable frame, part of the fourth chapter of Jonah (King James Version):

> *Who can tell if God will turn and repent, and turn away from his fierce anger, that we perish not?* [3:9] *But it displeased Jonah exceedingly, and he was very angry. And he prayed unto the Lord, and said,* I pray thee, O Lord· . . . for I knew that thou art a gracious God, and merciful, slow to anger, and of great kindness, and repentest thee of the evil. Therefore now, O Lord, take, I beseech thee, my life from me; for it is better for me to die than to live. *Then said the Lord, Doest thou well to be angry?* . . . *And he said,* I do well to be angry, even unto death.

Chambers would write to me:* "The Bible is, I suppose, the single greatest anti-intellectual book ever put together, but it is full of those magical simple phrasings—bread on the water, etc. It is full of them, of course, because it is, at its best, about simple life; because Job's question ('Why me?'), the central issue, remains unan-

---

* *Odyssey of a Friend* (New York: G. P. Putnam & Sons, 1969), p. 61.

swered, and because Jonah does not lie, but says, 'I do well to be angry.' "

Earlier Chambers had let me know what Jonah meant to him. He was speaking, in the late fifties, of his general desolation over the turn of international events (Khrushchev had sent the tanks in to crush the students in Budapest, and the West had done nothing). When he left Communism in 1938, Chambers recalled,

I had, and have, no illusions, or few. This is at the root of my endemic hopelessness, made deceptive to most people by my temper-amental buoyancy. It is part of the climate that has taken vengeance on my heart—overweight and work are only incidental factors, though of the kind that the secular world puts its faith in. This, too, was at the root of much of my vacillation in the past. I have, for years, been fascinated by the Book of Jonah, and I said to a few at the time that it was the pattern of the Hiss case. Therefore, in a sense, I fled to Tarshish with the dread words in my ears: "Go up unto Nineveh that great city, etc." But when the tempest rose, and it became a question of myself or the crew, I had also to say: "Take me up and cast me unto the sea, because it is for my sake that this trouble is come unto you." That is why Jonah's words in the belly of the whale [*"The water compassed me about even to the soul; the depth hath closed 'round about; the sea hath covered my head. I went down to the lowest parts of the mountains; the bars of the earth have shut me up for ever . . ."*] also appear in . . . *Witness*—by intention, the only biblical quote in the book. But, in the end, I did go unto Nineveh, and when nothing really happened (noth-ing did), and when the . . . worms and others had eaten up the cucumber vine, and God had asked: "Do you well to be angry?" I answered and still answer: "I do well to be angry, even unto death."

I had written to Chambers, after first meeting with him, to remark what I thought his singular purity. He quickly put aside the compli-ment, but did say this, that what I wrote was justified to this extent. "Against the clear and forceful evidence of my own mind, I will always give my body to be burned if, by so doing, our children are given even that slightly better chance against the falling night. And the sure knowledge that that is what God is demanding of me in not permitting me to die is the seed of my private agony and the secret of my heart attacks. For only I know what God has said to me, and I have told no one, not even a priest.''

Said what? Promised what?

To visit on the West the fate it deserved? Even as Nineveh deserved the fate Jonah had been sent to proclaim? To visit on the Communist world the fate its leaders had earned? ''Those collapses which the world sees are due to the tension between my feeling that I do not have, as a man, the strength to do what will be laid on me, and the horror of knowing that, when it is laid on me, I shall do it.''

I understood Chambers to be saying that, like Jonah, he could not, except at a distance that brought him no personal satisfaction, understand the immeasurable mercy of God. He was also saying that resistant though he was to God's incontinent mercy, even so—like Jonah—he felt himself an instrument of God, however unwilling; because he understood the nature of the philosophical imperative.

Obviously the meaning Chambers found in Jonah isn't exactly public tender. But it is an instructive example of the subtlety of biblical passages that exegetes spend lifetimes analyzing. Whittaker Chambers almost certainly was not aware of Arnold Lunn's disparagement of Jonah when he wrote as he did about the special meaning the book had for him.

5a. An Ending Word on Scriptural Literalism

Arnold Lunn concluded his case: ''If every part in the Bible is equally inspired, we are forced to identify the God of the Psalms, the God of Isaiah, and the God of St. John with the barbarous and anthropomorphic Jehovah—a god who is angry and who repents, a god who demands blood sacrifices, a god who approves of the murder of women and children, a god who, in brief, represents at every point the most complete contrast with the God of the New Testament.'' Lunn cannot believe that God lent Himself to such an enormous and superfluous deception.

Knox moves in massively. *Providentissimus Deus* is not an infallible pronouncement. Even so, it doesn't follow that a papal utterance is quite simply mistaken. Assume that the grace of the Holy Spirit is behind the words written in the Bible—even so, these words were written down by men who were less, one takes it, than divine transcribers. Moreover, it's wrong to speak of the "plain meaning" of passages whose meaning can reasonably be disputed. It is exactly for this reason you need a church to tell you what is in fact *the* "meaning" of a biblical passage variously interpreted. You can't simply jettison those parts of the Bible that do not seem to you to dovetail with salient Christian dogma. If any part of the Bible is subject to "error," as distinguished from misinterpretation, then the whole of it must be so regarded.

Knox put it this way: "I should say now that the whole of the Bible is immune from error in its own right; although it is only the Church's teaching which makes that fact known to us."

Knox is telling us that the Church's manifest reluctance to engage in selective validations must be held responsible for such (incautious) edicts as the *Providentissimus* cited by Lunn. A and B can differ in their interpretation of a given passage. A says it is literal, B says it is poetical, pseudonymous, parabolic, prophetic, allegorical. We can go only so far as to say that in the present state of our knowledge it would not be right to teach in seminaries any one of B's alternatives as the authorized way of explaining the sacred text. It's obvious that much of the Bible needs interpretation. If we needed to take literally the preachments of the Bible, one would have to suppose that God had eyes, ears, and hands. It comes down to this: since we cannot know the true meaning of any particular passage unless the Church has pronounced on the matter—as it has, for example, on the virginity of Mary, her assumption into Heaven, the trinitarian nature of God—the well-instructed Christian has primarily the negative responsibility of declining to endorse, absentmindedly, an assertion that a biblical passage, as set down, is other than inspired by the Holy Spirit.

• • •

Arnold Lunn drops the last question. "I have tried to show that the Catholic Church officially claims for the Bible a degree of inerrancy which the Bible does not in fact possess."

A stalemate. "On the major point," Knox writes, "we must agree to differ."

Theirs was not, in my judgment, a conclusive exchange on the half dozen Christian doctrines challenged, refined, and defended. *Difficulties* isn't to be likened to Lincoln's decisive moral defeat of Douglas, or Socrates' of his accusers. Yet in my own study of the exchange my mind focused on the deeper problems of Protestant Christianity, given that there is no magisterium to pronounce conclusions by which the faithful are bound. There are here and there calcified differences in Protestant and Catholic interpretations of the Bible. For Catholics, "This is my body . . . this is my blood" signifies a transubstantiation of the Species: the priest and communicants consume, exactly as the Apostles once did, what they were told was, is, precisely the body and blood of Christ. For many Protestants, communion deals only symbolically with the body and blood of Christ.

Who is correct? Catholics rely on an institutional church. Knox is intellectually convinced that by that way, and that way alone, can Christians be protected against a misreading of the divine word.

My own reasoning is that if the inquirer is prepared to believe in apostolicity, prepared to believe that the Church founded by Christ is the Church from which Roman Catholicism is descended, then it is to cavil whether Rome is on time, ahead of time, or behind time in attaching a more widely appealing significance to any single episode or stricture in the Bible. Accept the Bible as divinely inspired, all Christians need to do. To accept the interpretive authority of Rome requires loyalty to the Church of Ronald Knox, admirably defended during the stressful period that Arnold Lunn labored, with resourcefulness and eloquence, over his *Difficulties*. I rejoice over a theological exchange I find enduringly illuminating. I have at this moment, at my side, a copy of that book. It is inscribed, in his hand, "For Bill

Buckley, with affectionate greetings from Arnold Lunn. Mürren, March 12, 1968.''

Two years after *Difficulties* was published, Arnold Lunn was received into the Catholic Church by—Ronald Knox. Fourteen years later, *Difficulties* was republished with a profoundly moving final exchange between Lunn and Knox. ''I had no real conception of all that is implied in submission to divine authority,'' Lunn wrote to his sometime antagonist, by now an old friend. ''I can illustrate what I mean by a story. Some little time before I was received my wife said to me, 'I can't think how you can become a Catholic without finding an answer to the points which you put in your letter to Father Knox about the difficulty of reconciling omniscience and free will.' To this I replied, 'If God came into this room and said to you, ''I *am* omniscient and *you've* got free will,'' you would have to accept both statements.'

'' 'No, I shouldn't,' said my wife; 'I'd assume that I hadn't heard him correctly.' ''

That, of course, is the problem. We cannot, carousing about in our potty little planes of reason, confidently assume that we have heard correctly the word of God as given to us in the Bible. That word is best likened to the Lost Chord about which Arthur Sullivan wrote, the chord perhaps accidentally, perhaps providentially, struck one day by the discursive fingers of the organist. He struggles to finger again the same notes that produced that sound, musically, spiritually, orgasmic. He does not, in Arthur Sullivan's account, ever succeed. It is a Christian postulate that those who struggle to decipher that chord will one day hear it. Anyone who is looking for God, Pascal said, will find Him.

AN OBITUARY NOTICE

Arnold Lunn, R.I.P.

Lunn died in London, on June 2, 1974. I draw on the obituary from *National Review.*

At eighty-six he was undaunted, though the flesh had become very weak. He was at work for the next issue of *Ski Survey,* an essay on the Olympic Committee's official history of the Games. Also, on a book on Lakes Thun and Brienz; on several articles, including one for *National Review;* and he was eagerly expecting, in America, the reissue of his book *Spanish Rehearsal,* a book written about Spain during its civil war. His most recent article had appeared in the *Tablet* only the day before and his son Peter, and his wife Phyllis, read it aloud to him in the hospital. I can imagine his chuckling over his own words, which always amused him, as they did everybody else save possibly their victims. They, come to think of it, probably made up a majority of his readers. He took an unrestrained, unaffected pleasure in his work, which was amiably sarcastic, in the meiotic British tradition, wonderfully well-turned, unrelenting but good-natured. He was a most serious man who saw the humor in every situation.

His career began only months after graduating from Harrow, a few years after Winston Churchill. He wrote *The Harrovians,* an exposé of sorts of public school life—tame stuff, by the standards of *The Fourth of June* by David Benedictus, which came along fifty years later about life at Eton; but enough to launch him as a radical young writer. His interest in sports and mountaineering dominated him in those days; and one summer before he was twenty-two he fell while on a solo climbing expedition. For several hours he was without help; then they found him, took him to the hospital, and he blessed himself (a) that the anesthetist was incompetent and (b) that he understood Welsh, because he was awake when he should have been unconscious, enough so to hear the doctors preparing to amputate his leg. This, from his strapped-down position on the operating table, he forthwith forbade, summoning all the authority he could in his youthful voice.

The result was a leg deformed, slightly shorter than the companion leg. Athletes and mountaineers of the world wondered what the competition would have been from Lunn if he had had intact legs, because he scaled every mountain in Switzerland that ever challenged mountaineers, and raced with the early British ski teams. He was made president of the Ski Club of Great Britain fifty years before his death, and he founded the prestigious Kandahar Club in Mürren. It was in those days that he conceived the idea of the slalom, which he introduced into Olympic competition where it has been a fixture ever since. As the years went on he found skiing more and more difficult, but he persevered, and I skied with him when he was seventy-five years old.

He lived in Mürren during the winter, a ski eyrie that faces, across the Lauterbrunnen valley, the Jungfrau and the dreaded Eiger. At Mürren he was visited by princes and paupers in his little suite at the Jungfrau Lodge, made available to him by the hotel's owner who recognized that Arnold Lunn had done more for mountaineering and skiing than any Swiss (indeed he was knighted in 1953 by Queen Elizabeth in acknowledgment of those achievements), and that he was broke. To reach him one rose by funicular, or took the new, awesome lift, developed just in time to be exploited in one of the James Bond movies.

In Mürren, where there are about 300 residents, he was the most illustrious of them all, and the most beloved and most indulged. When he was eighty-four, Lady Lunn left to visit very briefly her aged mother. She gave Arnold detailed instructions on how he was to behave during her absence. He listened with great attentiveness and apparent docility; and the moment she was off and away on the funicular, he picked up the telephone in his hotel room and ordered the concierge to produce his skis. The concierge reported back forty-five minutes later that he had assiduously looked for Sir Arnold's skis, but in vain: they must have been lost, after ten years of neglect. Ten minutes later, very nearly in tears, the concierge appeared and confessed that he had hidden them at the express instructions of Lady Lunn, who suspected her husband might be just mad enough to try them on.

Sir Arnold used to say that all of mankind is divided inflexibly in two classes. There are the "helpers" and the "helpees." He had discovered early in life that he was a member of the latter class and that no marriage was successful that united two members from the same class. His first wife, Lady Mabel Northcote, was a helper; and when she died, in 1959, after forty-six years' marriage, he wed Phyllis Holt-Needham who, in addition to all her other qualities, was also a born helper: so he knew he was licked on the question of mounting his skis.

Disconsolate, he set out, using the two walking sticks on which he now depended, across the snowy path to the Jungfrau's dining room when, suddenly remembering his wife's several admonitions on departing, he found his hand slipping down his front to verify that he had remembered to button his fly. But experiencing nothing there at all, he realized that he had his pants on backward.

It was all he could do to survive the three days of her absence, and she was never absent again, and was with him when in the early afternoon, failing to rally, he died in the Catholic Hospital of St. John and St. Elizabeth, near London.

He must have found it an inconvenient time to die. Two days later he was to have spoken at a golden jubilee dinner of the Kandahar Ski Club, of which he had been the central figure since its founding. "Phyllis has told me not to be controversial in my speech," he had written me. "I must be amusing. I thought after the president had proposed my health as founder of the club to begin my speech saying, 'Phyllis tells me I must not be controversial. So I will begin by expressing cordial agreement with all the very nice things the president has said about me.'" He'd have laughed greatly, telling his friends this. I think he must have spent half his life laughing. During the other half, in addition to the usual things, he wrote fifty-four books, discovered Christianity, and, for his friends, reminded us more than any man I have ever known what is meant when one talks about the irrepressibility of the human spirit.

His road to orthodoxy was, as so often is the case, the road of the militant agnostic. During the 1920s he engaged in spirited debate with believers. It was thought the exchanges with Father Ronald Knox were so brilliant and of such general interest that they warranted publication as a book. This was done and Lunn and his votaries were satisfied that they had had the better of the argument. But Knox's arguments, not inconceivably by grand design, overcame Lunn himself, and presently he left the comfortable world of skepticism for a career as a brilliant and persuasive Christian apologist. (His book *Now I See,* published in 1933, was a part of the incidental reading of the critic Hugh Kenner when he was a boy, and thirty years later he wrote Lunn to tell him he, Kenner, had succumbed to its arguments.) It was the failure of his contemporaries to concern themselves for the evangelistic mission of Christianity that Arnold Lunn could never understand, and against which he railed to the end, criticizing altar boys and Popes. He remarked in one letter to me, "I expect to be the first Catholic excommunicated for orthodoxy."

He was always writing, in his private and published letters, about the Christian mission and about the importance of individual protest. As a high functionary in the skiing world during the period of Hitler he had succeeded in applying pressure in behalf of Jewish athletes. Why are things now so different? he wondered, in a letter to the *Times.*

His letters, even on the most solemn matters, almost always ended with a smile. "P.S. Could you tell me whether it is improper to address an American on an envelope as A. B. Smith, Esquire, rather than as Mr. A. B. Smith? A newly appointed American concierge here at the hotel in Switzerland thought that 'Esquire' was a family name and assumed it must be a very large family, to judge by the number of letters addressed to different persons of the Esquire clan. All such letters were filed under 'E.' It was only when his 'E' partition was overflowing that he asked the manager just when would all these different members of the Esquire clan be arriving."

I am a member of the Kandahar Ski Club. In order to qualify it is required that you descend that terrible mountainside in less than a specified number of minutes—too much for a skier who came to the sport in middle age. "Why are you not a member?" Sir Arnold asked me one day. I explained. Sitting at his desk, he executed a form, asked me for three guineas, gave me a club receipt and the envied badge for my ski parka. "You are now a member." How? I asked. "Under Rule 13, my dear Bill. Nepotism."

When I say I treasure my Kandahar badge, I use the word loosely—I haven't any idea where it is, as a matter of fact. But I treasured the gesture, in the context of Arnold's unfailing good humor during the afternoons and evenings we spent together at Mürren, and on one occasion I wrote him to this effect.

"You have occasionally implied that I have tendered you a service," he wrote back. "I have tried very hard—for it makes me more comfortable to believe you—to recall any real service that I have ever rendered to you. Of course I have sometimes made you laugh, and that is a trivial service of sorts. Our friendship dates from a banquet at which I claimed that we in England are more democratic than you in the U.S.A., that whereas you provide careers only for the talented in Congress, the House of Lords provides a career for the untalented. Well, well, if my alleged service to you is as one who has made you laugh, never in all time has a laugh-maker been more rewarded. And the greatest reward is all that your friendship has meant to me."

Gratitude was the source of his energy, and of his faith, and of his humor. After commenting, in a letter written before his last Christmas, about the indifference of men toward the plight of each other, he closed with an uncharacteristic solemnity, a valedictory. "Every night when I curl up in bed I try not to take for granted that I have a roof over my head and a pillow below my head, and to contrast my immense good fortune in love and friendship with the millions in misery and the millions persecuted, and my letter to the *Times* is not only intended to awake Christian conscience but as a trivial token to quiet my own."

Surely Arnold Lunn rests in peace.

CHAPTER SIX

Disruptions and Achievements

of Vatican II

When Arnold Lunn wrote to say he might become the first Catholic to be excommunicated for orthodoxy, he was making a jocular reference to whatever had freshly been brought in from the Second Vatican Council while he was writing. The Council, as noted, was convened in 1959 by Pope John XXIII, and met between 1962 and 1965. It was the primary event within the Catholic Church in my lifetime. It is greeted almost universally as a success. Its implications are not fully realized, granted. For me, it seemed at first a little aimless (in fact, it was—many who participated in it weren't exactly sure where they were going). It was the perfect time to persuade ourselves that the Council was being guided by the Holy Spirit. It gave some of us pause.

The Council had for the average Catholic a few immediately visible manifestations, and these were not everywhere welcome, some drifting in after the Council had ended. In 1966 Pope Paul VI abruptly ended by apostolic decree the traditional requirement to forgo eating meat on Fridays. I remember, just before the word went out from Rome, reading the menu on a TWA flight. Immediately below the tenderloin-of-steak listing appeared in small type some such wording as, "Roman Catholics on this flight, by agreement reached between TWA and the Vatican, are exempted from dietary obligations on Fridays." (How would Pan Am, in hot competition in those days with TWA, do better with the Vatican?) I passed off the dispensation as an interesting diplomatic initiative by TWA and wondered idly just how management had set about convincing the Vatican that to serve passengers something other than meat on Fridays was an unreasonable imposition on the crew and on the passengers. I knew—my brother Reid, who lived in Spain, had explained it to me—that during the Spanish Civil War food was so haphazardly available that the Vatican, or perhaps it was the bishops (it wasn't clear), had exempted the Spanish people from Friday absti-nence. That wasn't hard to understand: if food is scarce, then whatever turns up on Friday—fish or fowl—must be consumed.

But I did find it hard to understand why the Vatican was now (1966) dispensing with this weekly offering (to use the word common in Christian usage). I had thought Friday abstinence—I think it safe to say that *most* Catholics so thought it—a very slight deprivation, yet one that served as a palpable reminder that Friday had a special significance for us.

The no-meat-on-Friday rule had been very firm. I remembered a passage from one of Arnold Lunn's books:

[Dick] is an extremely attractive young man and does not always find it easy to resist those whom he attracts. His uncle and mother had been worried about a siren who had succeeded in having an affair with him but who had failed to lure him into marriage. That episode had just come to mind when I saw [his uncle] Oliver.

"What puzzles me about Dick," said Oliver, "is that he's so fussy about going to Mass. Nothing would induce him to miss Mass. Does he really suppose that it's a greater sin to cut Mass than to have an affair with a siren like that . . . adventuress? It seems to me hypocritical to turn up at Mass every Sunday and break the rules about sex during the rest of the week."

"Why hypocritical?"

"Oh, because it's staking a claim to be religious when you're not behaving religiously."

"It doesn't strike a Catholic that way. We don't cease to believe when we cease to behave. If the Communists seized control in England, Dick would cheerfully die in defense of the Church."

"Then why doesn't he live for the Church? Why doesn't he keep the rules about sex?"

"Because they're infernally difficult to keep. On the other hand the obligation to attend Mass is easy to observe. You seem to think that because a Catholic can't keep all the commandments he should, to prove his consistency, keep none of them. I dare say Dick hopes that God will make allowance for those who lack the heroic virtue which alone enables a young and very attractive man to avoid the sins of the flesh, but Mass is like cutting an important parade. It's bad manners, and as good manners are easier to acquire than good morals, bad manners are in some ways more inexcusable."*

Christianity is unmistakably asking us to believe certain things we can understand and to accept others not so readily understandable, some of these tempting, in impious moments, to make sport of, indeed easy to do so. Oh how we laughed when Aloïse Heath, my oldest and most reverently irreverent sibling, told us about an encounter with a tweedy cosmopolitan skeptic who taught her children history in grammar school. The scene was a teacher-parent tea, and Aloïse, who was then about forty-five, was offered hors d'oeuvres while talking with the history teacher. She dabbled with her fingers

* *And Yet So New* (Sheed and Ward, 1958), pp. 55–56.

and pulled up one that had cheese on it, maneuvering around those that had ham, salami, or bacon. The teacher smiled at her. "What happens if you eat meat on a Friday?"

"Why," answered Aloïse—as matter-of-factly as if the question had been, What would happen to a car if it ran out of gas?—"I'd go to Hell."

The young teacher thought that wonderfully amusing and pursued his interrogation. Did Mrs. Heath believe that when the Virgin Mary died she went straight up (he pointed at the ceiling) to Heaven?

Aloïse loved it. She put down her glass and said, "Why yes. I not only believe that, I believe that if at the moment the Blessed Virgin Mary began to rise, the earth, rotating on its axis, was"—with her hands, Aloïse turned an imaginary globe—"upside down, then she traveled"—she thrust her hand to the right, then up, then to the left, then up again—"like that!"

It's probably true that the sin of pride sometimes played a part when, on Friday, Catholics declined the meat dish. Our mother had coached us on proper manners when offered meat by an unknowing or careless hostess. (*"Just cut off a little piece, darling, and put it somewhere on the plate, and just leave it there."*) If absolutely necessary to guard against embarrassing the hostess, then it was okay to nibble. In fact, back then hostesses who entertained on Fridays routinely served meatless entrées. It became instinctive to guard against the high possibility that one or more Catholics were at the dinner table; routinely, fish was served. And then of course at restaurants there was always something other than meat, except when airborne on TWA.

The denial had served as a weekly reminder that the Catholic Christian was, at least nominally, just that—someone who accepted the Church's rules. Like wearing your veteran's or Red Cross insignia on relevant occasions. Once upon a time to identify oneself as a Catholic could be terminally provocative (in England, Catholics were not given the vote until 1829). It was no longer that in the United States, though it did set one apart, as for instance at Millbrook, the boarding school I attended, as recounted above (see chapter 3). It was a Protestant school in which the four or five Catholic boys went to

Mass on Sundays instead of attending the Protestant service obligatory for other boys. Meat was not served on Fridays at the school dining hall; indeed, many Protestants practiced abstinence on Fridays. What passed through my mind when the Vatican abolished the Friday-no-meat convention was, simply: Why?

The Vatican II reforms came thick and fast, the most conspicuous of them liturgical. Fr. David Tracy, now a renowned (liberal) theologian teaching at the University of Chicago, was in those days a young curate at St. Mary's Church in Stamford, where I attended Mass on Sundays. He was placed in charge of the new liturgical arrangements and asked me if I would agree to serve as "lector" at the eleven o'clock Mass. The new Mass called not only for a lay lector but for a lay "commentator," who would read some of the opening prayers in the Mass, leaving it to the lector to read the Epistle. I agreed to do so.

A few years later, in January, my sister Aloïse died, aged forty-nine, eldest of ten children, mother of ten. The family—her children and her siblings—were catapulted into a dumb grief. We took refuge in our conviction that our separation from her was impermanent. It was for us acutely the time not merely to recall the promises of Christ but to invoke their magical capacity to mitigate grief. We wanted to relive, in the funeral ceremony, the liturgical experience we had all grown up with—indeed, what had been the universal practice up until a few years before—the Mass in Latin. This request the priest we dealt with gladly granted.

And so on January 18, 1967, the weather in the little town in northwestern Connecticut, at subzero, in the homely brick church we had all known since childhood, the priest recited the Mass of the Dead and the organist accompanied the soloist, who sang the Gregorian dirge in words the mourners did not clearly discern, words which, had we discerned them, we could not exactly have translated; and yet we experienced—not only her family but her friends; not alone the Catholics among us but also the Protestants and the Jews—something akin to that spiritual transport which, in the late sixties, many restless folk were finding it necessary to search out in drugs or from a guru in Mysterious India.

Six months later (we were in the storm center of Vatican II) Aloïse's oldest daughter was married. With some hesitation (one must not petition exorbitantly) Ben Heath, her widower father, asked the same priest whether this happy ritual might also be performed in the Latin. The priest replied, with understanding and grace, that unhappily that would not be possible inasmuch as he would be performing on this occasion not in a remote corner of Connecticut, but in West Hartford, practically within earshot of the bishop. We felt wicked at having attempted anything so heterodox—Latin in church!—so to speak within the walls of the episcopacy; and so the wedding Mass was conducted according to the current cant, with everybody popping up and kneeling down and responding, more or less, to the stream of objurgations that issued from the nervous and tone-deaf young commentator: All together now, *who do we appreciate?*—Jesus! Jesus! Jesus! *Jezus*—it was awful. My Protestant wife, to whom I had been beholden for seventeen years and who had borne with me countless weddings of my countless relatives, was with me, alongside. She had in January clutched my hand during the funeral service of the bride's mother. Now she turned to me early in the new liturgy to express utter incredulity, wondering whether something was especially awry. Defensively I rebuked her, muttering something to the effect that she should not be so ignorant of what had been going on in my Church for three years; she turned her head away from my asperity.

She was right, I utterly wrong. How could she, an innocent Anglican, begin to conceive of the liturgical disfigurations of those years? My own reaction had been the protective reaction of the son whose father, a closet drunk, is spotted outside his household unsteady on his feet.

All of those daffy innovations did not matter, to be sure, in any Benthamite reckoning: the sacraments of the Mass, its canon, were undeniably still there. But as with the new rules for Friday, the obvious question came to mind: What goal was being served by the new liturgy? On one point I—and other dissenters—were ready to yield from the first moment the liturgy was changed. It was incontestably right that the vernacular should displace the Latin if by so doing the rituals of Catholic Christianity brought greater satisfaction to the laity along with a deeper comprehension of what was going on at the altar. Though even then I'd continue to cherish the bodkin Arnold Lunn inserted so deftly in the soft tissues of the revisionists' argument: "If it is so," he wrote in a letter addressed to the London *Times,* alongside Evelyn Waugh and a few others pleading for one (1) Latin Mass each Sunday in the larger churches, "that the Latin Mass is only for the educated few, surely Mother Church, in all her charity, can find a place even for the educated few?"

Having agreed to participate in the new liturgy as a lector, I hoped that something was about to unfold before me that would vindicate the progressives. I hung on as lector/commentator doggedly for three years, until the day came when I felt obliged to act on my reservations. I wrote to my pastor (Fr. Tracy had left for the academy at the University of Chicago) that I no longer thought it right to continue. During those three years I had observed the evolution of the new Mass and the reaction to it of the congregation (at the time the largest in Connecticut). Much emphasis had been put by Vatican II on involving the congregation in the Mass. In our diocese four hymns were prescribed every Sunday. They were subsequently reduced to three, even as, in the process of distillation, the commentator's job would be absorbed by the lector.

At our church perhaps a dozen people out of a thousand joined in singing the hymn. In the ensuing thirty years this ratio did not materially change. Granted, St. Mary's is atypical: a church that large tends to overawe the uncertain singer. In other Catholic churches, congregations tend to join a little more firmly in the song. In none that I have been to is there anything like the joyous unison that the bards of the new liturgy thrummed about in the anticipatory literature, the only exception being the highly regimented Benedictine school my son attended, in which the reverend headmaster had the means to induce cooperation in whatever enterprise struck his fancy.

In the thirty-odd years since my sister's funeral, alterations have been made in the Mass. The idea of recruiting the congregation into hyperactive participation simply hasn't worked. Catholic parishioners just don't sing out, as many Protestants are accustomed to doing, nor do they join lustily in common prayer. And then whatever the spiritual advantages traceable to incorporating the congregation in the brick-by-brick architecture of the Mass, we are left with a troublesome trade-off not frequently raised, which is the difficulty the individual celebrant now has in dogging his own spiritual pursuits in the random cacophony. In an aggressive essay written at the time (for *Commonweal,* 1967), I referred to

> the fascistic static of the contemporary Mass, during which one is either attempting to sing or attempting to read the missal at one's own pace, which we must now do athwart the obtrusive rhythm of the priest or the commentator; or attempt to meditate on this or the other prayer or sentiment or analysis or exhortation in the Ordinary or in the Proper of the Mass only to find that such meditation is sheer outlawry standing in the way, as it does, of the liturgical calisthenics devised by the Central Coach, who apparently judges it an act of neglect if the churchgoer is permitted more than two minutes and 46 seconds without being made to stand if he was kneeling, or kneel if he was standing, or sit—or sing—or chant—or anything if perchance he was praying, from which anarchism he must at all costs be rescued. *"Let us now recite the Introit Prayer"* says the commentator: to which exhortation I find myself aching to reply in that "loud and clear and reverential voice" the manual for lectors prescribes: "Let us *not* recite the Introit Prayer!"

Overheated? No doubt. A voice from the sixties, the counter-counterculture. But the tremor of a dismayed reaction worth recalling, even thirty years after the first shocks. And we continue to ask, in a calmer voice, about the dogged insistence on the use of the vernacular to the exclusion of the Latin. The substitution, I continue to believe, was grounded on wobbly hypotheses, as also the sudden enthusiasm for the Mass done not alone by clergy but here and there jointly with the congregation. For a long while, for instance, we were instructed to say the Introit Prayer (now the Entrance Antiphon) together. Why? It is difficult to know the reason for joint utterance of prayers that are different from those which, like the Pledge of Allegiance, presuppose a communal approach. Is sufficient thought given to the demands, anxieties, curiosities of the worshiper who, before it all happened, might begin the prayer five seconds before, or ten seconds after, the celebrating priest—who, himself enjoying the privacy granted him at Trent, pursued his prayers in his own way, at his own speed, ungoverned by the metronomic discipline of a choirmaster? It used to be that there were stretches of several minutes during the Mass when worshipers were, so to speak, on their own, left to follow the missal, in English or in Latin; or indeed to ignore the liturgical stagecraft and ponder, muse, inquire, worship. This was no longer possible.

And then of course, the matter of the English into which the Latin has been translated. There are several versions (I hope) of what, in the churches I attend, I am given to read and made to hear. John Cardinal Wright served, at Vatican II, as the learned prefect of the Sacred Congregation for the Clergy. He was a personal friend, and I professed my concern to him in the mid-sixties, citing one or two specific, bewildering usages. He did not defend the then-current translations. "Happy" (as in, "Happy as those who do not see, and yet believe") simply doesn't mean the same thing as "blessed," I remember his acknowledging. But mistranslation is one thing, he said, the use of the vernacular another. He had himself voted for the vernacular after hearing from Cardinal Wyszynski that the government of Poland, in pursuit of the Communists' eternal war against Christianity, was progressively limiting the forums in which the use of the Bible was permitted. Most lately (the mid-fifties) the government had outlawed any use of the Bible in Polish schools—"so that the Polish people are left substantially with only what they hear spoken in their churches." It was not edifying, under the circumstances, Cardinal Wright* argued, to restrict to Latin the prayers heard by the Polish people.

The premise here is, I think, that prayers spoken at Mass are

---

* There is every reason to assume that what Vatican II germinated went further than what Cardinal Wright contemplated. There was concern elsewhere. From the Spring 1997 issue of *The Latin Mass* magazine, an excerpt from a previously unpublished letter (January 3, 1965) from Evelyn Waugh to John Heenan, Archbishop of Westminster: "You sent me away reassured that the novelties about to be introduced would be much mitigated. I do not know how things are in Westminster. In the provinces they are *tohu bohu* (if you will forgive a quotation from a language otherwise unknown to me)."

instantly understood if they are read or heard in the vernacular. But I don't think that's true of many, perhaps even most prayers. The language of much of the Bible and of many of the prayers spoken at Mass is beyond any instant understanding of the parishioners, or the lector, or, indeed, every priest; or, for that matter, every theologian. There are passages in the Bible Delphic in construction. If clarity were the paramount purpose of liturgical reform—the *ultima ratio* for going into English; the whole reason for the vernacular—then the intended reform of the liturgy has not been accomplished because it cannot be accomplished. If clarity were the desideratum, one would need to jettison, just to begin with, much of St. Paul, whose epistles are in some respects inscrutable to some of the people some of the time, in most respects inscrutable to most of the people most of the time. To translate them from the Latin or from the archaic grandeur of the Douay into John-Jane-Gyp contemporese is quite simply undoable. Now add to the textual difficulty that of metrical recitation. The very first day I served as lector the liturgy specified the following, introduced, with my ordaining, "LET US NOW RECITE THE INTROIT PRAYER." Followed by, *Judge me, O God, and distinguish my cause from the nation that is not holy; deliver me from the unjust and deceitful man.*

"Judge-me-O-God / And-distinguish-my-cause-from-the-nation-that-is-not-holy / Deliver-me-from-the-unjust-and-deceitful-man." Why was it thought that such words as these are better understood, appreciated—*felt*—when rendered metrically in regimented marches with the congregation? Who, thinking to read these holy and inspired words reverently, submits happily to the iron rhythm of a formulaic joint reading? It's one thing to chant together a doxological refrain (*Lord deliver us / Lord save us / Grant us peace*). But the extended prayer-in-unison is a forced unison that defies the proffered justification of the exercise, if indeed the objective is to cultivate an understanding of Scripture. The rote saying of anything is the enemy of understanding. To reduce to unison prayers whose meaning is elusive to begin with is virtually to assure that they will mean nothing to the reciter, denied the time to ponder their meaning according to his own resources or desires.

Even when spoken in English by a single voice, the scriptural passage is not readily penetrable, let alone pellucid. *"Brethren: Everything that was written in times past was written for our instruction, that through the patience and encouragement afforded by the scriptures we might have hope. I say that Christ exercised His ministry to the circumcised to show God's fidelity in fulfilling His promises to the fathers, whereas the Gentiles glorify God for His mercy, as it is written: 'Therefore will I proclaim you among the nations, and I will sing praise to your name.' "* These were words with which I accosted my fellow parishioners from the lector's pulpit at St. Mary's in Stamford. I do not even now comprehend this passage well enough to give its meaning with absolute confidence. And yet the instruction manual informed me that I was precisely to pronounce the words I spoke "clearly" and "confidently." And—together— the congregation would recite similar such passages in (what was then) the Gradual.

In 1962 Evelyn Waugh wrote and asked me if *National Review* would "wish to publish"—his words—an essay he had just completed entitled, "The Same Again Please: A Layman's Hopes of the Vatican Council" *(NR,* December 4, 1962). It was plain that he wanted a decision without submitting his manuscript to a probationary reading. Of course we would like to publish it, I wrote him, as who would not have?

Mr. Waugh didn't mean us to assume that he opposed *all* Church reforms. He listed some as plainly desirable—for example, the abolition of the Index of proscribed reading (though it had its uses: "Sartre's presence on the list provides a convenient excuse for not reading him"). But he dismissed the notion that modifications in Catholic practice were greatly overdue and that the replacement of the Latin by the vernacular would enhance ecumenism. "Few believe that moment to be imminent. The Catholic aspiration is that the more manifest the true character of the Church can be made, the more dissenters will be drawn to make their submission."

But no such movement is around the corner:

There is no possibility of the Church's modifying her defined doctrines to attract those to whom they are repugnant. The Orthodox Churches of the East, with whom the doctrinal differences are small and technical, are more hostile to Rome than are the Protestants. To them the sack and occupation of Constantinople for the first half of the thirteenth century—an event which does not bulk large in the historical conspectus of the West—is as lively and bitter a memory as is Hitler's persecution to the Jews. Miracles are possible; it is presumptuous to expect them; only a miracle can reconcile the East with Rome.

And on the liturgy:

. . . there is a persistent rumour that changes may be made in the liturgy. . . . There is a party among the hierarchy who wish to make superficial but startling changes in the Mass in order to make it more widely intelligible. The nature of the Mass is so profoundly mysterious that the most acute and holy men are continually discovering further nuances of significance. It is not a peculiarity of the Roman Church that much which happens at the altar is in varying degrees obscure to most of the worshipers. It is in fact the mark of all the historic, apostolic Churches. I think it highly doubtful whether the average churchgoer either needs or desires to have complete intellectual, verbal comprehension of all that is said. He has come to worship . . . I lately heard the sermon of an enthusiastic, newly ordained priest who spoke, perhaps with conscious allusion to Mr. [Harold] Macmillan's unhappy phrase about Africa, of a "great wind" that was to blow through us, sweeping away the irrelevant accretions of centuries and revealing the Mass in its pristine, apostolic simplicity; and as I considered his congregation, closely packed parishioners of a small country town of whom I regard myself as a typical member, I thought how little his aspirations corresponded with ours.

Waugh was wrong. The vernacular swept through the Church like a tornado. Although from time to time the Vatican reminds us that it was never intended that the Latin Mass should die, dying is exactly what is happening, notwithstanding efforts here and there to keep it alive. One reason some bishops are reluctant to encourage the Latin

Mass is that to do so is to encourage, even posthumously, the movement of Archbishop Marcel Lefebvre, who defied the Vatican even to
the point of ordaining priests in his schismatical order. In my town of
Stamford, Connecticut, there are thirteen Catholic churches. The
Bishop of Bridgeport, a learned Latinist as it happens, permits only a
single church in Stamford to conduct one Mass in Latin, on the first
Sunday of the month. But Bishop Edward Egan is not indifferent to
plain mistreatment in translations from the Latin. "Take just one example," he said at a meeting of bishops in Rome convened to review
liturgical texts presented by the International Commission on English
in the Liturgy. "The prayer to which the speaker before me referred
contains twenty-two words in Latin. Nine of them are not translated at
all. This is not 'translation' in any serious meaning of that word. This
is 'invention,' 'composition,' 'revising,' or something of the sort."
Bishop Egan strongly protested the attempted "inculturation" of the
original Latin texts into the "American context." "We are to 'translate,' that is, convert the same thoughts from one language to another.
If we were to find in the Latin texts of the Church universal elements
which we believe cannot be squared with 'American culture,' we have
no course but to discuss and resolve the problem with those in Rome
who wrote what we are to translate."

I have viewed the liturgical reform, or revolution, as vexing. My
understanding of arrangements, as a boy and up until the Council, was
that the congregation of the laity was gathered together primarily for
the convenience of the priest, who could hardly go from household to
household to administer the sacraments and deliver homilies. In the
days of the catacomb, and under modern persecutions, the assembly
was an empirical requirement. Churches are houses of God and, here
and there, exquisite architectural and artistic creations. But I never
thought of the Mass, when only I was present (and such things happened, every blue moon), as an incomplete experience for want of
fellow worshipers. The individual at Mass is witness to the stunning
patrimony of Christ. If we followed the missal and read to ourselves
the same prayers the priest was saying, then we felt an intimacy with

the individual Mass. Those who chose might recite the rosary or read divers prayers while the priest was following the liturgical score; but everyone, even those inattentive, was witness to what was happening at the altar. The priest was the executor of the act of transubstantiation. He stood, appropriately, with his back to the parishioners, the better to absorb himself in his divine mission.

But now the priests were instructed to face the congregation and to conduct their thaumaturgical rites so to speak under the widest public scrutiny. It was not only the priest's privacy that was invaded—the parishioners would now be reminded every few minutes of the congregational nature of their celebration. "The new Catholic cathedral in Liverpool," Mr. Waugh wrote, "is circular in plan: the congregation are to be disposed in tiers, as though in a surgical operating theater. If they raise their eyes they will be staring at one another. Backs are often distracting; faces will be more so. The intention is to bring everyone as near as possible to the altar. I wonder if the architect has studied the way in which people take their places at a normal parochial Mass. In all the churches with which I am familiar it is the front pews which are filled last." I somewhere opined that Evelyn Waugh's death on Easter Sunday in 1966, the Sunday before the reformers promulgated the Kiss of Peace, was evidence that the Holy Spirit was in fact behind it all, but merciful in His afflictions: no imagination is so vivid as to visualize Mr. Waugh yanked from prayerful thought to clasp the hand of the pilgrim to his right, to his left, ahead, and behind him.

And it is reasonable to meditate on the loss of Latin to the Church. The author Alexander Stille wrote a marvelous long essay for the *American Scholar,* "Latin Fanatic: A Profile of Father Reginald Foster" (autumn 1994). Fr. Foster is the principal Latinist at the Vatican. His enthusiasm for Latin and Latin literature consumes him and inspires the hundreds (thousands?) of men and women who have voluntarily taken his classes. I remember the amazement I felt at age thirteen on learning that the faculty of St. John's conversed in Latin when they met together formally. Mr. Stille corrects me—there was no reason to be surprised:

> Not only was the Mass said in Latin, all of Foster's classes—theology, philosophy, canon law, archaeology, and Church history—were taught in Latin. All priests were required to take seven or eight years of Latin, and everyone in the Catholic Church, from San Francisco to Sydney, had some degree of proficiency in Latin. International Vatican meetings were conducted in Latin. Popes, cardinals, and bishops corresponded and sometimes conversed in it. The current Pope, Karol Wojtyla, wrote his doctoral dissertation in Latin when he was a student in Rome.

Here, then, was a manifest utilitarian benefit: all Catholic religious knew the language and, with varying degrees of skill, could communicate with one another. What does startle us is the speed with which the bond was disbanded.

> Even fifteen or twenty years ago [Stille writes], the Vatican could effectively use Latin as its principal tool of communication and expect that prelates around the world would understand it. Increasingly, Latin has been reduced to merely ceremonial or decorative functions—like the colorful uniforms worn by the Pope's Swiss guards or the elegant calligraphy that adorns official Vatican invitations. There is some talk about eliminating the calligraphy department as an unnecessary extravagance, and Foster is worried that one day in the not-too-distant future the same will happen to the Latin department. "There is no illusion about Latin taking off. It's not," Foster says with disenchanted realism. "It's definitely going down." At a recent synod of European bishops, Pope John Paul II chose to give his final address in Latin, but, says Foster, most people didn't have any idea what he was saying.

The technology of the computer age will not leave anyone who cares to communicate with someone of another tongue without the means to do so. And one must suppose that priests can make do studying in translation the work of St. Augustine, St. Thomas Aquinas, Erasmus, St. Thomas More, Descartes, Spinoza, Galileo, Newton, and Leibniz, who wrote part or all of their work in Latin. But what has the layman lost?

The Catholic churchgoer might have studied Latin seriously in high school and college, though this would be so only of a very few. But a substantial number were exposed to Latin at school—two years of it, as a rule. They would remember a few phrases, and could follow the Ordinary passages of the Mass. An elderly woman minding the little bookstore at the narthex of the Farm Street Church in London smiled when I asked her a dozen years ago if she still carried Latin missals. The mere request brightened her, and in the low tone of voice one tends to use inside a church she divulged her awful disappointment at the disappearance of all Latin. "I thought, if *only* the priest were allowed to say *Corpus Christi* when administering Communion—just that." (We get, instead, "Body of Christ.") Most Catholics would have recognized the meaning of Corpus Christi, one supposes, though perhaps even that is asking too much. Perhaps the residents of Corpus Christi, Texas, don't know what the name of their city means, no more than the non-Hispanic residents of Los Molinos in California can be expected to know what a *molino* is.

But what of the majority of churchgoers, or at least that large number of them who had never studied Latin at all? Who couldn't go much further than to translate for themselves the meaning of *Ave Maria?* Have *they* lost anything from the alteration? In place of what was once rapidly spoken Latin by the priest, or even silently read Latin, we get now rapid English, spoken by the priest, and at a more moderate tempo, here and there joined by the congregation (some members of the congregation). The words spoken in English are taken from the missal for that Sunday, and in this sense the situation has not changed: before Vatican II those who wished to use missals did so and they found in the missals the English on the left column of the page, the Latin on the right column.

The question before the house: Is the congregation absorbing more

Scripture than under the old system? Clue: Why, if it is now needed only to listen to the words spoken by the priest, are most parishioners seen using the missal for that Sunday?

The loss of the universal Latin, together with the efforts to congregationalize the liturgy, has not, in my judgment, inspirited the Mass, and certainly has not brought converts to the churches. Not only has the size of the laity diminished, but also the size of the clergy. Given the spiritual acedia throughout Christendom, what happened can't be laid on the shoulders of the liturgical reforms of Vatican II. But inasmuch as the reformers can't hold up empirical successes as justification, an observer old enough to have experienced the old ways is entitled to judge the two experiences—the old and the new Mass—as they affected him; and on this matter I side with Mr. Waugh. Hugh Kenner, the distinguished critic, himself a convert, never knew the Latin Mass while growing up and does not (therefore?) object to current procedures, while wincing at the translations one finds in the pews. Perhaps if poetry were permitted in the vernacular translations, the loss would be felt less keenly.

But of course Vatican II was an event of enormous sweep. Particular criticisms of it are just that, particular criticisms of changes most visibly encountered. The Council was greeted with enormous enthusiasm by the overwhelming majority of priests and laity. For a little while it seemed that the Church had vaulted over encumbrances that had consolidated unreasonably and lay in the way of a sophisticated acknowledgment of ecumenism, pluralism, and decentralization. The Council ran into one event that took the wind out of it. This of course was the encyclical of Pope Paul VI denying the permissibility of birth control. That was a complicated pronouncement, profound in its implications, and in its effects, a matter on which I'll dwell. Meanwhile, there was the other, acid test. Did the reforms transfuse a great enthusiasm into the clergy? Into the laity? Into Catholic schooling?

In the United States:

Seminarians	1965: 48,992
	1995: 5,083
Infant baptisms	1965: 1.3 million
	1995: 1 million
Annulments	1968: 338
	1983: 52,000
Brothers teaching	1965: 5,868
	1995: 1,528
High school students, diocesan and parish	1965: 698,000
	1995: 379,000
Priests	1965: 58,632
	1995: 49,551
Brothers	1965: 12,271
	1995: 6,578
Sisters	1965: 179,954
	1995: 92,107

CHAPTER SEVEN

_____

In Search of Advisers: My Forum

of Converts

After spending time on the exchanges between Lunn and Knox I felt a need to inquire further, as who wouldn't? I wanted to know how some of these questions had weathered when examined by people for whose thought I had respect, in some instances affinity. I resolved to pass along my questions not to men who had published their theological catechisms, but (mostly) to men who hadn't.

I wanted, obviously, men of learning, but I wasn't looking for professional scholars. I wanted, also, people whose work, or whose spoken words, I was either formally or informally familiar with. I didn't want—not this time, not in this rather intimate book—an alien presence. And then I thought to invite only men and women who had become Catholics during their adult lifetimes. Such as these made passages into the faith that remain more vividly in the mind than those brought up, as I was, a practicing Catholic.

I had thought, when the idea first crystallized, to conscript Clare Boothe Luce, a very old friend, to join what I would call the Forum. It mattered slightly that she would give a woman's perspective, whatever that might bring; mattered greatly that she had one of the liveliest minds I ever knew. But Clare was sick. Her final illness was protracted, and I thought even of intruding on it, to ask her to look at some of the questions I would finally formulate for my stable. I told myself that that energetic, animated, and original woman hated idle moments. But I delayed, until it was too late. She had designated me, and her stepson, to deliver the eulogy at her funeral service. Soon after, I put together an hour's *Firing Line* tape drawing on five hours she had done with me on the program over the years. Hearing her arguments, experiencing her spice, I missed all the more her participation here. I probably would not have gone along with her analysis, but that would not matter. I wanted the feel of the Forum's analysis, in order to reify my own.

My second delinquency was failing to accost Malcolm Muggeridge in time. I say in time because in the last three or four years of his life he was suddenly still. No more articles, reviews, books, television interviews. I learned of his death during a sailing passage across the Atlantic, in November 1990. I will recall him and his work in a later chapter.

There was no woman (other than Luce) who met all the criteria above, and I regret this, while continuing to resist the generality that men and women, when accosting such questions as I had in mind to put to them, think or perform differently.

I learned from Lunn/Knox that when religion is being explored, the manner in which a question is addressed can be critically important. I bore this in mind as I sat down to frame my queries. I thought immediately to dwell on two broad questions. The first, What *about* Jesus of Nazareth? The second, Do you believe his miracles were conclusively documented? I held back on the crowning event, the Resurrection. I wished to pay special attention to it. I was not here conducting a plebiscite (yes, everybody believed that Jesus of Nazareth was a historical figure), but I savor the way in which each answered that question, and the one that came immediately after, about the miracles.

—Richard John Neuhaus—scholarly, dogged, genial. I met him when he was still a Lutheran pastor. In 1987 he wrote *The Catholic Moment* (HarperCollins). The book speaks of the heady opening he saw at hand for Christianity, brought on by the collapse of Marxism and by the general fatigue in Western culture. Notwithstanding that book— with its provocative title—I was surprised when, just two years later, he told me he had decided to become a Catholic. (Not much later he was a priest.) He had done, as Lutheran pastor, parish work in black communities in New York. Before his conversion, he began his full-scale career as an author and editor. He is the Editor-in-Chief of *First Things,* a Christian-oriented monthly.

Do you consider that the advent of the person of Jesus Christ is historically established beyond reasonable doubt?

Fr. Neuhaus:

Assuming you mean the first advent, the answer is certainly yes. And I do mean "beyond reasonable doubt," not merely "the preponderance of evidence." The evidence for Jesus of Nazareth is much, much better than for many other figures of antiquity whose existence is not questioned by reasonable people.

Another assumption is that you mean Jesus of Nazareth, not "the person of Jesus Christ" theologically considered. That this Jesus is the Christ, the promised Messiah, cannot be *historically* established beyond reasonable doubt. Some nineteenth-century liberal thinkers argued against the event of the historical Jesus, but that was widely recognized as an awfully strained labor that demanded too much credulity, and the effort has been entirely abandoned and discredited among reasonable people today.

Whether the early followers—those who came to be called Christians—were right about who they say Jesus was and is, that is quite another question and is eminently debatable. New Testament scholars today, Protestant and Catholic, tend to drive a sharp wedge between the historical Jesus and the Christ of faith. I think that is utterly wrongheaded (the Holy Father addresses this in passing in his encyclical *Redemptoris Missio,* explicitly stating that the Jesus of history and the Christ of faith are one figure and one concept).*

Of course the truth of the entirety of the Christian proposition depends upon the *second* advent of Jesus the Christ. Christians proleptically experience the fulfillment of that promise. In this sense, Christians are the people ahead of time; the people who are saying now what one day all will acknowledge—when "every knee shall bow and every tongue confess that Jesus Christ is Lord" (Philippians 2).

Fr. Neuhaus went on to remark the work of Josef A. Piper, and to draw special attention to his concept of the entirety of the Christian life as the life of faith, assuming the form of hope *(status viatoris)*. I think this engaging and not outside human understanding, conventionally applied. The legendary wife on the widow's walk was there every day scanning the horizon, testimony to her hope that one day her husband's ship would come into view. That in fact he might have been lost at sea didn't mean to me that hope had to be abandoned, discounted in deference to empirical reality.

* For further comment on the Jesus of history/Christ of faith question, see Fr. Neuhaus's "Reason Public and Private" in the February 1992 issue of *First Things.*

I savor Fr. Neuhaus's formulation. We concede that Jesus-the-Christ—Jesus-the-Savior—isn't something you submit for validation to the Bureau of Weights and Measures. We therefore think of him, as all Christians must, "proleptically," i.e., in anticipation of a comprehensive acknowledgment of him, as Him. And this gives additional romance to Christian belief, as is fitting for those who sit waiting, forever and ever, yet confident that the third act will be transporting.

And on the subject of miracles,

In your judgment, is the evidence in the Gospels that He committed miracles convincing?

Fr. Neuhaus calls up the difference between Newtonian and contemporary physics. The physics of the Enlightenment demanded exact validations of any event that contradicted natural physical laws. How could this have happened? Why not? It is, really, a derivative question, isn't it? "If God, the source and end of all that is, entered history in human form, I should think that there would be some rather stunning signs that something remarkable had happened. Signs very much like those recounted in the Gospels."

We have left the Enlightenment behind. "We live in a world within worlds, and apprehend but a very small part of reality." Fr. Neuhaus seemed to me correct in pointing out that "contemporary science is increasingly directed toward mystery rather than, as was thought at one time, cognitive closure." And the deductive point. If Jesus, then . . . "One works backward from one who believes Jesus. Then the miracles seem both entirely plausible and fitting. The central question in apologetics is now as it was when Jesus posed it to His Disciples, 'What think ye of the Christ?' When one gets the right answer to that, miracles and much else fall into place."

But what does this say to the skeptic? If he disbelieves in Jesus, obviously he disbelieves in his miracles. These were at the time tactile phenomena—they ate the bread He created and drank the wine. But there was no Zapruder on the spot with the probative camera lens. How much of Christianity rests on reason's acceptance of the miracles? Is it historical arrogance to doubt what was so widely recorded as having happened? Where is the greater strain on faith, that all those things did happen? Or that they didn't?

—George Rutler, whom I met not when he was a Lutheran pastor, but when he was an Anglican priest, is shy of manner, soft-spoken, resplendently learned with a fine capacity to amuse and to be amused. After ten years as an Anglican, he became a Catholic priest (in 1981). He does parish work in New York City and writes books and articles. On Jesus of Nazareth his judgment was essentially the same as Fr. Neuhaus's. I liked his formulation that the "historicity of the Christ is a matter of faith [only] because it transcends historical experience." The point is arresting. Faith that the sun will rise tomorrow is regularly validated. Faith that Caesar was killed calls for reliance on historical material.

On the matter of the miracles he wrote,

The order in which the miracles happened varies, in the Gospel accounts, as does their selection. But Christ clearly was a miracle worker: that was a ground of the accusations made against him (in particular the raising of Lazarus). What is most fascinating is the reasons for the miracles.

They are totally different from the typical stunts performed in those days to give the illusion of a miracle in order to create a following. The Messianic miracles were carefully planned as "signs" of the coming Kingdom. Those of healing were done reluctantly, out of compassion, and were something of an embarrassment to Christ himself: he even ordered that they be hushed up. The "Messianic" signs were carefully planned to point to the Passion (beginning with the Miracle at Cana). There is nothing like them in pious literature before or since. Moreover, the early Church had conspicuous success largely because of the miraculous powers of the Apostles. The book of Acts is the most reliable historical account we have of the period, and the miracles are consistent with political and social developments attendant upon them.

This analysis would seem to increase the odds in favor of belief. To deny the miracles is to suggest massive and orchestrated imposture. Would answers from men not of the cloth be very different?

—Russell Kirk (1918–94), author of *The Conservative Mind* and twenty other books, was the academic dean of the conservative movement in America. He was hugely informed, stern in his judgments, shy in person, emphatic in style, and something of a storyteller. Soon after he married a devout and spirited Catholic, he joined the Church. We learn from his posthumous autobiography, *The Sword of Imagination: Memoirs of a Half-Century of Literary Conflict* (Eerdmans, 1995), that he had felt a strong religious inclination for many years.

On Jesus:

Nothing in the history of the ancient world is better established than the life of Jesus of Nazareth. We have four separate accounts by four witnesses, contemporaries; also the Epistles of St. Paul, a brief account by the Jewish historian Josephus, and various mentions of Jesus and his followers by Greek and Roman writers. By contrast, of Socrates we have accounts by only two ancient writers, Plato and Xenophon, who knew him; and of some of the great men included in Plutarch's *Lives of the Noble Greeks and Romans,* we have inherited next to no account except Plutarch's own. It has been pointed out that it would be no more absurd to maintain that Napoleon Bonaparte was a figure merely of myth than to argue that a real Jesus never walked the earth. We even have the Shroud of Turin [quite possibly] Jesus' burial garment, with its scientifically inexplicable image (like a photographic positive) on the linen. Nobody challenges the existence and the deeds of Augustus or of Herod, Jesus' contemporaries of his early years; why try to maintain that the Carpenter of Nazareth was a figment of the imagination, and that the Christian religion, which swept across the world, had no founder at all?

The question, Was there a historical Jesus? I thought closed, though the way in which the serial affirmations of my Forum were made, interested and gratified me.

And on the miracles:

For Jesus' "Great Works" we have chiefly, of course, the Synoptic Gospels and certain traditions recorded in Eusebius' *History* and lesser gospels of the early centuries. Astounding wonders appear to have been worked. That nobody works such wonders near the end of the twentieth century of the Christian era is no reason for disbelief: by definition, miracles are rare exceptions to the ordinary operation of the laws of nature. See C. S. Lewis's little book *Miracles*.

If the Word became flesh a second time, presumably such miracles as the Great Works would be held again. It is said that faith works miracles, and that miracles are worked in order to rouse faith. Were miracles worked in medieval times at the shrine of St. Thomas Becket in Canterbury Cathedral, or at the shrine of the bones of St. Andrew in St. Andrew Cathedral, Scotland? And if so, why did those miracles cease to occur well before the coming of the Reformation? Is it perfect faith that conjures up the miracle? Why is it that no miracles have been recorded at the splendid shrine of the most wondrous of all relics, the Shroud of Turin, but a good many are said to have come to pass at the shrine of the girl-saint Bernadette Soubirous? [see below, chapter 9] Are miracles, like beauty, in the eye of the beholder? I do not doubt that Jesus worked his miracles; yet how long the results thereof endured, and whether what the witnesses beheld was physically "real," we have no means of knowing. Oh for a revelation!

The great ache, the absence of which all Christians experience, requiring us to acknowledge that the God we believe in feels no compulsion (perhaps the opposite) ostentatiously to confirm the faith.

. . .

—Jeffrey Hart is emeritus professor of English at Dartmouth. He is vastly learned in literature and philosophy and cultural history and athletics, the author of a half dozen books. He has been for thirty years a senior editor of *National Review* and we worked side by side during most of those years, when he wrote about every subject on earth—but not religion (excepting poetical columns at Christmastime, in his nationally syndicated column). He became a Catholic while in his forties. He is divorced and remarried, for reasons unexplored by the author. He dove with gusto into the question of the historicity of Jesus of Nazareth.

I certainly consider that the historical presence of Jesus Christ has been established beyond a reasonable doubt. I know that late-nineteenth-century and earlier twentieth-century biblical criticism cast doubt upon the "historical Jesus." Albert Schweitzer provided a good account of this in his *The Quest for the Historical Jesus,* which ended up concluding that the historical Jesus is difficult to establish and represents a sort of vanishing point. At the same time, the theology of Karl Barth and his many followers made a virtue of these negative conclusions. Barth was in a sense conservative, in that he pushed the "faith" dimension of Protestantism to its extreme conclusion. Historical arguments, for Barth, were beside the point. What mattered was the encounter with the utterly transcendent God, who would always be Other. Meanwhile, Rudolph Bultmann was "demythologizing" the Scriptures, that is, bringing them into line with nineteenth-century presuppositions about what is possible in the cosmos.

However, and as summed up conveniently in Stephen Neill's *The Interpretation of the New Testament 1860–1960* (Oxford, 1966), more recent serious work has pointed in a different direction. Neill concludes that the biblical narratives are worth far more as history than earlier scholars thought, that we know more—historically—about Jesus than about other figures in the ancient world. This receives support as archaeology moves on. For example, some scholars even doubted the historical existence of Nazareth. Then archaeologists dug it up. Archaeology is now constantly turning up confirmation of sites and events in the Old Testament. (The existence of Troy was doubted by scholars until a German businessman named Schliemann, using Homer's narrative as a guide, found it.)

It is very difficult (impossible?) for skeptics about Jesus to get around 1 Corinthians 15. Paul there is speaking to an audience that agrees with him on the nature of historical fact. Corinth was not some backwoods, but well within the Hellenistic ambience. He appeals to the testimony of witnesses, "most of whom are alive at this day"— that is, you can check it with them. And uses a blatantly historical argument to affirm the life, death, *and* resurrection of Jesus.

Once more, a ringing affirmation, done by a scholar trained in the science of evaluating data. Jeff Hart edges into the critical question of the Resurrection. . . . And in respect of miracles:

The Gospels include narrative accounts of His miracles, but usually do not provide evidence. The Resurrection of course is a miracle. Therefore I regard the Gospel miracles as derivatively credible, on the argument that the spiritual force that could accomplish the Resurrection could certainly accomplish lesser miracles. The Resurrection I take to be a reexpression of the original divine creative energy that made the universe in the first place. [I take this to mean that the Resurrection, in Professor Hart's view of it, was something on the order of a divine assertion comparable to the creation of the universe.] David Hume's comment on miracles has always been something of a puzzler to me, and I notice that Robert Fogelin, in his book of essays, devotes one to this argument. Briefly, Hume, as I understand him, argues that if someone reports a miracle, it is more probable that (a) he is lying than that (b) the miracle occurred. That is a good approach to ask of some extraordinary report—for example, that Eisenhower was an atomic spy. But it does not seem to touch the question of miracles. No one ever said miracles are *probable*. Actually,

Hume is very tricky. In his famous *Dialogues Concerning Natural Religion,* the skeptical position defeats the argument from design too easily, I think, but does not touch the argument from faith (Demea). The dialogue in effect concedes that there is or at least may be a realm to which the probabilities of the phenomenal world do not apply.

I heard from Jeff Hart what I hadn't thought I would so much welcome, namely the *plausibility* of the miracles. If a movement that would soon absorb the Western world was launched by a few dozen men and women all of whom thought themselves witnesses to miracles, isn't the burden of disbelief tougher? We can, after viewing the movie by Oliver Stone, and reading tracts in the tradition of skepticism, believe that the man who shot Kennedy was firing from the grassy knoll. But the abundance of evidence to the contrary would seem to me to make a skeptic of the grassy knoller, rather than of the host of others who accept overwhelming evidence that pointed to Lee Harvey Oswald.

—Ernest van den Haag, distinguished sociologist and legal scholar, an intellectual of renowned analytical lucidity and wit, responded laconically to my questionnaire with an introductory warning, ''Note also that I am a convert in substance but not in form. I stayed away for a long time from the Church except in the most formal sense and I am only now making my way back.'' He is welcome. We have been close friends for forty years. He agreed on the question of the historical Jesus—that he was indisputably there—and on the miracles he underscored Neuhaus on modern scientific curiosity.

Note that the very notion of miracle—a supernatural event—rests on a conception of nature no longer held by science. Natural (physical) law was thought to be immutable and without exception. Therefore exceptions could only be—supernatural. Today natural laws are observed with recurrent irregularities, statistical in nature. Hence ex-

ceptions are incorporated. This does not actually contradict the supernatural factor but requires of it a bit of reformulation.

The insight is refreshing. Science does not pretend to know how to
account for phenomena which it nevertheless acknowledges, permitting us, within the bounds of scientific discipline, to denominate the
cause of any particular phenomenon as supernatural. But it seems to
me that this introduces terminological sophistry. If the cause of that
eruption cannot be divined by scientific investigation, the scientists
then say, and it would seem to me properly, that the experience
denotes nothing more than the insufficiency of their resources, not a
supernatural whim.

—Wick Allison is a young Texan, the nonacademic member of my
Forum; a bright and enterprising graduate of the University of Texas
who leaped into the publishing business while in his twenties. He
served briefly as publisher of *National Review* and in his spare time
edited a fresh edition of the Bible first put together in the thirties by
Ernest Sutherland Bates. It is called *The Bible Designed to Be Read as
Living Literature* and was assigned by Mr. Pulling, the headmaster of the
Millbrook School, to his students at Bible class at the time I was there
(see chapter 3). Allison made a relatively neglected point about the
bearing on our inquiry of the loyalty Jesus himself inspired among his
followers.

> Even if there were little external evidence of His life, the actions of
> His disciples and the written record produced by His followers hardly
> seem possible without a real person to inspire and motivate them.
> The fact that many of His early followers, including the Apostles
> themselves, were put to death on account of their fidelity to the
> mission they believed He had sent them on seems inconsistent with
> the notion that He was a fabrication.

I had always thought this point very difficult for the skeptic to cope with: the utter loyalty of the company of Jesus, and the harmony of their integration of him as the Christ that had been promised by Scripture.

And on miracles:

At times the Gospel writers themselves seem a little flustered about what they are reporting, and I find this charming. Of course explanations can be invented to explain some of the miracles, such as Lloyd C. Douglas's rendering of the loaves and fishes (people who brought food with them were embarrassed to eat around people who had brought nothing until Jesus started to share His own food, and the "miracle" was that everybody started to share). It could well have happened that way, but the healing miracles require a little more work: "I was blind and now I see." These are hard to explain for the simple reason that there were so many witnesses and that the early ones were the basis for Jesus' fame spreading throughout Galilee. People came to see Him because they knew someone who had been cured. The villages were small; if someone had been lame for thirty years and suddenly could walk, everybody was bound to know it.

Another insight into the question *What is the preponderance of the evidence that comes down to us?*

My own thoughts on the subject, better consolidated thanks to my Forum, are, happily, not novel. If Jesus never existed as a historical figure, the great vacuity would long since have been isolated. If He had been (as more than one critic has urged) an illiterate but charismatic fanatic, He would not have inspired the perdurable faith He did among His followers. Seductive fanatics we know all about; but when they die, their shadows quickly dissipate. That of Christ soon enveloped the entire Western world. Erwin Goodenough, the renowned religious historian at Yale (himself a skeptic), acknowledged in conversation with me twenty years ago that he simply could not explain (and therefore nobody could, he invited me to conclude) how Christianity managed to survive Christ. There were dozens, even hundreds, of start-up religions during those centuries, all over the world. Those who reject the explanation of Jesus Himself, that not even the gates of Hell would prevail over His Church, will have to go on looking for an explanation of Christianity's hold on great thinkers, and billions of disciples.

The episodic nature of miracles continues to confound Christians . . . Why at Lourdes? Why not as spectacularly—if at all—in many other shrines? I see no refuge here, beyond the Butler Escape ("If I had been put in charge of the incidence of miracles, I'd have orchestrated them differently"). It would be nice to have one very conspicuous miracle, in every—major—country, on Christmas Day. That isn't the way God goes about things. Evelyn Waugh said it simply in his essay quoted in the preceding chapter: miracles happen, but it is presumptuous to expect them.

CHAPTER EIGHT

———————

The Crucifixion Examined,

and Imagined

I invoked my Forum on this question:

In your opinion, is Christ's Resurrection critical to your faith? Critical to Christianity? If so, why?

—Fr. Neuhaus:

Utterly critical, for the reasons that St. Paul gives in 1 Corinthians 15. That the promised "new creation" has already broken into history in

Jesus is the core of the Christian good news, or gospel. It inescapably has everything to do also with eschatological promise. The alternative to His being raised, never to die again, is that He did die again; and therefore our hope (for eternal life) is in vain.

—Fr. Rutler agrees:

Like the Oxford don who said he was "inclined to agree with St. Paul," I have to agree with the Apostle that the Resurrection is *the* reason for Christianity.

What if it hadn't happened?

—Russell Kirk asked that we look at Christianity assuming Christ were *not* divine:

The Resurrection lacking, what we call Christianity would be a mere congeries of moral exhortations, at best; and exhortations founded upon no more authority than the occasional utterances of an obscure man whose hints of divinity and half-veiled claims of power to judge the quick and the dead might be regarded as manifestations of delusions of grandeur. Many false prophets are gone forth into the world. It is no wonder that the Pharisees regarded with suspicion—nay, horror—the Nazarene who advised them to resist evil. But the Resurrection in the flesh—which some now hint was bound up with nuclear disintegration and reintegration, our solid flesh being known now to consist of innumerable electrical particles held in coherence by means of which we know nothing—proved that indeed Jesus the son had transcended matter and was divine. Without that Resurrection, which prefigures our own resurrection and life everlasting, one might as well turn again to the gods of the Greeks, or to Epictetus, Marcus Aurelius, and Seneca. The Resurrection is critical both to my personal faith and to the whole elaborate edifice called Christianity. It is now more rationally possible to believe in the Resurrection than it was in Saint Paul's time.

I was surprised by Kirk's closing point, that but for the Resurrection we might just as well turn to the gods of the Greeks, or whatever. If, *per impossible,* it were established that Christ did not rise, I would myself instantly enlist in the Judaic faith, whose heaviest burden would then be not Jonah and the whale, but the blemish brought on Judaism by the fake Jesus who went around citing the Old Testament as his patrimony, claiming he was God. I would then, in Judaism, still be united with the prophets, and settled down for the promised incarnation, sometime in the future.

Jeffrey Hart returns to the evidence, insisting on its conclusiveness:

I know that demythologizing theologians try to make of the Resurrection a spiritual rather than a physical event, suggesting that a movie camera at the tomb would have photographed no event, etc. But Paul is not speaking about something that happened only in the minds of the Disciples. He is not flimflamming the Corinthians. He is talking about a risen Jesus who was *seen,* and he specifies seen by whom.

For Wick Allison the Resurrection

is indeed everything. Not only the theological construct. Not only the mythic resonance. The whole business. And it's not just because a hundred other Jewish rabbis before, during, and after Christ have preached many of the same things He did, and we've never heard of them. While the Resurrection was immensely important in spreading the "good news," it was more important than that: the Resurrection *was* the good news. God came to man to suffer like a man, to be killed for His trouble, and to give an imperishable sign of hope. This is the entire message of the Gospels. All else Jesus gave us were signposts to guide us along the way, to enable us to behave as hopeful people and to enable us to remain faithful.

It surprises almost no one that Christians believe in the Crucifixion of Jesus Christ and in His subsequent Resurrection. What isn't easily dramatized is the mind-numbing scene on Calvary. I remember that Fr. Burke, our parish priest in Camden, South Carolina, read out one Good Friday when I was a boy a technical description, done by a pathologist, of the pains inflicted on Christ. I was much moved by the recitation. It is easy to forget pain—it is healthy to do so, the mother's transcendence of childbirth pain serving as the standard metaphor. At Millbrook School, Nathaniel Abbott coached junior varsity football, taught Latin, conducted the Millbrook orchestra, and gave a class in music appreciation. A feature of his music class was a look—a very long look—at J. S. Bach's *St. Matthew's Passion.* On the day he began it he told his dozen-odd students that in the succeeding six class sessions we would be listening to all four hours of the *Passion,* a kind of twitch-anticipating warning which had exactly the results Mr. Abbott could predict, having seen the same thing happen to a generation of boys—general dismay at the prospects of six hour-long sessions of Baroque boredom.

The boys would sit through it, as I did, only because we had no alternative. At the outset of the hour Mr. Abbott would read out the scriptural verses Bach set to music, giving us some narrative orientation of what the music was up to. He knew that many of the students would pass the experience by . . . One more exposure to a great work, ho hum, and on to livelier things.

But Mr. Abbott knew also that some of the boys would be taken by what in my experience is the most compendiously moving extended piece of music I ever heard. The artistic climax is the chromatic movement toward the depths of desolation as Christ dies (*"et sepultus est"*), leading to the brassy triumph of His Resurrection (*"Et resurrexit"*). Bach did this in a composition quite simply overpowering, infusing in the recitative, followed by the aria, followed by the chorale, an intimate sense of the pain, the sorrow, and the joy.

My nephew Fr. Michael Bozell thought to send me a few years ago some pages from Maria Valtorta, Italian writer and mystic (1897–1961). She wrote a huge five-volume book called *The Poem of the Man God,* and one part of the fifth volume was her fancied vision of the

Crucifixion. She got into trouble with the authorities in the Vatican because she insisted that what she had written about the Crucifixion was what actually happened.

Oh? How did she know?

A private vision.

"The subject of mystical visions is always a touchy matter," Michael's accompanying note read, "because sometimes you're dealing with pathological problems rather than supernatural manifestations, and it is almost impossible to make a definitive judgment. That judgment will inevitably hinge on two things: the saintliness of the visionary's life and the integrity of the doctrine implicitly or explicitly contained in the visions. It takes a while for a consensus to materialize. In the meantime, the fate of this or that work can fluctuate."

My friend and theological consultant Fr. Kevin Fitzpatrick, who is also a doctor of theology, was a little alarmed at the prospect of my using Valtorta. Not so much because her work was, for a while, on the Index of prohibited reading—that kind of thing happens, and there is often life after death. He wrote me:

> My main problem is the use of any private revelations not approved by the Church. This is not a legalistic concern, but a concern based on some experience of people who, to be blunt, are not satisfied with Revelation which ended with the death of the last Apostle. Some people consume books like this out of what can only be described as a lust for details of the life of Our Lord and Our Lady. They are dissatisfied that the Gospels give so little. They don't understand that they were not written as biographies of Christ, but as proclamations of the "god-spell," the Good News of our salvation. All we know and will ever know about the life of Christ and His Mother is in sacred scripture and, unsatisfying as that may be to those who want full-fledged biographies, there is nothing to be done about it. As private material for mental prayer and meditation, [such material] can be used by mature and prudent people.

Well, then, is there scriptural conflict? Fr. Michael had written me, ". . . I have poked around to some extent in volume five, from which the enclosed passages are culled, and I have only found one scene which I found difficult to mesh with the Gospel.''

Not quite enough. Fr. Kevin wrote:

In fact, Valtorta seems to have solved the Synoptic problem that's been plaguing scholars for centuries, viz., the contradictions between Matthew, Mark, and Luke. She has St. Dismas, the Good thief, blessing Christ; Matthew (xxvii.44) has him reviling Him (Luke and Mark do not); she has Our Lord drinking gall mixed with vinegar (Mark xv.36 has Him drinking just vinegar). I was amused to see Joseph of Arimathea boldly traversing the line of fifty soldiers and the angry Jews in order to get near the Cross, since in Mark (xv.43) we're told he "took courage" to go to Pilate to retrieve the body. In John (the non-Synoptic Gospel), Joseph is a disciple of Christ's, but "secretly, for fear of the Jews" (v.38).

Fr. Michael warned me that the literary genre "varies notably from visionary to visionary. I have read several volumes of Katherine Emmerich's *Life of Jesus Christ,* another compilation of visions (nineteenth century), and find the whole approach to be other than Valtorta's. Whereas Emmerich's account is nothing less than psychedelic, Valtorta reads like a James Michener novel. But even what they *'see'* varies. In my mind this does not discredit their testimony, because two witnesses to the same event don't necessarily look at or record the same things. What's more, a vision seems to be heavily imprinted with the seer's subjectivity.'' Knox and Lunn agreed, in passages not reproduced above, that the slight variations in the accounts of the Crucifixion rather validate, than otherwise, an event which, had all reports of it been identical, would have raised a suspicion of collusion.

The account by Valtorta, or at least that much of it that deals specifically with the suffering endured, would be painful reading describing any death by crucifixion. Valtorta is excruciatingly absorbed by physical detail. Either she was once a medical student or else she studied anatomy, bone by bone. The language is crude, sometimes convoluted. Basic theatrical skills are almost clinically absent. She felt a need for repeated ejaculations of dismay, indignation, fury, reverence.

And yet when I first read it, the words of the Negro spiritual I heard so often growing up in South Carolina sang out in my memory. *Were you there when they crucified my Lord? / Were you there when they nailed Him to the Cross? / Sometimes it causes me to tremble, tremble, tremble. / Were you there when they crucified my Lord?*

My decision, then, is that in the only book on the faith I will ever put together I don't want to deprive the reader of what I view, notwithstanding its crudity—perhaps because of it?—as an artful portrayal of the great historical event that preceded, and led to, the Resurrection, a depiction if not inspired by God, inspiring nonetheless.

THE CRUCIFIXION, AS SEEN, OR IMAGINED, BY MARIA VALTORTA*

Four men, seemingly more worthy of death on the cross than the condemned men, jump from a path onto the place of the execution. They are wearing short sleeveless tunics and in their hands they are holding nails, hammers, and ropes, which they show to the condemned men, scoffing at them. The crowd is excited with cruel frenzy.

The centurion offers Jesus the amphora, so that He may drink the anaesthetic mixture of myrrhed wine. But Jesus refuses it. The two robbers however drink a lot of it. Then the amphora, with a wide flared mouth, is placed near a large stone, almost on the edge of the summit.

The condemned men are ordered to undress. The two robbers do so without shame. On the contrary they amuse themselves making obscene gestures towards the crowd and in particular towards a group

---

* The English translation I was given is not always idiomatic. I have for that reason taken a (very) few editorial liberties. The extract from THE POEM OF THE MAN-GOD by Maria Valtorta is granted by permission of Centro Editoriale Valtortiano, 03036 Isola del Liri (Fr.), Italy. North American distributor, Librarie Mediaspul, 250 Nord Boulevard St. Francois, Sherbrooke, Quebec JIE 2B9, Canada.

of priests, who are all white in their linen garments and who have gone back to the lower open space little by little, taking advantage of their caste to creep up there.

The executioners offer the condemned men three rags, so that they may tie them round their groins. The robbers take them, uttering horrible curses. Jesus, who strips Himself slowly because of the pangs of the wounds from His flogging, refuses them. Perhaps He thinks that He can keep on the short drawers, which He had on during the flagellation. But when He is told to take them off as well, He stretches out His hand to receive the rag of the executioners, to conceal His nakedness.

But Mary has noticed everything and has removed the long thin white veil covering her head under her dark mantle, on which she has already shed so many tears. She removes it without letting her mantle drop and gives it to John so that he may hand it to Longinus for her son. The centurion takes the veil without any objection. He sees that Jesus is about to strip Himself completely, turning to the side where there are no people, His back, furrowed with bruises and blisters, to the crowd. The back is covered with sores and dark crusts that are bleeding again. The centurion gives Him His mother's linen veil. Jesus recognises it and wraps it round His pelvis several times, fastening it carefully so that it will not fall off. And on the linen veil, so far soaked only with tears, the first drops of blood begin to fall, because many of the wounds, covered with blood-clots, reopened again as He stooped to take off His sandals and lay down His garments, and blood is streaming down again.

Jesus now turns towards the crowd and one can see that His chest, legs, and arms have also been struck by the scourges. At the height of His liver there is a huge bruise, and under His left costal arch there are seven clear stripes in relief, ending with seven small cuts bleeding inside a violet circle, a cruel blow of a scourge in such a sensitive region of the diaphragm. His knees, bruised by repeated falls that began immediately after He was captured, are dark with hematomas and the knee-caps are torn, particularly the right one, by a large bleeding wound.

The crowds scoff at Him in chorus. "O Handsome! The most handsome of the sons of men! The daughters of Jerusalem adore you!" And in the tone of a psalm they chant:

"My beloved is fresh and ruddy, to be known among ten thousand. His head is purest gold, His locks are palm fronds, as silky as the feathers of ravens. His eyes are like two doves bathing in streams not of water, but of milk, in the milk of His orbit. His conversation is drenched with sweetness and He is altogether delightful."

And they laugh and shout also: "The leper! The leper! So have you fornicated with an idol, if God has struck you so? Have you mumbled against the saints of Israel? Are you the Son of God? . . . Certainly not. You are the abortion of Satan! At least he, Mammon, is powerful and strong. You . . . are in rags, you are powerless and revolting."

The robbers are tied to the crosses and are carried to their places, one to the right, one to the left, leaving the place destined for Jesus. They howl, swear—particularly when the crosses are carried to the holes, making the ropes cut into their wrists—curse out their oaths against God, the Law, the Romans, the Judaeans.

It is Jesus' turn. He lies on the cross meekly. The two robbers were so rebellious that, as the four executioners were not sufficient to hold them, some soldiers had to intervene to prevent them from kicking away the torturers who were tying their wrists to the cross. But no help is required for Jesus. He lies down and places His head where they tell Him. He stretches out His arms and His legs as He is told. He takes care only to arrange His veil properly. Now His long, slender white body stands out against the dark wood and the yellow ground.

Two executioners sit on His chest to hold Him fast. A third one takes His right arm, holding Him with one hand on the first part of His forearm and the other on the tips of His fingers. The fourth one, who already has in his hand the long sharp-pointed quadrangular nail, ending with a round flat head as big as a large coin of bygone days, watches whether the hole already made in the wood corresponds to the joint of the wrist. It does. The executioner places the point of the nail on the wrist, he raises the hammer and gives the first stroke.

Jesus, who had closed His eyes, utters a cry and has a contraction because of the sharp pain. He opens His eyes, flooded with tears. The nail penetrates, tearing muscles, veins, nerves, shattering bones.

Mary replies to the cry of her tortured son with a groan that sounds almost like the moaning of a slaughtered lamb; and she bends, as if she were crushed, holding her head in her hands. In order not to torture her, Jesus utters no more cries. But the strokes continue, methodical and hard, iron striking iron . . . it is a living limb that receives them.

The right hand is now nailed. The executioners pass on to the left one. The hole in the wood does not correspond to the carpus. So they take a rope, they tie it to the left wrist and pull it until the joint is dislocated, tearing tendons and muscles, lacerating skin already cut into by the ropes used to capture Him. The other hand must suffer as well, because it is stretched as a consequence of the movement, and the hole in it widens round the nail. Now the beginning of the meta-carpus, near the wrist, hardly arrives at the hole. They resign them-selves and nail the hand where they can, between the thumb and the other fingers, just in the middle of the metacarpus. The nail penetrates more easily here, but with greater pain because it cuts vital nerves, so that the fingers remain motionless whilst those of the right hand have contractions and tremors that denote their vitality. But Jesus no longer utters cries, He only moans in a deep hoarse voice with His lips firmly closed while tears of pain drip onto the ground after falling on the wood.

It is now the turn of His feet. At two metres and more from the foot of the cross there is a small wedge, hardly sufficient for one foot. Both feet are placed on it to see whether it is in the right spot. It is a little low and the feet hardly reach it, so they pull the Martyr by His ankle bone. The coarse wood of the cross rubs on the wounds, moving the crown that tears His hair once again and is on the point of falling off. One of the executioners presses it down on His head again with a slap.

Those who were sitting on Jesus' chest get up to move to His knees because Jesus, with an involuntary movement, drew up His legs on seeing the very long nail, twice as long and thick as those used on his hands, shine in the sunshine. They place their weight on His flayed knees and press on His bruised shins while the other two are performing the much more difficult operation of nailing one foot on top of the other, trying to combine the two joints of the tarsi.

Although they try to keep the feet still, holding them by the ankles and toes on the wedge, the foot underneath shifts away by the vibrations of the nail and they almost have to draw the nail out. The nail, which has pierced the tender parts of the right foot and is already blunt, is to be moved a little closer to the centre. And they hammer, and hammer, and hammer . . . Only the noise of the hammer striking the head of the nail is heard, because all Calvary is nothing but eyes and ears to perceive acts and hear noises, and to rejoice.

The harsh noise of iron is accompanied by the low plaintive lament of a dove: the hoarse groaning of Mary, who bends more and more at the sound of each stroke, as if the hammer were wounding her. She is about to be crushed by such torture.

The cross is now dragged near the hole and it jerks on the uneven ground shaking the crucified person. The cross is raised. Twice it slips out of the hands of those raising it; the first time it falls with a crash, the second time it falls on its right arm, causing terrible pain because the jerk He receives shakes His wounded limbs.

They let the cross drop into its hole. Before being made fast with stones and earth, it sways in all directions, continuously shifting the body hanging from three nails. The weight of the body lurches forward and down and the holes in the hand widen, particularly the one on the left hand, and the hole for the feet widens, and the blood drips copiously. The blood of the feet trickles along the toes onto the ground and along the wood of the cross, the blood from the hands runs along the forearms, as the wrists are higher than the armpits, and trickles down the sides from the armpits towards the waist. When the cross sways, before being fastened, the crown moves, because the head falls back knocking against the wood and drives the thick knot of thorns at the end of the prickly crown into the nape of the neck, then back on the forehead, gouging it mercilessly. At long last the cross is made fast and there is only the torture of being suspended.

They raise the robbers who, once placed in a vertical position, shout out as if they were being flayed alive. The ropes cut into their wrists and cause their hands to turn dark with the veins swollen like ropes.

Jesus is silent. The crowd is no longer silent. The people resume bawling in a hellish way.

Now the top of Golgotha has its trophy and its guard of honour. At the top there is the cross of Jesus. At the sides the other two crosses. Half a Roman century of soldiers, in fighting trim, is placed all round the summit; inside this circle of armed soldiers there are the ten dismounted soldiers, who throw dice for the garments of the condemned men. Longinus is standing upright between the cross of Jesus and the one on the right. And he seems to be mounting a guard of honour for the Martyr King. The other fifty soldiers, at rest, are on the left, along the path and the lower open space, under the orders of Longinus's adjutant, waiting to be used, in case of need. The indifference of the soldiers is almost total. Only an odd one now and again looks up at the crucified men.

Longinus, in contrast, watches everything with curiosity. He makes comparisons and judges mentally. He compares the crucified men, observing Christ in particular, and then looks at the spectators. His piercing eye does not miss any detail. To see better, he shades his eyes with his hand, because the sun is annoying him.

The sun is in fact strange. It is yellow-red like a fire. Then the fire seems to go out all of a sudden, because of a huge cloud of pitch that rises from behind the chains of the Judaean mountains and soars swiftly across the sky, disappearing behind other mountains. And when the sun comes out again, it is so strong that the eye endures it with difficulty.

While looking, he sees Mary, just under the slope, with her tormented face raised towards her son. He summons one of the soldiers who is playing dice and says to him: "If his mother wants to go up with her other son, let her come. Escort her and help her."

And Mary, with John, who is thought to be her "son," climbs the steps cut in fucaceous rock, I think, and passes beyond the cordon of soldiers and goes to the foot of the cross, but a little to one side, to be seen by, and to see, her Jesus.

The crowd, associating her with her son, showers abuse on her. But with trembling white lips she tries to comfort Him with an anguished smile but tears come down which willpower cannot restrain.

The people, beginning with priests, scribes, Pharisees, Sadducees, Herodians and the like, amuse themselves by going on a kind of roundabout, climbing the steep road, passing along the elevation at the end and descending along the other road. And while they pass at the foot of the summit they repeat their blasphemous words to the dying victim.

"Well you—Savior of mankind!—why do you not save yourself? Has your king Beelzebub abandoned you? Has he disavowed you?" shout three priests. And a group of Judaeans shout, "You, who not more than five days ago, with the help of the Demon, made the Father say—ha! ha! ha!—that He would glorify you, how is it you do not remind Him to keep His promise?" And three Pharisees add: "Blasphemer! He said that He saved the others with the help of God! And He cannot save Himself! Do you want us to believe you? Then work the miracle! Hey, are you no longer able? Because your hands are now nailed and you are naked." And some Sadducees and Herodians say to the soldiers: "Watch His witchcraft, you who have taken His garments! He has the infernal sign within Himself!"

A crowd howls in chorus: "Descend from the cross and we will believe you. You who want to destroy the Temple . . . Fool! . . . Look at it over there, the glorious and holy Temple of Israel. It is untouchable, O profaner! And *you* are dying." Other priests say: "Blasphemer! You the Son of God? Come down from there, then! Strike us by lightning, if you are God. We are not afraid of you and we spit at you."

Others who are passing by shake their heads saying: "He can but weep. Save yourself, if it is true that you are the Chosen One." And the soldiers remark: "So, save yourself! Burn to ashes this cross! Yes!

You are the ashes of the empire, you Judaean rabble. Do so! Rome will put you on the Capitol and will worship you as a god!''

Some throw stones, shouting: ''Change these into bread, since you multiply loaves.'' Others, mimicking the Hosannas of Palm Sunday, throw branches and shout: ''Curses on Him who comes in the name of the Demon! Cursed be His kingdom! Glory to Zion that cuts Him off from the living!''

The Magdalene lowers her veil again—she had raised it to speak to the revilers—and goes back to her place. The other women join her.

But the robber on the left hand side continues to insult from his cross. He seems to have summarized all the curses of the other people and he repeats them all, and ends by saying: ''Save yourself and save us, if you want people to believe you. You the Christ? God does not exist. I do.''

The other robber, who is on the right hand side with Mary almost at his feet, looks at her almost more than he looks at Jesus, and for some moments has been weeping, murmuring: ''My mother says: 'Be silent. Do not fear God—even now that you suffer this pain.' Why do you insult Him who is good? And His torture is even greater than ours. And He has done nothing wrong.''

But the other robber continues to curse.

Jesus is silent. He is panting, as a result of the effort He has to make. Because of His position, because of His fever and heart and breathing conditions, the consequence of the flagellation He suffered in such a violent form, and also of the deep anguish that had made Him sweat blood, He tries to find some relief by reducing the weight on His feet, pulling Himself up with His arms and hanging from His hands. Perhaps He does so also to overcome the cramp that tortures His feet and is revealed by the trembling of His muscles. But the same trembling is noticeable in the fibres of His arms, which are constrained in that position and must be frozen at their ends because they are higher up and deprived of blood, which arrives at the wrists with difficulty and trickles from the holes of the nails, leaving the fingers without circulation. Those of the left hand in particular are already stiff and motionless, bent towards the palm. Also the toes of the feet show their pain, especially the big toes that move up and down and open out, probably because their nerves have not been injured so seriously.

And the trunk reveals all its pain with its movement, which is fast but not deep, and tires Him without giving any relief. His ribs, wide and high as they are because of the structure of His perfect body, are now enlarged beyond measure as a consequence of the position taken by the body and of the pulmonary edema that has surely developed inside. And yet they do not serve to relieve the effort in breathing, any more than the abdomen, with its movement, helps the diaphragm, which is becoming more and more paralyzed.

And the congestion and asphyxia increase every minute, as is shown by the cyanotic color that emphasizes the lips, which the fever has made bright red, and by the red-violet streaks that tinge the neck along the turgid jugular veins and widen out as far as the cheeks, towards the ears and temples, while the nose is thin and bloodless and the eyes are sunken in a circle, which is livid where no blood has trickled from the crown.

Under the left costal arch one can see the throbbing imparted by the point of the heart, an irregular but violent palpitation, and now and again, owing to an internal convulsion, the diaphragm has a deep pulsation, which is revealed by a total stretching of the skin, for what it can stretch on that poor wounded dying body.

The face already has the aspect we see in photographs of the Holy Shroud, with the nose diverged and swollen on one side, and the likeness is increased because the right eye is almost closed, owing to a swelling on this side. The mouth, however, is open, with the blood on the upper lip by now turned into a crust.

His thirst, caused by the loss of blood, by the fever and by the sun, must be burning, so much so that with automatic movements He drinks the drops of His perspiration and His tears, as well as those of blood that run down from His forehead and He wets His tongue with them.

The crown of thorns prevents Him from leaning against the trunk of the cross to help the suspension on His arms and lighten the weight on His feet. His kidneys and all His spine are curved outwards, detached from the cross from His pelvis upwards owing to force of the weight that makes a body, suspended like His, hang forward.

The Judaeans, driven beyond the open space, do not stop their insulting, and the unrepentant robber echoes their insults.

The other one, who now looks at the mother with deeper and deeper compassion, and weeps, and answers the other thief sharply when he hears that she also is included in the insult. "Be silent! Remember that you were born of a woman. And consider that our mothers have wept because of their sons. And they were tears of shame . . . because we are criminals. Our mothers are dead . . . I would like to ask mine to forgive me. But shall I be able? She was a holy woman . . . I killed her with the sorrow I gave her . . . I am a sinner . . . Who will forgive me? Mother—Mary—in the name of your dying son, pray for me."

The mother for a moment raises her tortured face and looks at him, the poor wretch who through the remembrance of his own mother and the contemplation of the Mother moves towards repentance, and she seems to caress him with her kind gentle eyes.

Disma weeps louder, which raises even more the mockery of the crowd and of his companion. They shout: "Very well. Take her as your mother. So she will have two criminal sons!" The latter aggravates them and they say: "She loves you because you are a smaller copy of her darling."

Jesus speaks for the first time: "Father, forgive them because they know not what they do."

This prayer overcomes all fear in Disma. He dares to look at the Christ and says: "Lord, remember me when you are in your Kingdom. It is just that I should suffer. But give me mercy and peace hereafter. I heard you speak once and I foolishly rejected your word. I now repent. And I repent of my sins before you, the Son of the Most High. I believe that you come from God. I believe in your power. I believe in your mercy. Christ, forgive me in the name of your Mother and of your Most Holy Father."

Jesus turns round and looks at him with deep compassion, and He smiles a still beautiful smile with His poor tortured lips. He says: "I tell you: today you will be with me in Paradise."

The repentant robber calms down, and as he no longer remembers the prayers he learned when a child, he repeats as an ejaculation: "Jesus Nazarene, king of the Jews, have mercy on me; Jesus Nazarene, king of the Jews, I hope in you; Jesus Nazarene, king of the Jews, I believe in your divinity."

The other robber continues cursing.

The sky becomes duller and duller. Now the clouds hardly ever open to let the sun shine. On the contrary they cluster on top of one another in leaden, white, greenish strata, they disentangle according to the caprices of a cold wind, which at times blows in the sky, then descends to the ground, and then drops again, and when it drops the air is almost more sinister, sultry and dull than when it hisses, blowing, biting, and fast.

The light, previously exceedingly bright, is becoming greenish. And faces look strange. The profiles of the soldiers, under their helmets and in their armour, which were previously shining and have now become rather tarnished in the greenish light and under an ashen-gray sky, are so hard that they seem to be chiseled. The Judaeans, the complexion, hair and beards of whom are mostly brown, seem drowned people, so wan are their faces. The women look like statues of bluish snow because of their deadly paleness, accentuated by the light.

Jesus seems to be turning ominously livid, because of the beginning of putrefaction, as if He were already dead. His head begins to hang over His chest. His strength fails Him rapidly. He shivers, although He is burning with fever. And in His weakness He whispers the name that so far He has only uttered in the bottom of His heart. "Mother! Mother!" He murmurs it in a low voice, like a sigh, as if He were already lightly delirious and thus prevented from holding back what His will would not like to reveal. And each time Mary makes an unrestrainable gesture of stretching her arms, as if she wished to succour Him. And the cruel people laugh at such pangs of Him who is dying and of her who suffers agonies.

Priests and scribes climb up again as far as the shepherds who, however, are on the lower open space. And as the soldiers want to drive them back, they react saying: "Are these Galileans staying here? We want to stay here as well, as we have to verify that justice is done to the very end. And from afar, in this light, we cannot see."

In fact many begin to be upset by the light that is enveloping the world and some people are afraid. Also the soldiers point to the sky and to a kind of cone that seems of slate, so dark is it, and that rises like a pine-tree from behind the top of a mountain. It looks like a water-spout. It rises and rises and seems to produce darker and darker clouds, as if it were a volcano belching smoke and lava.

It is in this frightening twilight that Jesus gives John to Mary and Mary to John. He lowers His head, because the Mother has gone closer to the cross to see Him better, and He says: "Woman, this is your son. Son, this is your mother."

Mary looks even more upset after this word, which is the will of Jesus, who has nothing to give His mother but a man, He who out of love for man deprives her of the Man-God, born of her. But the poor mother tries to weep only silently, because it is impossible for her not to weep. Tears stream down her cheeks notwithstanding all the efforts to refrain them, even if on her lips there is a heartbroken smile to comfort Him.

Jesus' sufferings increase more and more. And the light fades more and more.

It is in this sea-bottom light that Nicodemus and Joseph appear from behind some Judaeans, and they say: "Step aside!"

"You are not allowed. What do you want?" ask the soldiers.

"To pass. We are friends of the Christ."

The chief priests turn around. "Who dares profess himself friend of the rebel?" ask the priests indignantly.

And Joseph replies resolutely: "I, Joseph of Arimathea, the Elder, and noble member of the Supreme Council, and Nicodemus, the head of the Judaeans, is with me."

"Those who side with the rebel are rebels."

"And those who take sides with murderers are murderers, Eleazar of Annas. I have lived as a just man. And now I am old and close to death. I do not want to become unjust, while Heaven is already descending upon me and the eternal Judge with it."

"And you, Nicodemus! I'm surprised!"

"So am I. And of one thing only: that Israel is so corrupt that you cannot even recognise God any more."

"You disgust me."

"Move aside, then, and let me pass. That is all I want."

The officer examines them and says to the soldiers: "Let the two men pass."

And Joseph and Nicodemus approach the shepherds. I [the narrator adopts *now* the first-person point of view] do not even know whether Jesus can see them in the fog that is getting thicker and thicker, and with His eyes that are already veiled by agony. But they see Him, and they weep without any respect for public opinion, although the priests now abuse them.

The sufferings are worse and worse. The body begins to suffer from the arching typical of tetanus, and the clamour of the crowd exasperates it. The death of fibres and nerves extends from the tortured limbs to the trunk, making breathing more and more difficult, diaphragmatic contraction weak and heart beating irregular. The face of Christ passes, in turns, from very deep-red blushes to the greenish paleness of a person bleeding to death. His lips move with greater difficulty because the overstrained nerves of the neck and of the head itself, that for dozens of times have acted as a lever for the whole body, pushing on the cross bar, spread the cramp also to the jaws. His throat, swollen by the obstructed carotid arteries, must be painful and must spread its edema to the tongue, which looks swollen and slow in its movements. His back, even in the moments when the tetanising contractions do not bend it in a complete arch from the nape of His neck to His hips, leaning at extreme points against the stake of the cross, bends more and more forward because the limbs are continuously weighed down by the burden of the dead flesh.

The people cannot see this situation very clearly, because the light now is like dark ashes and only those who are at the foot of the cross can see well.

At a certain moment Jesus collapses forward and downwards as if He were already dead. He no longer pants, His head hangs inertly forward, His body, from His hips upwards, is completely detached from the cross, forming an angle with its bar.

Mary utters a cry: "He is dead!" A tragic cry that spreads in the dark air. And Jesus seems really dead.

Another cry of a woman replied to her, and I see a stir in the group of the women. Then some ten people go away holding something. But I cannot see who goes away so. The foggy light is too faint. It looks as if we are immersed in a cloud of very dense volcanic ash.

"It is not possible," shout some of the priests and of the Judaeans. "It is a simulation to make us go away. Soldier, prick Him with your lance. It is a good medicine to give His voice back to Him." And as the soldiers do not do so, a volley of stones and clods of earth fly towards the cross, hitting the martyr and falling back on the armour of the Romans.

The medicine, as the Judaeans say ironically, works the wonder. Some of the stones have certainly hit the target, perhaps the wound of a hand, or the head itself, because they were aiming high. Jesus moans pitifully and recovers His senses. His thorax begins to breathe again with difficulty and His head moves from left to right, seeking where it may rest in order to suffer less, but finding nothing but greater pain.

With great difficulty, pressing once again on His tortured feet, finding strength in His will, *and only in it,* Jesus stiffens on the cross. He stands upright, as if He were a healthy man with all his strength, He raises His face, looking with wide open eyes at the world stretched at His feet, at the far away town, which one can see just indistinctly as a vague whiteness in the mist, and at the dark sky where every trace of blue and of light has disappeared. And to this closed, compact, low sky, resembling a huge slab of dark slate, He shouts in a loud voice, overcoming with His will-power and with the need of His soul the obstacle of His swollen tongue and His parched throat: "Eloi, Eloi, lama sabachthani!'' [My God, my God, why hast thou forsaken me?] (I hear Him say so.) He must feel that He is dying, and in absolute abandonment by Heaven, if He confesses His Father's abandonment, with such an exclamation.

People laugh and deride Him. They insult Him saying: ''God has nothing to do with you! Demons are cursed by God!''

Other people shout: ''Let us see whether Elijah, whom He is calling, will come to save Him.''

And others say: ''Give Him some vinegar, that He may gargle His throat. It helps one's voice! Elijah or God, as it is uncertain what this madman wants, is far away . . . A loud voice is required to make oneself heard!'' and they laugh like hyenas or like demons.

But no soldier gives Him vinegar and no one comes from Heaven to give comfort. It is the solitary, total, cruel, also supernaturally cruel agony of the Great Victim.

The avalanches of desolate grief, which had already oppressed Him at Gethsemane, come back again. The waves of the sins of all the world come back to strike the shipwrecked innocent, to submerge Him in their bitterness. And above all what comes back is the sensation, more crucifying than the cross itself, more despairing than any torture, that God has abandoned Him and that His prayer does not rise to Him.

And it is the final torture. The one that accelerates death, because it squeezes the last drops of blood out of the pores, crushes the remaining fibres of the heart, ends what the first knowledge of this abandonment has begun: death. Because of that, my Jesus died, O God, who have struck Him for us! Because after your abandonment, through your abandonment, what does a person become? Either insane or dead. Jesus could not become insane, because His intelligence was divine, and since intelligence is spiritual, it triumphed over the total trauma of Him whom God had struck. So He became a dead man: the Dead Man, the Most Holy Dead Man, the Most Innocent Dead Man. He who was the Life was dead. Killed by your abandonment and by our sins.

Darkness becomes deeper. Jerusalem disappears completely. The very slopes of Calvary seem to vanish. Only the top is visible, as if darkness held it high up to receive the only and last surviving light, laying it as an offering, with its divine trophy on a pool of liquid onyx, so that it may be seen by love and by hatred.

And from that light, which is no longer light, comes the primitive voice of Jesus: "I am thirsty!"

A wind in fact is blowing, which makes even healthy people thirsty. A strong wind that now blows continuously, and is full of dust, cold and frightening. And I think of what pain its violent gusts must have caused to the lungs, the heart, the throat of Jesus, and to the frozen, benumbed, wounded limbs. Everything has combined to torture the martyr.

A soldier goes towards a jar in which the assistants of the executioner have put some vinegar with gall, so that with its bitterness it may increase the salivation of those condemned to capital punishment. He takes the sponge immersed in the liquid, he sticks it on a thin yet stiff cane which is nearby, and offers the sponge to the dying victim.

Jesus leans eagerly forward towards the approaching sponge. He looks like a starving baby seeking the nipple of its mother.

Mary who sees and certainly has such a thought, leaning on John, says with a moan: "I cannot give Him even one of my tears. O God, why did you abandon us? A miracle for my son! Who will lift me up so that I may quench His thirst with my blood, since I have no milk? . . ."

Jesus, who has greedily sucked the sour bitter drink, makes a wry face in disgust. Above all it must act as a corrosive on His wounded, split lips.

He withdraws, loses heart, abandons Himself. All the weight of His body falls heavily on His feet and forward. His wounded extremities are the parts that suffer the dreadful pain as they are torn open by the weight of the body that abandons itself. He makes no further movement to alleviate such pain. His body, from His hips upwards, is detached from the cross, and remains so.

His head hangs forward so heavily that His neck seems hollow in three places: at the throat, which is completely sunken, and both sides of the sternum. He pants more and more and interruptedly and it sounds more like a death-rattle. Now and again a painful fit of coughing brings a light rosy foam to His lips. And the intervals between one expiration and the next one are becoming longer and longer. His abdomen is now motionless. Only His thorax still heaves, but laboriously, with difficulty . . . Pulmonary paralysis is increasing.

And fainter and fainter, sounding like a child's wailing, comes the invocation: "Mother!" And the poor wretch whispers: "Yes, darling, I am here." And then His sight becomes misty and makes Him say: "Mother, where are you? Are you abandoning me as well?" And they are not even words, but just a murmur that can hardly be heard by her who with her heart rather than with her ears receives every sigh of her dying son. She says: "No, no, my son! I will not abandon you! Listen to me, my dear . . . your mother is here, she is here . . . and she only regrets that she cannot come where you are . . ."

And John weeps openly. Jesus must hear him weep. But He does not speak. I think that His impending death makes Him speak as if He were raving and that He does not even know what He says, and, sadly, He does not even understand His mother's consolation and His favourite apostle's love.

Longinus is no longer standing at ease, his arms folded across his chest, one leg crossed over the other to ease the long wait on his feet. He is now standing stiff at attention, his left hand on his sword, his right one held against his side, as if he were on the steps of the imperial throne. He does not want to be influenced. But his face is affected by the effort of overcoming his emotion and his eyes begin to shine with tears that only his iron discipline can refrain.

The other soldiers, who were playing dice, have stopped and have stood up, putting on the helmets that had served to cast the dice. They are near the little steps dug in the tufa, looking heedful and silent. The others are on duty and cannot move. They look like statues. But some of those who are closer and hear Mary's words mutter something between their lips and shake their heads.

There is dead silence. Then in utter darkness, the word: "Everything is accomplished!" is *clearly* heard and His death-rattle grows louder and louder, with longer and longer pauses between one rattle and the next one.

Time passes in such distressing rhythm. Life comes back when the air is pierced by the harsh breathing of the dying victim . . . Life stops when the painful sound is no longer heard. One suffers hearing it . . . one suffers not hearing it . . . One says: "Enough of this suffering!" and then one says: "O God! Let it not be His last breath!"

The two Marys are weeping, their heads leaning against the escarpment. And their weeping is clearly heard, because the crowd is now silent again, to listen to the death-rattles of the dying master.

There is silence again. Then the supplication pronounced with infinite kindness, with fervent prayer: "Father, into your hands I commit my spirit!"

Further silence. The death-rattle has become fainter. It is just a breath confined to His lips and throat.

Then there is the last spasm of Jesus. A dreadful convulsion that seems to tear the body with the three nails from the cross, rises three times from the feet to the head, through all the tortured nerves; it heaves the abdomen three times in an abnormal way, then leaves it after dilating it as if it were upsetting the viscera; and it drops and becomes hollow as if it were empty; it heaves, swells and contracts the thorax so violently that the skin sinks between the ribs which stretch, appearing under the skin and reopening the wounds of the scourges; it makes the head fall back violently once, twice, three times, hitting the wood hard; it contracts all the muscles of the face in a spasm, accentuating the deviation of the mouth to the right, it opens wide and dilates the eyelids under which one can see the eyeballs roll and the sclerotic appear. The body is all bent; from the last of the three contractions it is a drawn arch, which vibrates and is dreadful to look at, and then a powerful cry, unimaginable in that exhausted body, bursts forth rending the air, the "loud cry" mentioned by the Gospels and is the first part of the word "Mother" . . . And nothing else.

His head falls on His chest, His body leans forward, the trembling stops. He breathes no more.

CHAPTER NINE

————

Experiencing Lourdes

Is the Lord through with miracles?

I traveled to Lourdes in 1994. I was indulging not only the experience of a pilgrimage but a corollary curiosity about what exactly goes on there and what its impact might be on one first-time visitor.

One reason one doesn't hear so much about Lourdes these days (compared, say, to a generation or two ago) has to be that people don't really know what more there is to say. The inquirer whose mind turns for the first time to the subject begins by asking the questions one would expect, the first of which is of course, "Was there really an apparition?"

This translates to, "Did the little girl called Bernadette Soubirous actually *see* something? Or was what she reported no more than the product of an inflamed imagination?"

That question was first posed on February 11, 1858, to her family, whose reply was plainspoken: Bernadette's mother spanked her and put her to bed.

But there was something about the dogged sincerity in the fourteen-year-old's recounting of her experience that brought on a grudging acknowledgment, not that Bernadette had in fact come face-to-face with an apparition, but that *something* was going on worth investigating, even if it turned out to be nothing more than her mental health. Accordingly, three days later her mother gave her permission to return. Back Bernadette went, to the little grotto alongside which, on day one, Bernadette, a younger sister, and a friend had been foraging for firewood.

That was when Bernadette had suddenly stopped, immobilized for a full half hour. When she came out of her trance, she excitedly described "the lady in white," with the blue eyes, the smile, and the blue belt-sash hanging down the front of her white robe. Now, once again, she had stopped, transfixed.

On that second day at the grotto, once again in the company of her sister and their friend, she lost her composure while in communion with the apparition. The trance over, she opened her eyes and said that the lady in white had come and gone. But she could not rise, nor could her companions lift her up from the ground. They called on a neighboring miller for help. He handled her as a muscular aide might handle a heavyweight boxer who had been knocked unconscious in the ring. Bernadette's family ruled that the phenomenon was ridiculous and profane and once again forbade her to return to the grotto.

But of course she did. And her third visit, four days later, proved special because, for the first time, the lady in white spoke to her.

What had she said?

She had said that Bernadette should come back every day for the next two weeks.

Bernadette did so. And as one might expect, with each visit a larger number of villagers accompanied her, curious to witness the girl's catatonia and to hear from her own lips, after she came out of it, what it was that she had seen and heard.

Lourdes was (and still is, really) a small town, situated in the northern foothills of the Pyrenees. Charlemagne is said to have fought over it, laying siege to its imposing fort in the eighth century, when the Moors occupied it. He struck a bargain with them: they would be permitted to survive the siege provided they converted to Christianity. In the years that followed, Lourdes passed from conqueror to conqueror. France had it, Spain had it, England had it. Permanent French occupation came only in the fifteenth century.

Lourdes withstood attacks during the religious wars, remaining stoutly Catholic, so that Bernadette's neighbors were indisputably French and unflinchingly Catholic; but notwithstanding the fabled Gallic skepticism, they were hypnotized by the apparent transfiguration, before their own eyes, of the miller's oldest daughter. Whatever it was that was inducing those trances, the consensus gradually consolidated that they were not *self*-induced. For one thing there was nothing in the least theatrical in Bernadette's disposition, and certainly nothing in her background that would encourage anything of the sort. Her father was wholly unpretentious, a casualty of the Industrial Revolution—he was well on the way to bankruptcy because technology had come up with more economical ways of making bread than by grinding flour with roughly the same tools that were used at the time of Christ. In the single room that made up the home of M. Soubirous, his wife, and their four children, histrionic episodes, one confidently deduces, were neither expected nor countenanced. But Bernadette was seeing "something."

And then when Bernadette woke from her trances, her accounts were always direct and unambiguous. The lady in white usually did not speak to her, emitting only a smile. Seven times, during the eighteen apparitions, the lady broke silence. Once she called on Bernadette to relay to the people of Lourdes her plea for repentance—hardly an irrelevant request, in the south of France in 1858, or for that matter in the north of France in 1997.

Then came the second declaration: Bernadette was to pass on the word to the clergy: they must construct a chapel alongside the site at which the apparition was taking place. Next, she instructed Bernadette to dig in the earth a few feet away. She did so, and presently a stream of water sprang forth. It continues, 135 years later, to flow, at a rate of up to fourteen hundred gallons per hour. It is water from the Pyrenees mountains, emptying into the river Gave. It fills the thousands of receptacles in which it is collected by pilgrims. It is this same water that fills the baths in which over 1 million pilgrims have immersed their bodies, their motive to experience a cure for an infirmity, or else merely to perform a devotional act, even as, in the secular world, a line might form to kiss the Emperor's ring or curtsy to the Queen.

The elders of Lourdes were now prepared to acknowledge that Bernadette was seeing "something." But they were resolute in disbelieving that the lady in white was the Madonna: whatever the apparition was, surely it was something other than the Mother of Christ? The parish priest, a hardy skeptic during the entire fortnight, said repeatedly to Bernadette that she must ask the apparition to give herself a name: Who was she?

The priest's request was compliantly transmitted by Bernadette, but she reported that the lady only smiled in response—until the sixteenth apparition. This time the lady in white answered Bernadette. "I am the Immaculate Conception." Bernadette dutifully repeated these words to the priest and the general company. The reaction was electric: the lady in white had declared herself to be the Blessed Virgin, the Mother of Christ. The awe increased when Bernadette was closely questioned and it transpired that she had never before heard the term "Immaculate Conception," and had no idea what the words meant, or to whom they referred.

What followed was the usual sluggish reaction to any extraordinary event. (Thomas Edison brought on no headlines when he announced that he had harnessed electricity.) But the first stage was now complete. No one associated with her any longer doubted that Bernadette—who went on to a novitiate in a remote convent, where she died early from tuberculosis and the asthma she had contracted before the apparition—had truthfully described what she had seen and reported what she had heard.

In due course the chapel she had been instructed to propose was constructed. The basilica is very large, its satellites numerous. The lady in white had given no intimation that the little spring she had brought to life would have therapeutic effects on many who touched it or were touched by it, but it did have such effects. And even after her story had become nationally and internationally accepted—well before her death in 1879 at age thirty-five—few gave any thought to the canonization of Bernadette Soubirous (this happened in 1933). Certainly no one had any idea that one hundred years later several million people every year would travel to Lourdes to see the grotto where the lady in white appeared, to experience the waters that continue to flow from the spring she unearthed, and to return from their visit to Lourdes substantially—in many cases, critically—affected by the experience. It is a matter of record that there are cases of the lame and the halt who have returned whole from Lourdes, and for every one of them there are tens of thousands who return affected in other ways.

Oddly, English-speaking visitors cannot find Lourdes literature other than photographic books with slender textual matter.* The French, yes—their Lourdes library is copious. But even the cosmopol-

---

* Arnold Lunn, writing in 1958, lists as relevant to the phenomenon Jean Helle's *Miracles*, B. G. Sandhurst's *Miracles Still Happen*, Le Bec's *The Medical Proof of the Miraculous*, Izard's *The Meaning of Lourdes*, and Leuret's *Raisons Médicales de Croire au Miracle*. I have not seen these books and certainly they are not merchandised.

itan bookstores don't carry copies of *The Miracle of Lourdes,* written forty years ago by Ruth Cranston, and more or less updated in 1986. It is a useful volume, by a Protestant who became a devotee of Lourdes. The book is valuable primarily for its inclusion of basic data about the shrine. It records in considerable detail, for instance, a dozen of the cures attributed to Lourdes.

It is not surprising, but worth stressing, that there are no tribunals in existence more skeptical than those through which you need to pass if your claim is to have been cured of illness at Lourdes. One faces first the so-called Medical Bureau. It is a cadre of doctors who donate their time, spending periods of various lengths in residence at Lourdes. Their duty is to examine—their opportunity is to learn from—the phenomena that pass by. Only a minority of these men of science are professing Catholics.

When the bureau, after exhaustive investigation, places a stamp of approval on the claims of a "cure," it is saying formally that there is no known or hypothetical scientific explanation for the physical trans-formation the doctors have documented. The case goes then to a second medical examining body, an international committee with headquarters in Paris. If this body concurs, that validation is then referred to a canonical commission in the diocese in which the candi-date lives; and the skepticism here is not only scientific but theologi-cal—the Church has almost always been the last to believe that a miracle actually took place, though is of course prepared to believe that what took place might have been miraculous. In this respect the Church apes Thomas, who declined to believe in the Resurrection until the palpability of Christ's wounds overcame him. Do not ask the ecclesiastical tribunal at Lourdes to acclaim that you have been miracu-lously cured (unless you have been). You would have better prospects declaring yourself to be Anastasia, and presenting yourself at that bank in London that is said to store remnants of the Czar's treasury.

Before the International Medical Committee will agree to pursue your case further, sixteen questions are asked. Samples (using the language in Mrs. Cranston's book):

- Has the diagnosis been established by adequate objective examination?
- Does the comprehensive clinical picture rule out psychogenic overlay?
- Does the prognosis rule out the possibility of spontaneous remission, natural cure, significant improvement, or long-term remission?
- Has the sick person noticed the disappearance of subjective symptoms?
- Did the cure appear completely contrary to the prognosis?
- Was the cure sudden and consistent with the disappearance of objective pathological signs?

A completed questionnaire, every one of its questions and taunts answered as a miracle would require, will not satisfy everybody. Émile Zola, a devout, indeed consecrated atheist, went to enormous pains, practical and poetic, to affirm his animating axiom, which he once reduced to simple words: "Even if I saw a miracle, I couldn't believe it." So eager was he to affirm his disbelief that he based a work of fact/fiction on a Lourdes pilgrim. The story was taken from life and he coped with his problem of gainsaying what had been a cure by simply falsifying the documented record, poor Zola.

Every now and again a dedicated body of skeptics engages somebody's theatrical energies with the aim of faking his way through the Lourdes accreditation process in order to discredit it. My favorite of these is the young lady who arrived at Lourdes complaining of a lifelong affliction, getting worse as the years went by—an anal fistula. She took the baths and on emerging announced herself triumphantly as cured! She was taken to the Medical Bureau, where the doctors proceeded to put together her record—her family history, history of the illness, history of the cure. The paperwork having been done, the doctors were ready to go on to the next stage, a physical examination. The record gives us the ensuing exchange:

"Examine me?—but why?"

"In order to verify your cure, madame."

"And all that I have been telling you—that is for nothing?"

"For nothing, madame, if we do not examine you."

"But I do not wish to be examined."

"In order to verify a cure, we must examine the patient. If you do not consent, we shall tear up the record."

"Then I shall not be verified?"

"No, madame."

The dear lady faced a problem, and the chronicler, Mrs. Cranston, tells in her book what then happened:

"After much protesting and objecting, finally she yielded, and the examination took place, five or six doctors assisting.

"There was nothing whatever the matter with the woman, and never had been—certainly not the malady she described. When the doctors asked her to show them where the anal fistula was, she pointed to a little white scar (the vestige of an old cyst operation) quite high up on the back and in a spot where certainly no one ever had an anus."

Well, one does try. After protracted questioning the lady broke down. "She had been purposely sent by an anti-religious organization of one of the big departments in the middle of France to bring back a personal document showing that at the Medical Bureau of Lourdes they recognized miracles without even examining the patients." It is really quite charming, this confidence of the young lady imposter that no gentlemanly doctor would propose to examine that part of the body in search of mere medical evidence.

Fewer than one hundred "cures" have been certified by the Church as miraculous. But this number is much, much smaller than the number of "cures" plausibly claimed by men and women who have traveled to Lourdes but who for whatever reason (they did not care; they had not kept records; their local doctors would not cooperate) didn't submit to the rigorous examinations required, or else did so and did not pass these tests. Mrs. Cranston, who spent many years in residence at Lourdes and engaged in meticulous record keeping, estimates at ten thousand the number who have declared themselves cured. But even if her calculations are correct, that leaves us with one cure per ten or fifteen thousand pilgrims. The odds, one supposes without actually going to statistical archives, are not very different from what one might expect on buying a lottery ticket. People go to Lourdes for other reasons, and if my own experience is representative, they leave profoundly affected.

The book by Mrs. Cranston gives the record, as noted, of many documented cures. I select one, not because it is singular, but because it is, in essential respects, typical. Marie Bailly was a patient of a French doctor who, when finally he complied with the family request that he accompany his patient to Lourdes, wrote down, for the record, what would be the transformation he would need to see before acknowledging that any cure had taken place. He confronted, first, a general question: What kind of ailment would qualify as miraculously treated? His answer: "An organic disease: a cancer disappearing; a bone regrown; a congenital dislocation vanishing."

He went on in his contemporary notes to describe the plight of his patient, a young woman in the last stages of tuberculous peritonitis. "I know her history," he recorded. "Her whole family died of tuberculosis. She has had tubercular sores, lesions of the lungs, and now, for the past few months, peritonitis diagnosed by both a general practitioner and the well-known Bordeaux surgeon Bromilloux. Her condition is very grave. She may die right under my nose. If such a case were cured, it would indeed be a miracle."

One hour before Marie Bailly was carried to the grotto, he examined her yet again at one of the adjacent hospitals, remarking in his notes her white, emaciated face, her galloping pulse—150 to the minute—the distended abdomen, the ears and nails turning blue. He told the sisters, "She may last a few more days, but she is doomed. Her heart is giving out. Death is very near."

The doctor accompanied Marie Bailly to the grotto. There the doctor saw her face suddenly change color, losing its ashen hue. Her swollen abdomen flattened out under the blanket. Her pulse became calm and regular. She requested a glass of milk. Her respiration had become normal. Mrs. Cranston records the doctor's reaction. "The sweat broke out on his forehead. He felt as though someone had struck him on the head. His own heart began to pump furiously. It was the most 'momentous thing' he had ever seen."

The doctor roused himself from his trance and took his patient back to the hospital, where he examined her in the company of three other doctors. They confirmed what he knew already from his intimate knowledge of her case. His patient had been cured. The doctor told a colleague, "When one reads about such things one cannot help suspecting some kind of charlatanism. But here is a cure I have seen with my own eyes. I have seen an apparently chronic invalid restored to health and normal life. . . . Such cures cannot be brought about by natural means."

Of course. Yet one can't go any further than to say that (a) there was a cure, and (b) there is no *scientific* explanation for it. On the other hand, you cannot conclude, using scientific terminology, that the transformation was a "miracle." To do so would be to place oneself in the hands of the theologians. Miracle: "A marvelous event occurring within human experience, which cannot have been brought about by human power or by the operation of any natural agency, and must therefore be ascribed to the special intervention of the De- ity . . ."(OED)

The word is casually used in the modern world. "Miraculously, Silky Sullivan came from last place and won the race by a nose." But the dominant meaning is as given in the *Oxford Dictionary:* something caused by an act of divine intervention. If one is required to describe what happened to Marie Bailly as other than a "miracle," one needs to use words that don't come easily to the tongue. Was it a *thaumaturgical event?* But in ruling out a natural cause, we are required to acknowledge a supernatural cause. In formal logic, it would not need to be a Christian agent that brought about the miracle; but given the story of Bernadette, Christian factors do, well, come to mind; and anyway, the secular humanist is stuck because in his etiology there has to be a natural cause for every phenomenon. Those who seek relief from the quandary—*If it wasn't a natural cause that effected the cure, what did?*—will need to come up with a superforce of some sort. Who was it at the grotto in 1858? Allah? The skeptics run the risk of being ambushed by: God/Christ/the Immaculate Conception. The whole Christian package.

But the Christian, too, is without *explanation* for what happens at Lourdes, because we cannot reason to why Marie Bailly found relief while so many others do not. But then this only reminds us that what in the secular coinage we would think of as random chance *(Why the death-dealing volcanic eruption here? The pestilence there?),* religion ascribes to a divine order that countenances extemporaneous afflictions, natural and personal. God's ways are inscrutable. There is no Butler Escape.

So what is the skeptic left to think? To say? I thought of the liberating sentence of G. K. Chesterton in which he recounts that in his desperate search for a suitable cosmology, he had stumbled upon orthodoxy. It was by chance that I stumbled, the second evening at Lourdes, on this paragraph in a Chesterton essay. GKC was an ardent admirer of W. B. Yeats; indeed he and the poet were friends. Chesterton is here reflecting on the endless search for timelessness on earth. ''A very distinguished and dignified example of this paganism at bay is Mr. W. B. Yeats.'' He quotes a passage from Yeats's ''delightful'' memoirs:

I think [that Christianity] but deepened despair and multiplied temptation. . . . Why are these strange souls born everywhere today, with hearts that Christianity, as shaped by history, cannot satisfy? Our love letters wear out our love; no school of painting outlasts its founders, every stroke of the brush exhausts the impulse; pre-Raphaelitism had some twenty years; Impressionism, thirty, perhaps. Why should we believe that religion can never bring round its antithesis? Is it true that our air is disturbed, as Melarme [sic] said, ''by the trembling of the veil of the temple," or "that our whole age is seeking to bring forth a sacred book"?

Chesterton moves in:

Of course there are many minor criticisms of all this. The faith only multiplies temptation in the sense that it would multiply temptation to turn a dog into a man. And it certainly does not deepen despair, if only for two reasons: first, that despair to a Catholic is itself a spiritual sin and blasphemy; and second, that the despair of many pagans, often including Mr. Yeats, could not possibly be deepened. But what concerns me, in these introductory remarks, is his suggestion about the duration of movements. When he gently asks why Catholic Christianity should last longer than other movements, we may well answer even more gently: "Why, indeed?" He might gain some light on why it should, if he would begin by inquiring why it does. He seems curiously unconscious that the very contrast he gives is against the case he urges. If the proper duration of a movement is twenty years, what sort of a movement is it that lasts nearly two thousand? If a fashion should last no longer than Impressionism, what sort of fashion is it that lasts about fifty times as long? Is it just barely conceivable that it is not a fashion?

Pilgrims who travel to Lourdes make up their own schedules, in cooperation with the administrative office there. The routine of our group began one afternoon with Mass at the upper Basilica, one of the many churches. An odd sense of tranquillity settled on us. I can't offhand remember when last, other than at sea, I felt so little concern for timetables. On Friday there was a "Morning of Recollection" and the anointing of the sick at another chapel (St. Joseph's). There are three hospitals—more properly, hospices—all of them administered by volunteers. (Few of us were sick in any conventional sense, but we were reminded that from the day of birth, we are on our deathbeds.) In the afternoon, Mass at the Salle Notre-Dame, and in the evening a candlelight procession in front of the Rosary Basilica. It is not easy to imagine twenty thousand candles shaping a cross. The ensuing four days included a daily Mass in different churches; easy access to confessions, heard in six languages, throughout the day; the Stations of the

Cross, twice-life-sized bronze statuary, rising up a steep hillside, invoking the travail of Calvary. The schedule left several hours every day during which one could do as one chose (there are historical sites, including the birthplace of Bernadette, and the great, massive fort built during the Middle Ages), and one tends to choose to walk about, and to take keen pleasure in casual encounters.

The sense of the visit is rapidly communicated. There are thousands of gurneys (*voitures,* they are referred to) for the *malades,* the all-inclusive French word for the sick—again, propelled exclusively by volunteers. Perhaps every *malade* harbors the hope that he or she will be cured, but it is not reasonably expected; yet somehow it seems irrelevant as larger perspectives take hold. It is a part of the common faith that prayer can effect anything. (*"Remember, most gracious Virgin Mary, that never was it known that anyone who fled to thy protection, implored thy assistance, or sought thy intercession, was left unaided"*), but incantatory hyperbole is simply a ritualized form of docility. The sick who travel to Lourdes are there, yes, because of the undeniability of recorded miracles, but that isn't what brings as many as fifty thousand people a day to Lourdes, the great majority of them healthy. The reason so many people come, many of them on their second or tenth visit, is that what is effected is a sense of reconciliation, if not well-being. Hardly miraculous, unless one chooses to use the word as most appropriate for that buoyancy experienced on viewing the great processions, sharing with almost thirty thousand people an underground Mass, being lowered for three bracing seconds into one of the baths, suddenly noting the ambient serenity. These are Christians feeling impulses of their faith, and intimations of the lady in white.

They are in Lourdes because of this palpability of the emanations that gave birth to the shrine. The spiritual tonic is felt. If it were otherwise, the pilgrims would diminish in number; would, by now, have disappeared, as at Delphos, which one visits as a museum, not a shrine. What it is that fetches them is I think quite simply stated, namely a reinforced conviction that the Lord God loves His creatures, healthy or infirm; that they—we—must understand the nature of love, which is salvific in its powers; and that although we are free to attempt to divine God's purpose, we will never succeed in doing so. The reason is that we cannot know (the manifest contradictions are too disturbing) what is the purpose behind particular phenomena and therefore must make do with only the grandest plan of God, which treats with eternal salvation. Our burden is to keep the faith: to do this (the grammar of assent) requires the discipline of submission, some assurance that those who are stricken can, even so, be happy; and that the greatest tonic of all is divine love, which is nourished by human love, even as human love is nourished by divine love.

Waiting in the lounge to board the airplane to Paris, en route home, I found myself in the company of three *malades*. They could walk, else they'd have been on one of the trains, on stretchers. One young man had a face wretchedly distorted—it brought to mind one of the unpleasant pictures of Picasso. Around his neck the attendant had placed a plastic folder, his ticket inside, his travel arrangements upon landing at Orly explained. With heavy use of a heavy cane he could, so to speak, move his body. He was treated, by this company returning from Lourdes, as—a member of the family; which he was, as Lourdes manages to make plain.

CHAPTER TEN

Difficulties: The Love of God,

the Love of Man

Since this volume is by specification "personal," I have the advantage that what I include need meet no higher entrance qualification than that it engaged my attention. And, of course, the disadvantage that what engages one person as a religious problem may not so engage another. But if you will, hear me out, and see how the words of others have so greatly consoled and instructed me.

I begin by reiterating one more time what I have come to refer to as the Butler Escape, adduced above by Ronald Knox in answer to one of Lunn's criticisms of the world around us. It is that the world would be different if I had created it. If you had created it. To appeal to the Butler Escape is a means of abandoning the struggle to understand. Or, at least, to abandon the struggle to understand within the framework of human reason. We can't fully "understand" the love a mother has for her infant child, but we acknowledge that it is there.

A few years ago, when weekending with an old friend in the English countryside near London, the morning paper brought news of an earthquake in East Turkey that had the day before killed some four hundred men, women, and children. Years of experience had warned me to resist the impulse; even so, I gave in to it. *Why does He permit such suffering*—self-evidently unrelated to human misbehavior?

I tried on myself the argument of life-is-that-way and injustice-is-random. The death of four hundred human beings as the result of an earthquake isn't any more a sign of ad hoc divine neglect or disorder than death from cancer of four hundred people scattered about the globe. That is the way the world works. *(Father, forgive me, I have committed murder. How many times, my son?)*

But I threw away the cancer victim examples. They didn't help me on that Sunday morning. I tried something else: the furtive search for an intersection, God's will/human understanding of a phenomenon. Of course it didn't work . . .

If everything that happens serves a divine purpose, is it conceivable that the resourceful mind can come up with the point of intersection between that earthquake in East Turkey and God's intelligent, not to say benign, superintendence of human and natural affairs? We know one of God's ends, which is to give us each the opportunity for eternal life in His company. But we don't know all of the purposes of God. What else might He have had in mind for the Turks who died? Our answer is that He could not have had anything commendable in mind, unless it is so that the laws of congruity—what on earth did the Turks gain from their disaster?—are impossible to penetrate, without a divine perspective. In our world we can understand why a child gets burned when he touches the hot skillet: once burned, twice shy. We do not know why that child suffocated in the fire that burns down the house. It simply didn't pay off to speculate on what might have been God's purpose, benign *or* punitive, in permitting the earthquake yesterday in East Turkey.

Well, then, still another avenue of thought: Did He will it? Or merely countenance it? Was it a rogue act of nature, incidental yet intrinsic to the functioning of the earthly organism He created?

We don't know, and persistence isn't rewarding. If God had willed that geological convulsions should not occur, there would be none. It is certainly more prudent to acknowledge the barrier of mystery than to go to pieces searching for rational explanations beyond human reach. Do not seek to know the unknowable. Frustrate frustration by declining to divine divine purpose. Christian theology goes no further than to assure us that we will never be asked to believe anything, within Christian architecture, that contradicts reason. Earthquakes do not contradict reason. They just happen.

But human beings tend to search out moral meaning, and though fatalistic about tabloid atrocities, the mind begins to reel at something on the scale of Gulag. I remember the rabbi, or rather the erstwhile rabbi, who told us at a television forum in Chicago that when the details of the Holocaust were revealed, he forthwith renounced his faith in God, giving up his rabbinate. Yet it is easier to understand the Holocaust than the earthquake, because God did not create man with capacity for merely measured evil: the evil of man, plus electricity, could give us a Holocaust. The earthquake can't rationally be ascribed to man's evil.

My next question, that Sunday morning, asked whether, by permitting the earthquake in Turkey, God knew what would be the consequences. Well of course, God is all-seeing and knows, therefore, the consequences of everything, as Fr. Knox so patiently and conclusively explained to Arnold Lunn. So there is going to be human attrition in the love of God, in those, like the ex-rabbi, who hold Him accountable for that earthquake, that Holocaust. Since we live in a world in which earthquakes or their equivalents are everywhere around us, what of the man who feels correspondingly absolved of any need to love God? "It would be most unreasonable of the Church to demand the love of God as an essential condition for escaping hell," Fr. George Tyrrell wrote, going on to say, as noted, that "the love of God is the luxury of a few happy and imaginative temperaments. In the lump," to repeat, "man was not created nor designed for the love of God in that mystical sense, but for the love of man."

"God," Arnold Lunn concurred in his exchange with Knox, "has the right to demand obedience, but not love."

Yet on the point there is simply no question of God's law. *"Which is the greatest commandment in the law? Jesus said unto him, Thou shalt love the Lord thy God with all thy heart, and with all thy soul, and with all thy mind. This is the first and greatest commandment."*

The God of the random earthquake, as one might here put it, should not expect reflexive love, except by those who tabulate the odds. I promise I am not about to say that everyone who on that Sunday morning was *not* victimized by an earthquake figured that, on the whole, God was doing all right. No, but I *would* say to myself: the Christian needs to begin his adjudications by acknowledging an infinity of gratitude for being alive and a candidate for perpetual life. Ivan Denisovich* in the cold horror of the Arctic labor camp felt a rush of gratitude on that day when fate conspired to give him one extra ounce of bread. The conventional grace recited before beginning a meal cedes to our Lord the credit for furnishing the food we eat *("Bless us, O Lord, and these thy gifts which we are about to receive from thy bounty through Christ our Lord").* The visitors I saw at Lourdes were happy, and, in their perspective, grateful. Christianity asks that we *cultivate* the love of God. Some do so, one supposes, primarily out of fear. Christians know that God is to be feared, for He is the dispenser of eternal punishment. It is a common psychological phenomenon that those whom we fear we can also love, even as Ivan the Terrible was loved, or for that matter, Joseph Stalin. In analogous circumstances, they call this the Stockholm syndrome, love-thy-jailer.

Why does God desire—command—love? Because His benefactions are critical to day-by-day living and must be lovingly besought?

---

* Aleksandr Solzhenitsyn, *One Day in the Life of Ivan Denisovich* (Dutton, 1963).

Once again we run into problems. I remember a story relayed by my music teacher when I was a boy. She intended only an anecdote when she told me of a neighboring fifteen-year-old boy who undertook assiduously to cultivate a patch of earth alongside the spare dwelling in which he and his parents lived, to which end he devoted many hours, day after day, month after month. Eventually it bloomed with flowers and vegetables. The neighboring priest, stopping by one afternoon, exclaimed to him, "Conrad, that is a beautiful garden that you and God grew." Bringing from the boy the blurted response, "You should have seen it when just God was taking care of it."

The sequence here brings to mind not only the question, so to speak, of the division of labor between God and man (God made fertile the earth on which young Conrad worked) but also the question Arnold Lunn put to Monsignor Knox: What is the point in glorifying God when God—in the nature of things—is already the locus of infinite glory? From His infinity we cannot subtract, to His radiance we cannot add. And so the restless mind asks, Are such prayers as we devote to the glorification of God redundant?

And, in skeptical free fall, one's mind is tempted to go further. Is there, in such prayer, an element of sycophancy? (Sycophant: "A servile self-seeker who attempts to win favor by flattering influential people" *[American Heritage Dictionary].*) A committed Christian *seeks* to be servile to God. He seeks to win favor from God. God is an influential figure. Here is a fine example of a secular definition inapt when applied to God. Sycophancy, whether before headmasters or Emperors, is deplored. But the word is meaningless, is it not, in thinking about God?

Consider a passage from St. Augustine. I select it because it is more than mere cant-adoration, building as it does on the great paradoxes that attach to God the Creator. And I select it also because it was framed by someone at once a great metaphysician and a great poet. St. Augustine wrote:

What are Thou then, my God? . . . . Most highest, most good, most potent, most omnipotent; most merciful, yet most just; most hidden, yet most present; most beautiful, yet most strong; stable, yet incomprehensible; unchangeable, yet all-changing; never new, never old; all-renewing, and bringing age upon the proud, and they know it not; seeking, yet having all things. Thou lovest, without passion; art jealous, without anxiety; repentest, yet grievest not; art angry, yet serene; changest Thy works, Thy purpose unchanged; receivest again what Thou findest, yet didst never lose; never in need, yet rejoicing in gains; never covetous, yet exacting usury. Thou receivest over and above, that Thou mayest owe; and who hath aught that is not Thine? Thou payest debts, owing nothing; remittest debts, losing nothing. And what have I now said, my God, my life, my holy joy? Or what saith any man when he speaks of Thee? Yet woe to him that speaketh not, since the mute are even the most eloquent.

It is not for the mind harnessed by finite measurements to parse such language. It is rather for the mind disposed to worship, and worship requires emancipation from the boundaries of reason (". . . *seeking, yet having all things*"). The morning I read of the earthquake in Turkey I went to Mass at Stonor. It is the little chapel that lies one hundred feet from the hidden recess in the great house in which Edmund Campion hid from the Elizabethan militia commanded to find him and bring him to the Tower of London to answer for the treasonable activity of distributing the sacraments under Catholic dispensation. He would be tried and found guilty; and Fr. Campion, sometime protégé of Queen Elizabeth, would submit to days of crippling torture before being hanged, drawn, and quartered.

In that little chapel where Campion prayed during his seclusion the congregation read from the Preface to the Eucharistic Prayer for that Sunday:

Father in heaven, it is right that we should give you thanks and glory; you alone are God, living and true. Through all eternity you live in unapproachable light. Source of life and goodness, you have created all things to fill your creatures with every blessing and lead all men to the joyful vision of your light. Countless hosts of angels stand before you to do your will; they look upon your splendour and praise you night and day. United with them and in the name of every creature under heaven, we praise your glory as we say:

"Holy holy holy, Lord, God of power and might, heaven and earth are full of your glory. Hosanna in the highest; blessed is he who comes in the name of the Lord. Hosanna in the highest."

It is right that we should give you thanks and glory intimates, with that inflection of we-say you-say, that there are those who believe that it is *not* right that we should give Him thanks and glory. But why would some of His creatures be reluctant to give Him thanks and glory? Well, one reason might be that they believe in an omnipotent God and cannot understand why only a few hours ago He would cause an earthquake in a little town in Turkey; or if He did not cause it, they do not understand why He failed to prevent it.

They ask: Is such a God, who permitted such random violence, indeed the God to whom we owe thanks and glory? Yes; our God is the source of life and goodness, who created all things. But did He not also create that geological malformation that caused life and goodness sharply to end for four hundred of His creatures? Since God is perfect we cannot dismiss—can we?—the Turkish event as divine oversight? And inasmuch as countless hosts of angels stand before Him to do His will, why was not one angel dispatched to Turkey to appease the restive geological substratum? If God does not give us the analytical resources to descry a rational motive in that earthquake, then indeed, as the prayer says, He is an unapproachable light; but why, then, do we say that He illuminates the thought of the world with His life and goodness?

A host of angels looks upon His splendor and praises Him, night and day. But why does He seek praise? Why does He *tolerate* praise?

And isn't the question necessarily raised, Does it not demean these creatures of God, to lift our poor voices in praise, through that hail-storm of praise with which the elements themselves storm the throne of Heaven?

Or does the problem lie in the verb "to praise"? What exactly is it that we intend? To praise is to extol, commend, admire the subject's virtues or talents. But how is this applicable when the subject is already the essence of virtue, whose talents are indefinable, even as infinity is immeasurable? Doesn't it run the risk of belittling God—to proceed as if to praise Him were to enhance Him? If to praise Him is to augment Him, then He is not perfect. If praise cannot augment Him, how is He susceptible to praise? Is there a problem posed by Christian prayer? Does it summon human endeavor to exercises beyond human capacity, to an end unachievable?*

We arrive finally at a simple question: How, reasonably, can man be expected to praise that God which we have agreed to call the god-of-the-earthquake?

The answer, by no means obvious, has necessarily to do with the purpose of worship, which is not to magnify God, but to enlist ourselves as among the faithful. To recognize that we pray to the entity described by St. Augustine tells us that we are making strides in understanding the immensity of the divine undertaking, and the immensity of the human being for whom God sacrificed the pain, sorrow, and humiliation of Himself. To praise the asceticism of St. Francis of Assisi is to focus attention on the difference between his and your and my lifestyle. To ponder the glory of God is to worship a transcendence that gives us a measure of man, near-infinitely small on the scale of things, but infinitely great, as the complement of divine love. Who are you, buster? *I am the man Christ-God died for.*

Does reality, illuminated, generate love? That is not unreasonable, to love the person who sacrificed so much. But as we move from deduction (why we worship) past the hindrances of reason to ecstasy (why we love), then an element of mystery enters (why does it happen to Alice and not to Beth?), as also of grace (why has Alice the buoyant pleasure of spiritual life, and Beth not)? In a television exchange with Malcolm Muggeridge we arrived at this point: What comes after deduction? He answered,

"The deductive process is the means, but faith is the motive force

---

* "You have no need of our praise, yet our desire to thank you is itself your gift. Our prayer of thanksgiving adds nothing to your glory, but makes us grow in your grace, through Jesus Christ our Lord." Catechism 2639–40 (Preface IV) (Weekdays).

that takes you there. It's exactly like—Bill, it's exactly like falling in love. You see another human being and for some extraordinary reason you're in a state of joy and ecstasy over that person, but the driving force that enables you to express that and to bring it into your life is love. Without love, it's nothing; it passes.''

Christ said it directly, in answer to the question Which is the greatest commandment? And went on to prescribe the second commandment (Matthew 22:39): *"Thou shalt love thy neighbor as thyself."*

I have seen this point probed by asking, Just how much do you love yourself? Enough to satisfy the Lord's commandment? But this is theological wordplay. Still, if we treat our neighbor as well as we do ourselves, are we then living by the second commandment?

No, because to care for your neighbor does not require that you love him, and most of us love ourselves. I recalled the opening lines of the novel *Father Malachey's Miracle,* by Bruce Marshall. I read it soon after World War II, led to it by the enthusiastic notice given it by Albert Jay Nock, a scholar and litterateur (and anarchist), in his autobiography, *Memoirs of a Superfluous Man.* I cannot remember whether Nock paused over the meaning of the opening page of Marshall's words, but I did. There was the piquancy of the priest who found himself staring his duty in the face one day in a railroad car, as well as the delight in the language; but much after that by the challenge it spoke at a very deep level, a parable on one's attitude toward one's neighbor . . .

A fat man climbed into the same compartment as the little clergyman, a fat man with a face that was so red and pouchy that it looked like a bladder painted to hit other people over the head with at an Italian carnival. He sat down, or rather threw himself down, in the corner opposite the priest and began to read a pink paper in which the doings of horses and erotic young women were chronicled at length. He was followed by a middle-aged woman who had a peaky, shiny nose with a funny little dent in the middle and whose hat was one of those amorphous black affairs which would have been, at any moment, out of fashion in any country.

The priest was distracted from his meditation. It was impossible, he told himself, with a wry little mental smile, to think competently of the Father and the Son and of the Holy Ghost proceeding from both, with such a bulging, red face in front of him and such a peaky, peering woman placing her parcels here, there and everywhere. How hard it was, here below and with the material and the temporal crowding out the spiritual and the eternal, to love one's neighbour, how hard and yet how necessary. For the soul behind that bulging, red face had been redeemed by Christ just as surely as had his own, and Our Blessed Lord, while He hung on the cross, had seen the funny little dent in the middle of the peaky, peering woman's nose just as clearly as He had seen the broad, bland visage of Pope Pius the Eleventh, and so merciful was He, loved it just as much. And yet it was difficult to imagine bulge or dent in heaven unless, among the many mansions, there were one which should be one-tenth Beatific Vision and nine-tenths Douglas, Isle of Man. Of course, if it came to the point, it was difficult to imagine the majority of contemporary humanity in any paradise which did not syncopate Saint Gregory, and whose eternal sands were without striped bathing tents and casinos.

He closed his eyes again. If he must love his neighbour he would love him without looking at him. He closed his eyes, and not only did he close them, but he kept on repeating the reflex action in his brain so that, with the bulging red face and the peaky, peering woman, away went the compartment, the train, the station, the world; and, as Scotland went swinging after Scandinavia and Spain came scampering after and Australia flew to join the stars, he was alone with God.

A great nothingness was before him, a great nothingness that was Something, a great nothingness that was All; and in the warm freedom from the tangible he knew his Saviour and was absorbed by Him.

One knows what one should feel, why one should feel so, and how light our effort alongside the exorbitance of Christ's example. Still, sometimes it is easier to do with eyes closed.

So: we come to rest with the mysteries. We have the wonderful tabulation of them done by St. Augustine. In agreeing that that is what they are, we are not violating the rule of Ronald Knox to prefer mystery to vagueness. We do not abandon reason, we merely recognize its limitations. We reason to the existence of God, it is revealed to us that His Son was the incarnation, and that such was His love of us that He endured a torture excruciating in pain, and unique in aspect—the God of hosts, mutilated by His own creatures, whom He dies forgiving, loving. Can we do less? Yes, we do less, but must try to do more, until we die.

CHAPTER ELEVEN

The Eyes of Hollywood

Hollywood has made a movie starring Bernadette, of course, and, for that matter, several starring Christ. But the allure of scandal is more interesting than the celebration of saintliness, and this isn't a discovery any profounder than that man bites dog catches attention. But more than that is going on, and depending on the analyst's view of causation, this is Hollywood shaping public attitudes, or public attitudes shaping Hollywood. But the appetite for scandal can be thought of as constant. The way in which Hollywood plays to it tells us something about the moral malleability of its clientele—in America, almost everybody.

On the relatively direct question of how Hollywood treats religion—most specifically, the clergy—I draw from Professor Stanley Rothman, writing in *The American Scholar* ("Is God Really Dead in Beverly Hills—Religion & the Movies," spring 1996). Mr. Rothman charts the disposition in Hollywood over the years in portraying religious characters. "In the first decade [the fifties], only 15 per cent of the characters with religious ties are unsuccessful, compared to 33 per cent of non-religious characters. . . . Now the number of religious characters who fail to achieve their goals rises to 36 percent compared to only 28 percent of non-religious defeated characters. Religious affiliation today actually seems to increase the likelihood that a character will fail to achieve his or her objectives. . . . In the most recent decade, only three of six religious workers are presented positively."*

I carry in the memory the Hollywood treatment of *True Confessions,* the novel by John Gregory Dunne (1977). I said about it, soon after its release, that Robert De Niro, playing the role of the priest, was badly miscast. He was never entirely convincing, and here and there words were put in his mouth ("I've packed up my bags," when he announces he has cancer) that one wouldn't have thought wild horses could have dragged from the word processors of the talented screenwriters (Dunne and his wife, Joan Didion). The scenes are one cliché mounted joylessly on another, so that the unfolding of each reminds one progressively of the weakness of the predecessor.

But the point of it, in this perspective, was the ease with which

---

* Mr. Rothman proceeds to give us his interesting insight: "The kinds of movies that have filled the void have not ignored religion altogether but instead have recreated it in such a way that it loses much of its previous affirmative value. Insofar as we never fully succeed in mastering our violent anti-social drives, and insofar as a child continues to function within the adult, it can be argued that most human beings require some mythic structure if they are to function effectively as responsible adults. The myth of the inevitable triumph of good over evil may seem simple-minded to the sophisticated Hollywood producers and directors, who believe that they themselves do not need such myths. They are, in fact, little different from the audiences they serve. They cannot find a satisfactory substitute for religion, though they continue to try. Their failure is reflected in the plethora of films that document the triumph of evil, an evil which, as in 'Alien,' often emerges from the bowels of the victim. One suspects that these themes are, at least partially, symbolic of the fear of loss of control of the evil impulses within the self."

Hollywood now handles the theme of the thoroughly disreputable priest. Now, the priest in *True Confessions* isn't actually all that hateful, no more is his boss, the cardinal; nor, for that matter, is his brother Tom, the driven, cynical policeman. The priest-protagonist (Monsignor) Desmond Spellacy is ambitious. He has not one foot in this world, but two. In his dealings with the cardinal he is somewhere between docile and servile. He is bright enough to know what's really going on, and morally awake enough to know that what's really going on, shouldn't really go on. This is of course essential to effect scandal. If the protagonist doesn't know you're not expected to eat children for breakfast, it isn't scandalous when he does so. Hollywood knows how to snicker. Here is Mother Church in Los Angeles giving out one of those medals ("Catholic Citizen of the Year" or whatever) to a big, beefy, repulsive Angelino—because he has given big money for the construction of parochial schools. Never mind that all the cognoscenti of Los Angeles (and the noncognoscenti in the movie house) know that the honoree got his early money by pimping, is probably still connected with organized crime, and regularly devotes himself to the most pleasurable feature of the biblical injunction to go out and multiply.

It used to be, of course, that Hollywood clergy were Bing Crosby, going his way, and making ours lighter; or Spencer Tracy, telling the dead-end kid he was a good boy after all, with transmutational effect; or Ingrid Bergman, raising money for the bells of St. Mary's and, while at it, tingling the chimes within the human spirit. Yes, I thought, most moviegoers know that much of this was romance, that in real life Bing Crosby neglected his children, Spencer Tracy kept a concubine, and Ingrid Bergman not only looked after orphans but produced them.

Even so, the theatrical convention was there: that priests usually behave in such a way as to invite emulation. Between the fifties and the seventies no professional class (save possibly investigative journalists) was presumptively expected to engage in altruistic activity. The author Ben Stein wrote a book (*The View from Sunset Boulevard*, 1979) about a year in Hollywood during which he had come upon not a single "good" businessman, or, for that matter, a "good" military officer in the pulp forests of screenplays he had read for television and the movies. If John Gregory Dunne had sat down to write a book about a priest who behaved like Mother Teresa, he would not have been asked to make a movie based on his discovery, never mind that such a discovery might have made it into *The Guinness Book of World Records*.

The priestly calling is a theatrical victim of an age of skepticism and self-gratification; and it isn't entirely unreasonable that the theatergoer should take this in stride. For one thing there are all those thousands of priests and nuns who have been "laicized," a desertion no man may judge harshly whose own faith, whether in God, marriage, country, or politics, has ever been shaken. But desertion it was: i.e., one pledged one's life to a calling, most spiritual in aspect—and after a while the public recognized you as the fellow drinking beer with the wife and girlfriend while watching Monday night football, waiting your turn at the bowling alley. The stereotype of tenacious Franciscan asceticism was, it seemed to me, gone, perhaps irretrievably. The public expectations of the priestly calling are probably better defined by his behavior on the screen than at the altar. The impact on vocations would seem self-evident.

And then, too, in the eighties there was the ideologization of religion. It was easier, among Catholic clergy, to pick a fight over whether to send arms to the rebels in Nicaragua than whether the Shroud of Turin bears the marks of an extra-worldly implosion.

So John Gregory Dunne's colorful story about priests who have one eye on ambition, and cardinals who leave it to God to forgive the means by which the local philanthropists accumulated their money in the first place, could not reasonably have been expected to disrupt the rhythm of the movie audience munching its popcorn. The book, as it happened, is very much more shocking than the movie: but this is so not because the clergy in the novel are even more gravely corrupted, but because the language, particularly the words of the cop and his sidekick, are textured with a blend of profanity and obscenity which almost everywhere (I think of one or two lapses) moves the imagination to delights undiminished by the moral infrastructure. True corruption is when you are asked to believe that what used to be thought of as the differences between right and wrong no longer works, because there really aren't any differences. It is one thing to discover that the pious priest was really Elmer Gantry all over again—just one more chapter in the Playboy Scheherazade, the 1,001st night of pleasure in a world whose catechism is to the effect that philandering is good because anything that *feels* good *is* good—except maybe lynching and Jim Crow *(Playboy*—and Hollywood—have to draw the line somewhere). The book *True Confessions* shocks by the color and irreverence in language used by characters who know what it is they are doing and would not be surprised to spend an eternity posing for Hieronymus Bosch. Hollywood does it as blasphemous software, etiolated yet eager to wring at least a little fruit from its impiety. Still it is a relief of sorts that Hollywood lets the viewer know that *it* knows the difference between right and wrong. That is better than experiencing life as a nihilist. You could fit every Christian martyr in history in the moral chasm between *True Confessions* and *Last Exit from Brooklyn*.

But it is the cultural point that here arrests the attention. The voyage between Bing Crosby and Robert De Niro. Fifty years ago there was plenty of sin going on. In the Eurasian continent more people were killed, one ruminates, than in the three millennia of recorded history. Even so, for a period in popular culture, however brief, benign presumptions were indulged. Just as rabbis were "wise," priests were "benevolent." Drank a little too much, like Barry Fitzgerald maybe; but good fellows, professionally devoted to philanthropy of sorts. The viewer was only here and there teased into examining the underlying dogmatic solemnity of it all.

The Spanish filmmakers, back in the fifties, came up with a discreet little venture in evangelism *(Marcelino, Pan y Vino)* as charming and piquant as *The Hobbitt*. A little orphan boy, living in the monastery, is spotted by the camera spiriting away a loaf of bread and an occasional apple to hand over to the sad-faced man hanging on the crucifix in the attic where, before the dazed stare of the child, every night at exactly six o'clock, the incarnation is reenacted, and Christ takes the bread from the boy. Then of course, finally tabulating the missing loaves of bread, the monks' exploration freezes the figure back on the crucifix. A little Christian one-acter, innocent and engaging; nowadays unthinkable, unless a Fr. Merton were to produce a movie from one of his convents, to show to the nuns on Christmas Eve.

At the hot end of the theological prod, the viewer could see a movie with a dazzling blend of faith, triumphant over sacrilege *(Le Défroqué)*. Without faith there cannot, of course, be sacrilege; and here we had the sometime priest, become agnostic professor of philosophy, dining with his young former protégé, who had stayed true to their once-common faith and was now freshly ordained in the priesthood. In the noisy, bibulous tavern crowded with bons vivants, three violinists carry about the huge five-liter tankard of wine, plying away with their instruments on splashy and accelerando Gypsy-rhythmed music that is catalyst to happy frenzy, while one at a time guests chugalug competitively on the wine vat, the leader, up to the moment, a large-bellied Frenchman who, however, has succeeded in emptying only one-half of the seemingly bottomless vat.

It is routinely refilled and the violinists move exuberantly to the next table down, where the earnest young priest is chatting animatedly with his apostate mentor. The audience is distracted. The ex-priest seizes the moment, drawing the wine to him. Driven to black mass exhibitionism he quietly intones, in the hearing only of his freshly consecrated companion, the transubstantiating incantation: *Hic est enim Calix Sanguinis mei (. . . This is my Blood . . .)*. The violinists, unaware, noisily unaware, resume their routine. The young priest, dazed by his knowledge that apostate priests are not deprived of their sacramental powers, lifts the tankard—the blood of Christ—to his lips. He begins to drink. The applause at first is only routine. But the priest drinks on and the crowd goes wilder then breathlessly silent as the drama proceeds toward the impossible . . . the violinists sweat . . . the professor stands up in alarm. Now the boy-priest has emptied the great tankard; the crowd is delirious with admiration. The young priest, stumbling outdoors to the cheers of the crowd, suc-cumbs and, taken away by ambulance, dies. Flash-forward to the fu-neral Mass. It is being conducted by the professor, but he is dressed in clerical garb. Returned to the faith. A dramatic smash.

True Confessions (the movie, not the book) was not denounced by any remnant of the old Legion of Decency. Catholics don't have an effective Anti-Defamation League, for one thing; for another, there isn't anything there, in the tale of the Worldly Priest and his crooked brother, that is truly sacrilegious. Some priests will visit brothels as long as lust is given a fighting chance on earth, and it is the organizing Christian proposition that even Christ was tempted. Christianity in-spires great utterances, even as it provokes fervent mockeries. G. K. Chesterton, face-to-face with his time's version of Hollywood agnosti-cism—a humanism that seemed for a while to be endemic in philo-sophical faculties—concluded a major book by writing that "there are an infinity of angles at which one falls, only one at which one stands. . . . To have avoided them all has been one whirling adventure; and in my vision, the heavenly chariot flies thundering through the ages, the dull heresies sprawling and prostrate, the wild truth reeling but erect."

Those who were put off by *True Confessions* can remind themselves that much more serious stuff has always been leveled at the Church and its prelates. Over a century ago Charles Kingsley was writing such stuff as "The Roman religion . . . for some time past, [has] been making men not better men, but worse. We must face, we must conceive honestly for ourselves, the deep demoralization which had been brought on in Europe by the dogma that the Pope of Rome had the power of creating right and wrong; that not only truth and false-hood, but morality and immorality, depended on his setting his seal to a bit of parchment."

That kind of thing makes Hollywood's *True Confessions* taste like a no-cal Popsicle. But—caution! Kingsley, above, brought forth New-man's *Apologia pro Vita Sua,* the crushing masterpiece that British newspaper readers lined up to buy when it was serialized, a book that devastated Kingsley, leaving that urbane and witty skeptic sounding like the village atheist. Impiety can breed piety. That hasn't happened, but the dozen-odd years that have gone by are grains of sand in time. But meanwhile we do right to worry about the diminishing size of the religious orders, and ask whether the tradition of the celibate order is as firm as Pope John Paul would have it be.

CHAPTER TWELVE

Concerning Women as Priests, Divorce,

Birth Control, Remarriage

It is moderately easy to say that we must die trying to please the Lord and to abide by his laws. But earthbound people are discouraged by staring in the face of interpretations of God's law that strain reason as well as faith. The evidence is pretty plain that four practices of the Church—we pause, at least for the time being, before naming them doctrines of the Church—are primary causes of current dissension and concern. They are the Church's policies demanding priestly celibacy, granting ordination only of men, authorizing birth control only by the rhythm system, and affirming the indissolubility of marriage.*

At varying levels, these practices give rise to dissent between the Church and the laity. Birth control has caused a greater historical division than any other modern Church ruling. The demand for a married priesthood appears to increase. This is not surprising, in an age in which sensuality everywhere beckons, its promptings impossible to avoid, its favors progressively difficult to renounce. The sentiment in favor of ordaining women hasn't translated into a mass movement, but the right of married couples to practice birth control through the use of contraceptives is a major assertion, and the inflexibility of the divorce laws a major source of grief (universal) and defiance (widespread).

The Catholic Catechism, reedited and refined in 1994, is unambiguous on these matters:

Section 1577: "Only a baptized man (vir) validly receives sacred ordination."† Again, "The Lord Jesus chose men (viri) to form the college of the twelve apostles, and the apostles did the same when they chose collaborators to succeed them in their ministry."†† Again, "The college of bishops, with whom the priests are united in the priesthood, makes the college of the twelve an ever-present and ever-active reality until Christ's return. The Church recognizes herself to be bound by this choice made by the Lord himself. For this reason the ordination of women is not possible."††† And, finally, 1578: "No one has a *right* to receive the sacrament of Holy Orders. Indeed no one claims this office for himself; he is called to it by God. (69 Cf.

---

* I do not include abortion or euthanasia, since dissent on those questions is so rare among Catholic moralists as to leave them outside active analytical concern. The demand for a modification in the rules governing the other practices here mentioned is great. The demand to baptize abortion is very rare, the general position among Catholic dissenters being that those who do abort, or collude in bringing about an abortion, are yes sinners, but so is your old man.

† The scholarly references are supplied: 66—CIC 1024.

†† 67—cf. Mark 3:14–19; Luke 6:12–16; 1 Timothy 3:1–13; 2 Timothy 1:6; Titus 1:5–9; St. Clement of Rome, Ad Cor. 42.4, 44.3: PG 1.292, 300.

††† 68—cf. John Paul II, MD 26–27; CDF, declaration, Inter insigniores: AAS 69 (1977) 98–116.

Heb 5:4) Anyone who thinks he recognizes the signs of God's call to the ordained ministry must humbly submit his desire to the authority of the Church, who has the responsibility and right to call someone to receive orders. Like every grace this sacrament can be *received* only as an unmerited gift. . . ." And 1979: "All the ordained ministers of the Latin Church, with the exception of permanent deacons, are normally chosen from among men of faith who live a celibate life and who intend to remain *celibate* 'for the sake of the kingdom of heaven.' (70—Matthew 19:12). Called to consecrate themselves with undivided heart to the Lord and to 'the affairs of the Lord' (71—1 Corinthians 7:32), they give themselves entirely to God. Celibacy is a sign of this new life to the service of which the Church's minister is consecrated; accepted with a joyous heart celibacy radiantly proclaims the Reign of God (72—cf. PO 16)."

On birth control (2370): "Periodic continence, that is, the methods of birth regulation based on self-observation and the use of infertile periods, is in conformity with the objective criteria of morality. These methods respect the bodies of the spouses, encourage tenderness between them, and favor the education of an authentic freedom. In contrast, 'every action which, whether in anticipation of the conjugal act, or in its accomplishment, or in the development of its natural consequences, proposes, whether as an end or as a means, to render procreation impossible' is intrinsically evil" (158 HV *[Humanae Vitae]* 14).

On divorce (1650): "Today there are numerous Catholics in many countries who have recourse to civil *divorces* and contract new civil unions. In fidelity to the words of Jesus Christ—'Whoever divorces his wife and marries another, commits adultery against her; and if she divorces her husband and marries another, she commits adultery' (158 Mk 10:11–12)—the Church maintains that a new union cannot be recognized as valid, if the first marriage was. If the divorced are remarried civilly, they find themselves in a situation that objectively contravenes God's law. Consequently, they cannot receive Eucharistic communion as long as this situation persists. For the same reason, they cannot exercise certain ecclesial responsibilities. Reconciliation through the sacrament of Penance can be granted only to those who have repented for having violated the sign of the covenant and of fidelity to Christ, and who are committed to living in complete continence.''

I pretty much knew, ahead of time, how my Forum would ring in on these issues, but I expected, and got, inflections that catalyzed my own thinking. I had also a valuable exchange with Lance Morrow, who perfectly expressed the frustration of the Catholic who runs into the iron laws of the Church. My question:

Would you be disappointed—outraged?—defiant?—if the Church were to (a) authorize noncelibate orders; (b) withdraw its disapproval of birth control measures that don't require the use of abortifacients (e.g., condoms); (c) authorize divorce and remarriage?

It isn't quite fair, I subsequently reproached myself, to put such a question to a priest. Most priests make an effort to be loyal not only to the Church's regulation, as is natural, but to the Church's reasoning, except when to do so would violate their conscience. When that problem looms, a priest tends to go in one of two directions: The first, docility. We have seen that Monsignor Knox confessed to Arnold Lunn that at the time of his conversion Knox could not make himself believe in eternal damnation, and therefore dismissed his reservation as an act of deference to the wisdom of the Church. The second way for the priestly dissenter to handle unwelcome questions is to decline to answer them; or to answer them so abstrusely as to discourage the sound of contumacy. I say this not to characterize the responses by the two priests kind enough to serve on my Forum, merely to acknowledge a psychological burden I ran the risk of imposing on them.

Fr. Neuhaus joined most of the other respondents in saying that if ever a change were contemplated on the celibate priesthood, he would not want it to be now, when it would be seen so widely as yielding to social pressures. "Also, I think it's important to keep the discipline in place over the next few decades and see through [the question] whether the Church can generate" the required understanding of the "radical nature of vocation to the priesthood." Moreover, Fr. Neuhaus thinks himself informed by his own experience. "I was for thirty years in a church in which almost all clergy were married and I know that [a married clergy] does not 'solve' the problems that some Catholics attribute to the celibacy discipline. And it creates other very real problems that the Catholic priesthood does not presently have."

Fr. Neuhaus touches on a critical point, about which other respondents agreed unanimously (though Russell Kirk left himself room to maneuver). If the Church can be seen to be retreating from a position only because of public pressure to do so, it is undermining its own authority. Jeffrey Hart put it this way: "I suppose I could approve of a married clergy or female priests, but only on condition that it not be a capitulation to the *Zeitgeist*. Practically speaking, that means not for another fifty years or so if, for that matter, ever. The power of the Church is in its relation to the timeless. Transitory fashion is not welcome."

But Fr. Neuhaus's apparent willingness to see how it goes after another generation or two on the matter of priestly celibacy acknowledges that he sees no doctrinal barrier to a noncelibate priesthood. On the question whether a married celibacy will become necessary in order to staff the priestly orders, he defers to anthropological experience. We simply do not know, he is saying, whether a continuation of existing restrictions will leave the Church, in the days immediately ahead, with enough young men to serve the needs of the Church.

For reasons I can't explain, I never gave much thought to what it actually is that ignites a vocation. There were always priests around. I knew that the British tradition, for a couple of centuries, called upon the third son to look into holy orders. Two decades ago I remarked a special bustle at the eleven o'clock Mass I was attending, looked at the parish notes for that day, and learned that a young woman would be taking, at that service, perpetual vows to serve as a nun. The augustness of the occasion seemed to me at once frightening and glorious.

Across the way from where my wife and I lived (and still do) was a girl's convent, Convent of the Sacred Heart. Two of my sisters had been there to school, and two of my nieces were there now, where their mother had been. The twin sister of one of my sisters-in-law was there as a nun. The Sacred Heart order was reclusive, and the regimen so strict that when as an undergraduate at Yale I drove there to visit one sister, we needed special permission from the mother superior to drive away to a neighborhood drugstore to buy an ice cream cone.

I was asked to deliver a speech to the girls and alumnae and heard some of the lore. The beautifully placed convent had been the private mansion of the Stokes family, and (so the story went) a Sacred Heart nun searching for a site on which to situate a girls' school made an offer for the property and the choice half dozen acres in the 1920s, an offer of so much less than its commercial value as to bring only a smile from the aging owner, who suggested a price ten times that quoted by the nun. She replied that she would simply pray that, at some point in the future, the price would prove acceptable; which is what happened, two years after the Depression had razed the value of all property in that area and everywhere else.

The convent school flourished, about seventy-five girls from affluent Catholic families (I don't know how many scholarships were awarded to needy students). There was some criticism of the severities of life there, but they were accepted as a part of the discipline not alien, in those days, to boarding school existence.

What happened was so sudden, so startling, that it seemed, from the narrow perspective of the convent's neighbors and friends, something on the order of what must have been experienced by those who looked about in 1917 to discover that the Bolshevik order had set in. There was an interval, perhaps a year or two, when the new mother superior, carried along by the wildness of the sixties, reversed the protocols of convent life and suddenly the girls were given liberties as great as the local high school gave. Overnight—it seemed—the convent school closed down. The property was sold, soon converted into luxurious condominiums, the sisters dispersed (many of them, finding no call for their special training, released from their vows). From the window of our bedroom we look over at those large brick buildings and are reminded how very sudden these transformations can be.

But it wasn't like the disappearance of the Moral Majority or Moral Rearmament. Here now, twenty pews up from where I knelt, at Sunday Mass at St. Mary's in Stamford, a woman early in her twenties was pledging to spend the rest of her life teaching, doing missionary work, attending the sick, praying many hours of the day and the week. I would have a more direct experience with the access of a vocation years later, when a nephew (chapter 17) would become a priest in the Benedictine order in France.

It continues to happen, so to speak, right and left, even if in insufficient numbers. I have only twice heard priests, in Sunday sermons, remind their congregations of the need for vocations. One point made by a priest especially struck me. It was that young men and women, attracted to the idea of religious life, must not suppose that the calling is something that strikes in the night. It can be ambiguous in its address to the twenty-two-year old. A mere suggestion, followed by inquiry, followed still further by years (thirteen years, in the Jesuit order) of training and learning and spiritual exercises. By modern standards, in modern perspectives, an enormously serious commitment, a world away from the gratifications of the Playboy culture. Would any changes suggest themselves to the magisterium, interpreting such matters as celibacy and the restriction of the priestly office to men?

On the question of birth control, once again, I anticipated much of what my Forum would give me, but I was intensely curious about the formulations they'd use.

Fr. Neuhaus "would be grievously disappointed were *Humanae Vitae* [which reiterated the ban on contraceptive practices] to be modified." He does not reveal whether he thinks contravention a clearly readable defiance of scriptural doctrine, but he does say why he thinks it rings true. "I am persuaded that theologically, anthropologically, psychologically, it [*Humanae Vitae*] is a true account of human sexuality and marriage, as also of their attendant purposes, promises, and responsibilities.'' He acknowledges the wide disregard of the law against birth control, and has no notion what can be done about this. ''But to do anything that suggests the teaching is being retracted would be a terrible wrong.'' Nor does Fr. Neuhaus have an answer for the whole business of divorce, annulments, and remarriage. ''The question is a tough one, especially in its pastoral implications. But then it's not supposed to be easy to be a Catholic.''

Father Rutler, ever adamantine, which is to say, faithful to ortho-dox understanding, was in an I'm-glad-you-asked-me-that-question mood. ''On all three of the issues listed, I would be neither disap-pointed nor outraged nor defiant but incredulous. The Church cannot do the absurd because she is protected in essential matters by infallibil-ity. On priestly marriage the evidence is indicating more strongly all the time that priestly celibacy is more than a matter of juridical disci-pline. It has to do with the perfection of the sacrifice of Christ and the eternity of the Christian priesthood.''

The trouble with such explanations is that they do not explain. I am left thinking: the authority to interpret God's way in the matter is, in Catholic eyes, for the Pope to exercise. To say that celibacy is a sacrifice is plain. We like to assume that that sacrifice fortifies the spiritual reach and character of the Catholic priest, and if this is what is meant by ''the perfection of the sacrifice of Christ and the eternity of the Christian priesthood,'' good. But this is hardly a translucent finding.

And Fr. Rutler on birth control: ''It does pertain to natural law and the Church cannot undo nature. The level of commentary on this issue indicates the theological impoverishment of these days. Paul VI was a hapless and even tragic figure, but *Humanae Vitae* will be his one claim to Heaven and the prophet's mantle.''

Divorce and remarriage?

[They are] a total contradiction of our Lord's eschatological vision of conjugal love. As such, it cannot be altered without material heresy. However, the attempts of the Catholic Church in the United States to circumvent this by its abuse of the annulment process is dishonest and may lead a lot of Church bureaucrats to Hell. (More than 90 percent of all annulments, I believe, throughout the world, are granted [in] the USA.) This corruption is more perverse than anything the Protestant schismatics objected to. Its reform will be led by some other St. Charles Borromeo [a reformer], if we are lucky, or some other Martin Luther [a schismatic], if we are unlucky.

Father Rutler gives us the taste of the intransigent Church, but then he is entitled to ask whether we also think of God as intransigent.

Russell Kirk equivocated:

I would not be disappointed, outraged, or defiant at such changes, although I would think them misguided. The marriage of members of the clergy was not forbidden in the early centuries of the Western Church, and is common to the present day in the Eastern Church. It is desirable that ecclesiastics should not marry—for one reason: they are better able, if celibate, to devote their lives to their pastoral duties. But already the twentieth-century Church receives as priests married Anglican priests who have come over to Rome. If not enough celibates can be found for the Church to carry on its mission nowadays, doubtless it will be found unnecessary to require celibacy for all of them.

Birth control? "The rhythm method of birth control already being approved by the Church, it might be no very radical step to tolerate the use of contraceptives—not that I advocate aught of the sort." Remarriage? "Ease of Church annulment of marriages being notoriously loose nowadays, a limited indulgence of divorce and remarriage would not be astounding—though I would not readily approve it." Jeffrey Hart's responses are similarly accommodationist. He simply dissents from *Humanae Vitae,* whose arguments he finds "an overly precise application of the natural law." On divorce (Jeff Hart is, as noted, himself divorced and remarried), he skirts the issue: "The Church's practical position on divorce and remarriage has been made pretty elastic through the ease with which annulments now can be obtained."

Wick Allison would feel no sense of doctrinal betrayal with the advent of married Catholic clergy but he would be "disheartened" if the Church abandoned celibate orders altogether. "In the modern world we know realistically that if we introduced married clergy, we would soon be dealing with priests who need more money, priests who divorce, priests whose children are jailed for dealing drugs. On the flip side, I feel that the Catholic priesthood earns a respect that accompanies their great devotion and willingness to endure celibacy."

On birth control, Allison sees the Church's position as "intrinsic to its nature." "But then we are exploring such questions as whether it has become sinful to do something a Pope has proscribed."

And on divorce:

I am divorced. My marriage was annulled. If it had not been, I do not think I would have remarried, but who can say with certainty what I would have done under different conditions? All that I know is that it was my commitment to myself that I would not remarry. It seems to me that the great problem of the modern age is that we do not take sin upon ourselves. We refuse to be held responsible. Rather, we lobby to change the definition. We attempt to elevate our private problem into a change in a changeless teaching. The Church is only attempting—and a human institution only attempts—to uphold the very direct command of its Lord. It would be disgusting, and ultimately self-defeating, to retreat. And what would be the point? The Church gave up the English-speaking world over a divorce. Why back down now?

A spirited and devout defense of the traditional position.

•   •   •

In an early draft of this chapter I reflected that "Mr. Lance Morrow, the distinguished writer and journalist, took the Essay page of *Time* magazine in 1994 to catechize (right word?) the Church on the problems here scrutinized. His sanction was eyebrow-raising: if the Church would agree to make women priests and would allow birth control and would see the need for some divorces, Mr. Morrow would attend Mass more frequently. Since Lance Morrow has a fine eye for irony, it is not conceivable that he failed to see—and therefore to appreciate—the piquancy of his—what? Offering? Venture in reciprocity?"

In conversation with him, some time after his essay appeared, he told me he had reservations about what he had written. I sent him a draft of this chapter. In a return letter he said he had been "ruefully stimulated and chastened." And went on to say (I have his permission to quote him) those fearfully arresting things Catholics need to ponder.

Lance Morrow is a convert to Catholicism who divorced and remarried. He received "a ton of mail" after his essay appeared in *Time*. "Almost all the letters, both pro and con, urged me to go back to Mass, not to cut myself off from the Eucharist." He would like to do so. But as someone divorced and remarried, "I am of course not welcome at the table. . . . I might have tried to get my first marriage annulled, but I consider such exercises to be contemptible, insulting to all concerned, including the Church. Am I to have the Church declare that the first marriage, which was a real marriage, did not really exist, wink-wink, and that my sons are illegitimate?" (The Church has never "illegitimized" any child, whatever the circumstances of his conception.)

An annulment, in Catholic terminology, is a ruling that a marriage that ostensibly took place did not actually take place. This means that the partners to the ceremony were not capable of contracting the obligations of marriage. For instance, if there is a lack of "due discretion"—i.e., immaturity, or ignorance, or delusion, or mental incapacity—in either of the partners, the marriage oath cannot have been valid. Still another disqualifying feature would be intimidation—i.e., the exchange of vows was forced, not voluntary (a shotgun marriage).

I agree that the Church's stern policies do encourage people to stay with a marriage even long past the point at which they otherwise might have given up and drifted off to find new mates. And that emphasis on fidelity and sheer endurance is a good thing: sometimes by staying with it, a couple are able to break through into higher orbits or better territory—and in any case, they are able to obey Christ's injunction about the indissolubility of marriage.

But the effort to maintain his marriage had not availed him. "And here I am, forbidden to take Communion—"

Well one must gamble by the rules of the house. I am inclined to agree with those Catholics who say I have no business telling Catholics what to do because I am not entirely a Catholic myself. I am at best a kind of Shinto Catholic these days—well disposed toward the rocks and tree spirits of the Church, the surrounding ancestral atmospheres and mists, but irritated and even contemptuous of the fine print, the doctrinaire, litigious, management aspects of the Roman office. Is it true that God is in the details? I do not believe that God is a bureaucrat. It is hard for me to believe that I could be saved from the fires by going before the Church's annulment authorities in order to con them into thinking that my seventeen-year life with my sons' mother was . . . what?

My own sense is that life is always both mysterious and risky. I have a lot of trouble thinking that the brocaded eminences in Vatican City have any business telling me whether my first marriage was or (sleight-of-hand) *was not* "valid." . . . and so by extension, I have further trouble thinking that they have it in their power to cut me off from communion with God.

My thinking about the issue of contraception revolves around a similar sense of outrage at the indignity. For the Church, in its majesty, to apply needle-nosed casuistry to the question of contraception makes me think that betimes we are going to have encyclicals on wiping oneself. Abortion is clearly wrong, as I stated in my essay. But contraception is another matter. The Church badly needs some daylight, some common sense, on this issue.

Non serviam here does not mean *Non serviam Dominum,* but rather *non serviam* a delegitimized (in my eyes) Church bureaucracy. If I were in charge of managing the Church's position, I would nullify annulments—abolish the possibility, except perhaps in the rarest of cases. The problem (my problem anyway) would of course remain, but the position of the Church would at least be honorable and consistent. It is arguably neither now.

On the matter of divorce, we see the abrasion of empirical knowledge and experience on doctrine. Christ's ban was unambiguous. The Church shattered, in the sixteenth century, over the matter of divorce. The sequence stirs the memory. King Henry VIII requested a papal invalidation of his marriage to Catherine of Aragon so that he might marry Anne Boleyn. Pope Clement VII denied him an annulment. The King proceeded to remarry; and the rest is history, much of it chaotic. The progressive loosening of the marriage bond nurtured the question, especially in the United States during the sixties and seventies, Was the "marriage" in fact a marriage?

A professor at Yale who became a friend when I was a student asked me a few years after my graduation to travel to Hartford, the diocesan center, to make an appearance before the ecclesiastical body inquiring into his petition for the annulment not of one, but of two marriages. It isn't easy to testify usefully to the petitioner at such proceedings unless it happens that you were privy to the subjective commitments of the bride and/or bridegroom when they exchanged wedding vows, and know that these were substantially false. If Susie confided to you that she was going to marry Henry on Tuesday because otherwise her father would shoot her; or if she said, Whatever Henry thinks, I have zero intention of having any children; or if she said, Whatever words passed from my mouth, I have no intention of spending the rest of my life with him—then, by Church law, that marriage was not sacramentally effected; in which event Henry is free to marry someone else. If there were children, their civil status is of course unaffected, since the state does not grant annulments.

The scandal to which some members of the Forum point is the studied laxity of the Vatican courts for twenty years or so after the Vatican Council when, as Mr. Morrow points out, annulments were relatively easy to get. But where does that get us? Clerical permissiveness tells us nothing about the law, only about the looseness of its practice—and Pope John Paul is said to be closing that gate. We are left with the heart-rending problem of the failed marriage.

The conventional consequence of the failed marriage is separation. But no remarriage. If the Vatican courts hang tight, then most Catholics seeking annulment will fail to get one. What then? The following:

(1) Impulsive marriages will diminish. I.e., greater thought will be given to the indissolubility of marriage, and the corresponding need for greater caution and better deliberation. (2) More Catholics who have separated will leave the Church in order to marry again. (3) More Catholics who separate but remain faithful to Catholic law will cohabit with what would otherwise have been a new spouse. And (4) more Catholics will remain faithful to the Church and live alone, many of them suffering loneliness and, in some cases, attendant despair; and, of course, more children will be without two parents.

I cannot remember who told me about the concept of "psychic consummation." It sounds awfully accommodationist, but not indefensibly so, in my own judgment. The insight is that consummation of a theological character is not catalyzed on the wedding night by biological union. It happens (the theory holds) only after mutual experience ripens into a commitment of a kind that by definition cannot be made by newlyweds. The idea is that somewhere along the line, after three, perhaps five years, the man and woman married under the law, having experienced life together, engage each other with an informed solemnity that validates perpetual vows.

Obviously one problem with the idea is its arrant invitation to abuse. And then, too, it would seem to encourage "trial" marriages.

In any event, it has no franchise from the Church. Yet there are elements in the idea that are appealing, and the question before the house is whether Church doctrine makes room for a failed marriage. Present practice enforces celibacy even for those who early in their married life discover a gestating but conclusive incompatibility. Granted, in its tendency to absolutization, the Church is oddly comforting. No one has the figures, but it has to be true that apparently pointless marriages endure only because the Church offers no facile alternative; and—this is an assumption—perhaps as much joy, or, if not that, satisfaction, is engendered by the marriage that survives the potholes and the canyons of mutual irritation, or displeasure, or incompatibility as is expedited by user-friendly laws for those who want to end this marriage and try another.

I see the Church as echoing the word of the Lord on marriage (no remarriage, period) and seeking to muddle through where doctrine winks.

Members of the Forum join in arguing against any concession by the Church if prompted simply by public pressure. Church doctrines do not come and go like Italian prime ministers. But the Church must listen to its congregation. Its unalterable claim is that no authorized change reversed any doctrine that was ever an element of the deposit of the faith. It is then left to the doctrine-scanners to inquire: Would changes of the kind discussed here have the effect of reversing Church doctrine?

The Forum agrees, and history confirms, that the married priest is an anomaly. Either such priests as were married were forerunners, men who married before the institutionalization of celibacy, or they received holy orders in a different communion and were accepted as married priests when they converted to Catholicism. And of course the third exception, the Eastern rite, which established its own practices while subscribing to the same faith.

The question continues in the mind of restive Catholics: Is this particular practice of the Church—the celibate priesthood—one that might change in the years to come? Cardinal Hume of Great Britain spoke hospitably, in September 1996, on the idea of a married priesthood. Perhaps after the magisterium takes a third, fourth, one hundredth look at it, weighing abutting considerations (primarily, a shortage of priests)?

I see this as a looming challenge. A generation ago the priestly population in America was 56,628, which means one priest for 682 communicants, never mind the Church's missionary concern for the unbaptized. The ratio of priests to Catholics is reduced, in thirty years, to 1 for 1,222. Variabilities in priestly vocations have happened before. But what if the Church found itself so short of priests as perforce to be delinquent in its temporal duties? Seminarians are about 15 percent of their former number. Hollywood would handle this question by having the pious nun, eyes raised upward, comment: "God will take care of that problem." And Hollywood might have exactly the right answer—God may provide.

And so theologians are entitled to wonder out loud whether conventional restrictions on the priesthood are consistent with Christ's energetic mandate to feed the sheep and to cast out the net for more fish. The negative—no married priests, ever—would of course be permanently affirmed if the Pope were to invoke the mantle of infallibility; but as we have seen in the exchanges between Monsignor Knox and Arnold Lunn, infallibility is invoked so infrequently, it can safely be thought of as not more than the ceremonial confirmation of a doctrine already accepted by tradition and theological consensus as an immovable part of the Christian foundation.

Is a feminine priesthood likely?

One watches for papal emphases. When Pope John Paul pronounced on the question of holy orders for women in 1994, his language was not conciliatory. "All the ordained ministers of the Latin Church, with the exception of permanent deacons, are normally chosen from among men of faith. . . ."

Objections to the traditional practice are heartfelt. Mr. Morrow, in his essay, went on nicely to harpoon what he called the Fallacy of Incidentals. "Women are not ordained priests because Christ, in human form, was a man and chose male apostles. But surely maleness was incidental to the essence of Christ's teaching and importance?"

Morrow's point is that Christ's chosen ministers were only *incidentally* male. He had planted his major proposition and was off to the races: "Those who build cathedrals of principle, unassailable traditions, around an unimportant or incidental distinction—one that is rooted in custom of distant time and, interminably preserved, becomes essentially inhuman—are doomed."

But of course this criticism disintegrates if Christ *intended* that His priests should be male. The perspective of Mr. Morrow (and of others) is that the conventions of the age in which Jesus lived were heavily male-centered and for that reason, and only for that reason, the Apostles and their successor bishops were all male.

That conjecture, however, is based either on the assumption that Christ could not defy—or, rather, elected not to defy—conventions of time and place; or else that He Himself chose not to do so but cannot reasonably be held to have bound Peter and His successors to abide by the same restrictions.

But it is uninformed to assume that Christ felt bound by conventions. He let the prostitute wash and anoint his feet, labored on the Sabbath, denounced the tax collectors. His violation of convention was one reason for His death sentence.

How do we measure the consequences of the exclusion of women priests? It is at least instructive that although there are here and there women ministers in sundry denominations, the call to the life of the clergy hasn't been the same thing as, say, the clamorous call for coeducation. In the Episcopal Church, the movement to ordain women is heatedly resisted by married clergymen, among others, for the same reasons given above in the Catholic Catechism. Resistance among many Episcopal priests has been adamant to the point of schism: ironically it is a reason why many ordained and married Episcopal priests have fled to Rome.

If our perspective were entirely sociological, then curiosity focuses on what's happening and what is likely to happen that is directly traceable to the requirement that priests be male. Will the Lutherans and the Anglicans, admitting women into the clergy, flourish—in the sense in which Mr. Morrow speaks? Will they irradiate that life and health and joy that Mr. Morrow sees lacking in his own Church because it continues bound to an Incidental?

It's too early to tell—Lutherans first ordained women in Denmark in the 1950s; in the U.S., 1970. It may be that women's role will continue to be marginal, and only marginally exercised, like women's long-since-established right to smoke cigars. If so, it might gradually transpire that this is so because the ministry is, for women, *contra naturam*—especially for married women. It could even be argued that Christ knew this to be so.

The Forum is divided on the question of contraception. My own incomplete understanding of the natural law balks at the central affirmation of *Humanae Vitae,* even as I'd of course counsel dutiful compliance with it. It is difficult, at first blush, to understand why the sexual act during pregnancy is not blasphemous, nor after menopause, if sex is viewed as natural only in pursuit of conception. But that is not the point of the encyclical. The reason given for the prohibition is that intercourse is a "generational act" and must not be defiled. No impediment—the reasoning goes—should block a natural development of intercourse. In the nature of things, when the wife is pregnant, or after menopause, blockage is not in question—you can't blind a blind man—hence the theological irrelevance of sex with a pregnant wife.

Some forms of birth control (unlike the condom) are not designed to prevent insemination, but to nip the life of the fetus in the bud. Moral theologians argue on three levels. The first asks whether a principle ought to govern their reasoning *(Is the life of a creature made by God for that reason inviolable?).* A second, whether the principle being considered is *itself* arguable *(Thou shalt not kill).* A third, does that principle apply to a given situation *(Thou shalt not kill, but you may kill in self-defense)?* Theologian Janet Smith takes the question in hand.*

> The procreative good of sexual intercourse ought to be protected. But [theologians] might disagree intensely on the reasons that justify this principle; for instance, some would invoke natural law principles; some would invoke scriptural support (such as "be fruitful and multiply"); others would cite the coherence of this principle with personalist values. The most serious disagreement would, though, be on the absoluteness of this principle. Some claim that the procreative good of sexual intercourse is an absolute good, never to be violated. They would argue that contraception is an intrinsic moral wrong and thus could never be morally justified as a direct and deliberate moral choice. Others argue that procreation is not an absolute good and that thus it may be necessary to weigh other goods against the good of procreation. For instance, some may argue that the good of the spontaneous union of the spouses, or the good of prevention of pregnancy out of wedlock might supersede the good of procreation and that thus, at times, this good could be sacrificed to other goods.

The Catholic seeking to understand is not always the Catholic bound to observe. In 1966 the theologian Richard McCormick, S.J., wrote, "Contraception continues to be . . . the major moral issue troubling the Church." Meanwhile he counseled obedience. "The effect of repeated authoritative Church pronouncements on a matter of this importance is a presumptive certitude of their correctness." Two years later, the same theologian wrote, "The documents of the Papal Commission represent a rather full summary of two points of view"—i.e., for and against a ban on birth control paraphernalia. "They incorporate most of the important things that have been said on the subject of contraception over the past three or four years, plus a few very interesting and important nuances. The majority report [acquiescing on birth control] . . . strikes this reader as much the more satisfactory statement." This is an exercise in intellectual freedom—but also an invitation to contumacy. All of which leaves the Catholic,

* *Humanae Vitae a Generation Later* (Catholic University of America Press, 1991).

very enticingly, with a question: Which side to observe? But the answer, for a Catholic, has got to be: the position taken by the Pope, as spokesman for the magisterium.

We are left with a sociological problem very different from that of ordained women (who don't exist), or remarried men and women (they are denied the sacraments *pro forma*). It is that the law against contraception is quite simply ignored. No, not by everyone; but the data suggest that contraceptives are sold in similar quantities to Catholic and to Protestant men and women. There is no way to establish what percentage of Catholic women (or men) who use them confess to having committed a sin. And in any case, if absolution is not valid in the absence of the penitent's subjective determination not to sin again, one must assume—simply from one's view of crowded Communion rails—either that the sin is not being confessed or else that the determination not-to-sin-again is widely irresolute. When the Pope says that no woman shall be ordained, what follows is that no woman is ordained. When the Pope says that it is sinful to use contraceptives, he is left without visible means of enforcing his ordinance.

Now, this is true of most of the strictures of the Church. There is no mechanical means to measure faith, hope, and charity. But communicants do confess to not having attended Mass, to having lied, to having given bad example, to have harbored malicious thoughts or committed adultery. When there is reliable evidence that the faithful are simply ignoring a stricture of the Church, the loyalist reposes his hopes in the possibility that at some point in the future a Pope will modify the reasoning of Pope Paul (some time after Fr. Rutler has gone to his reward, let us pray!) or else that the principle being urged captures the moral imagination of the next generation of men and women, who will then abide by it.

Such an insight into moral resolution is not inconceivable in the matter of abortion. The advent of wholesale legal abortion (after *Roe v. Wade,* 1973) was a tormenting coincidence for American Catholics. *Humanae Vitae* (1968) had forbidden safeguards against human conceptions, the aborting of which was now legal. Though *Humanae Vitae* was heralded by many Catholics and a few non-Catholics (e.g., Malcolm

Muggeridge, not yet, in 1968, a Catholic), in many circles it was deeply deplored. For a while the word went around that *Humanae Vitae* was really about paradigmatic conduct; that sexual congress was especially sanctified by the natural law when in pursuit of progeny but that it is the counsel of perfection to sacrifice sex during fertile periods. I.e., only saints can be expected to forgo intercourse during fertile periods. But nothing said by the current Pope gives any encouragement to those who would relieve themselves of the problem by happily removing proffered halos from their heads. Prohibition appears (above) as a part of the Catechism of the Church, even though, evidently, it has not won the loyalty of all Catholics. As noted, many Catholics engage in contraception, and we do not know how many, for that reason, drop out of the Church, perhaps to rejoin after the use of contraceptives becomes biologically academic.

The orthodox observation on the matter, as I view it, is that it is expected that the faithful will sin, seventy times seven times. But the Church has much to ponder when, after pronouncing a practice anathema, the flock ceases even to wince. A sense of the sinfulness of an act is hugely important to the moral order. In its absence, there is a terrible void.

Malcolm Muggeridge, about whom more later, identified, and himself sensed, the commanding, demanding allure of the flesh. I get, on reading him, a kind of exultation from the mere memory of what he had, what he had yielded to; and the thrill he finally had from the crystallizing perspective of another joy, the knowledge that there is a preeminent vision, that it can prevail, and that in permitting it to do so, a special joy is to be had. There are many odes and sighs, in literature and in poetry, to the lure and demands of sexual passion which the Church, in this way and that, moves to put in place; which means, sometimes, to impose a hierarchy of concerns. I have not seen a more eloquent recitation, first of the special allure of the fleshly pursuit, and finally of the vision that replaces it, than Malcolm Muggeridge's:

When the Devil makes his offer (always open, incidentally) of the kingdoms of the earth, it is the bordellos that glow so alluringly to most of us, not the banks and the countinghouses, the boardrooms and the executive offices. We can easily resist becoming millionaires or privy councilors, but to swim away on a tide of sensual ecstasy, to be lost in another body, to fly as high as the ceiling on the wings of the night, or even of the afternoon—that, surely, is something. The imagination recoils from the prizes, or toys, of a materialist society. Who but some half-witted oil sheik or popular actor can go on desiring sleek yachts or motorcars or white villas perched above yellow sand? But what about the toys in living flesh? The Barbie dolls that bleed? The Hefner Playmates that move? The celluloid lover forever panting and forever young?

Sex is the mysticism of a materialist society, with its own mysteries—that is my birth pill; swallow it in remembrance of me! and its own sacred texts and scripture—the erotica that fall like black atomic rain on the just and unjust alike, drenching us, blinding us, stupefying us. To be carnally minded is life! So we have ventured on, Little Flowers of D. H. Lawrence; our Aphrodites rising, bikinied and oiled, from Côte d'Azur beaches; drive-in Lotharios, Romeos of the motorways, glowing and burning like electric log fires, until—cut! the switch is turned off, leaving the desolate, impenetrable night. Did I sometimes, staring sleepless into it, even then catch a glimpse, far, far away, of a remote shading of the black into gray? A minuscule intimation of a dawn that would break? You!

CHAPTER THIRTEEN

On Knowing Malcolm Muggeridge

I don't remember what it was, exactly, that brought Malcolm Muggeridge to my program, *Firing Line*. The taping was done in London, in February 1968, the high holy year of the countercultural revolution. That was the year when Martin Luther King was assassinated, when Eugene McCarthy challenged President Johnson in New Hampshire, Lyndon Johnson declared he would not run for reelection, Robert Kennedy leaped into the presidential ring and was assassinated, colleges and universities were in tumult. And that was the year when, in articles published in British journals, Malcolm Muggeridge divulged that he had embraced the Christian faith.

The counter-countercultural declaration of Mr. Muggeridge's movement was especially eye-catching given the great legions traveling in the opposite direction. He had been prominent for many years. His larger public knew him through his work as a television host and critic. But all of literate England, and much of America, knew him as a learned and incisive journalist who (in 1933) had written *Winter in Moscow.* It was a searing exposé of Communism, written after his year in the Soviet Union for the *Manchester Guardian,* the leading liberal daily. He had seen at first hand the torture and starvation of the kulaks in the Ukraine. After his exposé he continued with his books, wrote copiously for British periodicals, and was an instant hit on radio for the BBC (as he would be later on television). During the war he did hazardous duty in British intelligence in Mozambique and soon after the war became the editor of *Punch* magazine, the oldest English-language humor magazine in the world (1841–1992).*

It was just after leaving *Punch* that he wrote a funny and condescending article about young Queen Elizabeth (she was "frumpy, frowzy, and banal"), published on the eve of her visit (1957) to the United States in the *Saturday Evening Post,* then a U.S. magazine of enormous circulation. The article, which took a droll view of royal pageantry, outraged the British establishment. Muggeridge was eased out of *Punch* and shunned by the BBC, but by the early sixties he had reconquered England with his humor, skepticism, and acuity of expression. Everyone laughed, except that day's victims. His intellect and historical savoir faire gave his criticisms a very long reach. In America he made regular appearances as book editor for *Esquire* magazine. No Englishman, Evelyn Waugh having died, was a more mordant, more attractive wit.

It goes without saying that, as regards religion, he was an extrovert atheist (though, his biographers reveal, he had had an early interest in religion); in politics, a socialist (though never, since his experience in

* *Punch* was revived in the fall of 1996.

Moscow, pro-Communist). For those who hadn't been in personal touch and didn't know in what direction his mind was turning it was a shock when, in April 1968, the three BBC television documentaries were broadcast. Muggeridge had directed them and provided the spoken commentary. The cameras, shooting in and about Jerusalem, took the viewer to sites about which Muggeridge spoke.

"After his decisive dialogue with Satan," Muggeridge's voice came over the screen as the camera panned in to the city, "Christ very humanly chose to begin his ministry in Nazareth, where he was known and had grown up. There in the synagogue with, I daresay, his family present in the congregation, he chose to read the splendid passage in which the prophet Isaiah proclaims,

> *"The Spirit of the Lord is upon me,*
>
> *because he hath anointed me to preach the gospel to the poor;*
>
> *he hath sent me to heal the brokenhearted,*
>
> *to preach deliverance to the captives,*
>
> *and recovering of sight to the blind,*
>
> *to set at liberty them that are bruised,*
>
> *to preach the acceptable year of the Lord."*

Muggeridge then weighed in, which was his way, by unction and guile and excitement, grabbing his viewers by the hair and forcing them to consider his discomfiting words. "All would have been well if Christ had just left matters there. Nothing pleases the average congregation more—whether in synagogue, church, mosque, or other conventicle—than to be told about preaching deliverance to captives, healing the brokenhearted, etc., always provided nothing is expected of *them.* But Christ went on recklessly: *This day is this scripture fulfilled in your ears.* In other words, *he* was going to do it; the spirit of the Lord was upon *him,* Joseph's son, known to them all.

"It was intolerable. With one accord they rose up and turned him out of the synagogue and out of Nazareth. As far as we know, he never returned there."

Such was the temperament of Malcolm Muggeridge. His smile was ready, his blue eyes really did sparkle, his features exuded benevolence, he made his points in perfect diction, the historical and philosophical references were apt, his desire to communicate his insights earnest and engaging. When he came to *Firing Line,* commissioned to discuss "The Culture of the Left," I had not known about his turn to religion, which would be broadcast two months later on BBC. I did have the sense that something was exciting him. I would know soon what it was, and the world would know that this was not one of his passing fancies, because he lived in that excitement another twenty-seven years, about which one could reasonably say that they were a great modern pilgrimage.

In February of 1980 a wealthy Rumanian-Canadian approached me through an intermediary to ask if I would undertake an experimental documentary, exact size and shape undecided—that would be left in my hands. The single, and singular, asset of the Canadian, apart from his personal wealth, was exclusive access to the Sistine Chapel, on an appointed day one month away, for forty-eight hours. This privilege had never before been extended and I never learned how it came to be that the Canadian magnate had got it; but the invitation to me was to fashion two half-hour programs to be filmed in the Sistine Chapel.

I consulted with Warren Steibel, the producer of *Firing Line,* and asked him to serve as director. After a few meetings the idea evolved to reflect in each of the programs on one biblical parable. My idea was to feature their imperishable relevance.

It was expected (the entrepreneur's intermediary made this plain) that I would attract a star or two to participate. With only two weeks before the Sistine deadline, I approached David Niven, a neighbor in Switzerland (where I spend February and March), and Princess Grace of Monaco, who regularly vacationed with her family nearby and who, with Niven, spent occasional evenings at our house, painting in oils. By telephone I got to Charlton Heston, who had played Michelangelo in one movie *(The Agony and the Ecstasy),* John the Baptist in another

(The Greatest Story Ever Told), and Moses in a third *(The Ten Command-ments)* and so was enticed by the prospect of doing something in Michelangelo's primary shrine, adorned by the great painting of the Creation.

We would read, in the first program, the parable of the Good Samaritan and, in the second, the parable of the Prodigal Son. After the reading, the host would ask our guests to give from their own experience contemporary examples of the lessons of the Good Samaritan and the Prodigal Son at work. I telephoned to Malcolm Muggeridge in England and asked if he would serve as my cohost. He agreed instantly.

In the following week we spoke over the telephone several times, discussing details of the program. The Canadian entrepreneur was much taken by the formula I had come up with and wanted some indication whether, if the program succeeded, I would be willing to pursue in other renowned church sites other parables, with other luminaries. Muggeridge counseled that we put off a consideration of the question until after we saw what we had come up with.

A few days before we would meet in Rome, he called me on the telephone. I remember his words almost exactly. "Bill, in my life I have met with practically every important person and almost without exception I have regretted it. But I think the present Pope [John Paul II] is an exception. I think he is an immense personal and historical figure. I would like to meet him while we are in Rome. Can you arrange that?"

It was agreed he would use his own resources, I mine; and, on arriving in Rome, Malcolm and I were notified by written message that we had an appointment for a private audience with the Pope the following day at one o'clock. Malcolm's invitation was addressed directly. Mine, to "Mr. Buckley e due personi." That translated into: me, David Niven, and my wife, Pat. (Chuck Heston and Grace Rainier, who had not been told about our maneuver, would be leaving Rome at noon, after the film shoot, before the scheduled audience.)

. . .

It was shortly before midnight when we began shooting. The chapel, the most famous and intimate in the world, had been turned over to us only after closing time for visitors late that afternoon. The engineers and electricians and lighting men had been several hours getting things in order. It was mid-February, and there was no heating.

The half hour began with Princess Grace, radiant, modest in dress and mien, reading the Bible verse:

And a certain lawyer asked, "Who is my neighbor?" and Jesus, answering, said . . .

"A certain man went down from Jerusalem to Jericho and fell among thieves who stripped him of his raiment and wounded him and departed, leaving him half dead. And by chance there came down a certain priest that way, and when he saw him, he passed by on the other side. And likewise a Levite, when he was at the place, came and looked on him and passed by on the other side. But a certain Samaritan, as he journeyed, came where he was, and when he saw him he had compassion on him, and went to him and bound up his wounds, pouring in oil and wine, and set him on his own beast and brought him to an inn and took care of him. And on the morrow, when he departed, he took out two pence and gave them to the host and said unto him, Take care of him and whatever thou spendest more, when I come again, I will repay thee.

"Which then of these three, thinkest thou, was the neighbor unto him that fell among the thieves?" And the lawyer said, "He that showed mercy on him." Then said Jesus unto him, "Go and do thou likewise."

After the parable was done the camera turned to me. I said, "Although we speak from the sanctum sanctorum of the Roman Catholic Church, only two of the participants in this program are Catholics [Grace and me]. My cohost is Malcolm Muggeridge, the British writer, who in recent years has devoted his energies to examining the life of the spirit. Mr. Muggeridge."

He spoke without notes. "In the beginning was the Word. That's how the Fourth Gospel opens, intimating that since the world began, God the Creator has been communicating with men, His creation.

And what amazing diversity of communication there has been. Take, for instance, this Sistine Chapel, wherewith through the genius of Michelangelo, God has spoken to us. Or of course, the most sublime communication of all, [which] is in the first chapter of the Fourth Gospel. The Word dwelt among us and, full of grace, became flesh, whereby God, reaching down, became a man, Jesus Christ, in order that men might reach upward and relate themselves to God. So I find nothing strange or out of the way to be considering in this famous chapel the parables, their significance, their meaning, which played so tremendous a part in Jesus' ministry on earth.''

I then asked Princess Grace, seated, to come up with a parallel, a more or less contemporary Good Samaritan. She spoke of Henri Dunant, who during the War of the Italian Risorgimento and its ''bloody battle of Solferino'' (1859—forty thousand casualties) thought to institutionalize medical services to help the wounded. ''He founded what came to be known as the Red Cross.''

WFB: ''What happened to Dunant himself?''

GRACE: ''After ten years he met with bankruptcy, and he retired to a small village and he was almost forgotten. It was by chance that a newspaperman found him and sort of rediscovered him when he was almost forgotten. And in—''

WFB: ''Did the newspapers do their duty by him as Good Samaritans?''

GRACE: ''They certainly did. And as a result, Henri Dunant received the first Nobel Peace Prize, in 1901.''

Princess Grace thought the spontaneity of the act—caring for the wounded—was its distinguishing feature, though it seemed to me that the Good Samaritan must be expected to do the virtuous thing in every situation and that therefore, in the most commendable sense, his behavior was predictable.

Heston thought it significant that Christ had designated as a ''priest,'' and then as a ''Levite,'' the men who passed by without pausing to help the wounded traveler. Jesus must have astonished His listeners when He spoke of the Samaritan's intercession. ''The Samaritans, to Jesus' audience, were an outcast people, subject to all kinds of discrimination, and yet he makes the Samaritan the good man. Christ was saying: No, we must consider all men our own and charity is for all. And I think this is one of the distinguishing features of His ministry, one of His central teachings. And surely in the story of the Good Samaritan, that's why He had the Samaritan be the one that rescued the beaten man and succored him.''

David Niven spoke of the fear, in our litigious world, that many whose inclinations are philanthropic have of the lawyer-behind-the-bush. "[Even] doctors have to insure themselves before they give somebody a pill—they might get sued.'' He told then the engrossing story (I had never heard it) of a single episode in the chaotic flight from France after Dunkirk in 1940. One motley assembly, "Royal Air Force ground personnel who were trapped, Red Cross workers, women, ambulance drivers, and, finally, the embassy staff from Paris with their children—by the time they got to St. Nazaire at the mouth of the Loire, there were over three thousand of them and the British government sent an old liner called the *Lancastria* to come and take them away, with three destroyers to guard her. They were just pulling up the anchor when three dive bombers came. The destroyers did what they could, but one bomb hit, went down the funnel and blew a huge hole in the side, and she quickly took on a terrible list.

"In the hold there were several hundred soldiers. Now there was no way they could ever get out because of the list, and she was sinking. And along came my own favorite Good Samaritan, a Roman Catholic priest, a young man in Royal Air Force uniform. He got a rope and lowered himself into the hold to give encouragement and help to those hundreds of men in their last dreadful hour—''

WFB: "Knowing he couldn't get out?''

NIVEN: "Knowing he could never get out, nor could they. The ship sank and all in that hold died. The remainder were picked up by the destroyers and came back to England to the regiment I was in, and we had to look after them, and many of them told me that they were giving up even then, in the oil and struggle, and the one thing that kept them going was the sound of the soldiers in the hold singing hymns.''

• • •

It was weighty-thought time. I began with what became, in the edited film, a voice-over: "Inevitably when a text is examined and reexamined, the spirit of the exegete is aroused and the fine print comes into scrutiny. Were there hidden lessons planted in the parable? What did Christ mean when he spoke of a 'neighbor'? Malcolm Muggeridge [he was dressed in his overcoat to guard against the midnight cold of the Sistine Chapel] has, I'm sure, something to say on the subject."

Facing the camera, Muggeridge said that he understood the parable as "showing people reality." Christ didn't "accept human categories." He was not intending categorical slurs on priests or Levites, or special praise for Samaritans. "What he was saying really was that the people who are professionally compassionate—which those people were—when it comes to the crunch, often aren't. And that those who are not professionally compassionate are. And therefore I feel he was answering a trick question. He knew perfectly well this lawyer had no particular interest in what Jesus had decided was his true neighbor. The neighbor was the man who was compassionate, that's what He was saying."

A dialogue ensued on "Who is your neighbor?" It became, all too soon, a semantic excursion, but reached agreement that, in Christ's sense of the word, the neighbor isn't simply the man who lives next door. Muggeridge summed up. "Jesus would say if you want to know who your neighbor is, your neighbor is the man who is neighborly *in his behavior.* I mean, to me this is absolutely clear. He wasn't going to simply say to the lawyer, 'Well, a neighbor is a man who happens to live next door to you or up the road; you must love *him* as yourself.' Your neighbor is a man to whom you owe compassion, love, help. Insofar as you give it, you are loving your neighbor. Insofar as you don't give it, you are not loving him."

• • •

In the subsequent program on the Prodigal Son, Muggeridge had said, "I see the parable more than anything else as literature."

WFB: "Moral literature?"

MUGGERIDGE: "No, just literature. Life. Pictures of life."

WFB: "But I am surprised to hear you dispute that they are *moral* literature."

MUGGERIDGE: "All literature is in a sense moral. I mean——"

WFB: *"The Story of O* isn't. Well . . . in a sense it is."

MUGGERIDGE: "If in anything in literature, there is truth, then it's moral, whatever the scene might be being described. Jesus was taking us to the very roots of our existence with these stories. That's why they've interested artists and writers. If they were merely moralistic tales, then they wouldn't."

I asked Malcolm if he could come up with a parable whose meaning was unambiguous. Muggeridge replied that parables never ceased for him to be grounds for fruitful exploration. But he ventured on nonetheless. "Now here is a parable for you. It came to me one day. I was actually watching a caterpillar in the path of my garden, a furry caterpillar. And I thought to myself: Now, supposing the caterpillars have an annual meeting, the local society of caterpillars. They meet to discuss their affairs and how things are going. And my caterpillar, an older caterpillar, addressing them, says, 'You know, it's an extraordinary thing, but we are all going to be butterflies.' 'Okay,' the caterpillars say. 'You poor fool, you are just an old man who is frightened of dying, you're inventing something to comfort yourself.' [But] these are all the things that people say to me when I say I am looking forward to dying because I know that I am going to go into eternity. You see?"

Please explain, I asked.

"And so he——the caterpillar——abashed, draws back, but in a short time he is in his chrysalis, and sure enough, he's right. He extricates himself from the chrysalis, and he is no longer a creeper, which is what caterpillars are; he is flying away."

Muggeridge was inexhaustibly inventive. He volunteered a second parable. "Some very humane, rather simpleminded old lady sees the play *King Lear* performed and she is outraged that a poor old man should be so humiliated, made to suffer so. And in the eternal shade she meets Shakespeare and she says to him, 'What a monstrous thing to make that poor old man go through all that.' And Shakespeare says, 'Yes, I quite agree. It was very painful, and I could have arranged for him to take a sedative at the end of Act I. But then, ma'am, there would have been no play.' "

I ventured that King Lear might have preferred that there should have been no play than that he should have lived through Acts II and III.

"But then he would have been a cowardly man, and, of course, he did in fact have to go through that suffering in order to understand why there had to be a play; and, of course, in that marvelous speech of his—one of my favorite things in all Shakespeare—when he to Cordelia says, 'Come, let's away to prison'—you know—'and take upon us the mystery of things.' It's a beautiful phrase, isn't it? It expresses exactly what I mean. This affliction *has* to be, and that of course is why one is drawn irresistibly as a West European to the Christian faith and to Christ, because this is the central point: the Cross."

Muggeridge pressed on: "There's another parable I've often thought of. When St. Paul starts off on his journeys, he consults with an eminent public relations man: 'I've got this campaign and I want to promote this gospel.' And the man would say, 'Well, you've got to have some sort of symbol. You've got to have an image. You've got to have some sign of your faith.' And then Paul would say, 'Well, I have got one. I've got this cross.' The public relations man would have laughed his head off: 'You can't popularize a thing like *that* . . . It's absolutely mad!' "

And Muggeridge extemporized, with television cameras filming him, his haunting sentences. "But it wasn't mad. It worked for centuries and centuries, bringing out all the creativity in people, all the love and disinterestedness in people; this symbol of suffering, *that's* the heart of the thing. As an old man, Bill, looking back on one's life, it's one of the things that strike you most forcibly—that the only thing that's taught one anything is *suffering*. Not success, not happiness, not anything like that. The only thing that *really* teaches one what life's about—the joy of understanding, the joy of coming in contact with what life *really* signifies—is suffering, affliction.''

It hurt to think how many who had run into this theme of Malcolm Muggeridge would dismiss it, this quaint joy that comes to some from suffering. But *Schadenfreude* is pleasure taken from the suffering of others, and Muggeridge I thought of as engaged in a kind of total submission, on the order of what it was that gave Francis of Assisi the ecstasy he radiated.

It was some years after Malcolm died that I came upon a few lines of his in which I thought he captured beatifically the submission for which in his later years, animated by his meditation on the Crucifixion, he yearned. What he wrote I could not myself repeat with any pretense to projecting my own imperfect devotion, but reading what he said, I have as true an idea as ever I had of the saintly calling.

He had been writing of the impact on him of reading William Blake.

I can remember the first time my eyes rested on lines by Blake (actually, ''Ah, Sun-flower! weary of time''), and the extraordinary feeling I had of some unique distillation of understanding and joy, a unique revelation of life's very innermost meaning and significance.

I find it more difficult to recall and recount the feelings I had about the Cross even before it meant anything to me as such. It was, I know, an obsessive interest; something I avidly sought out, as in-flamed senses do erotica. I might fasten bits of wood together myself, or doodle it. This symbol, which was considered to be derisory in my home, was yet also the focus of inconceivable hopes and desires—like a lost love's face, pulled out and gazed at with sick longing. As I remember this, a sense of my own failure lies leadenly upon me. I should have worn it over my heart; carried it, a precious standard never to be wrested out of my hands; even though I fell, still borne aloft. It should have been my cult, my uniform, my language, my life. I shall have no excuse; I can't say that I didn't know. I knew from the beginning, and turned away. The lucky thieves were crucified with their Saviour; You called me, and I didn't go—those empty years, those empty words, that empty passion!

But the director was signaling. Our time was up.*
And the next morning we had an appointment with the Pope!

. . . It was wonderful! We were summoned to his private quarters at 12:45 for our 1:00 appointment. Wednesday was the day when during the morning, before any scheduled private audience, he met with pilgrims to Rome. We could see on the television screen in the private chamber where we sat that though it was after twelve—the appointed hour for the end of the public conference—John Paul II was still talking, making, in a half dozen languages, statements addressed to the curiosities of the large assembly. Finally he gave them his blessing and we were asked to stand abreast of each other; he would arrive soon now, and indeed presently he was there, the slight benign smile still on his face, though a fatigue was discernible (the next day he would be hospitalized with influenza). As in the auditorium, he wore his white cassock, on his head, the zucchetto. And, around his neck, the loose gold necklace with the pectoral cross. Several clerical aides were in attendance.

My wife, Pat, had been drawn slightly to one side by an attendant monsignor, the (correct) assumption being that she was not one of the

---

* No network bid for the Sistine Chapel programs. The coroners' principal finding (this was the judgment of Warren Steibel, Muggeridge, and me) was that too much was being asked of the viewer, who had exactly the same view of things in that epochal chamber that cardinals have when they are seated there with the august responsibility of electing a Pope. A camera's eye strolling over the arch of the Sistine Chapel is almost required to travel deliberately, lasciviously. But the viewer, his attention arrested by Michelangelo, was being asked simultaneously to struggle over what live human beings were having to say in a serious discussion about serious matters. And when the camera did level on the actors, the viewer found himself/herself staring at Grace Kelly, thinking thoughts like, *For gawd's sake—she hasn't made a movie in twenty years!* And at Charlton Heston, reciting lines different from any that had ever sounded from his lips, in a hundred-odd movies; and David Niven, a similar problem. And then there were Muggeridge and Buckley to cope with.

official party. The Pope passed by her, bowing his head in greeting. He approached Malcolm Muggeridge and extended his hand.

The words in the ensuing exchanges are etched exactly in my memory.

The Pope now addressed Muggeridge, in his serviceable though highly accented English. "Yes. You are radio?"

What possible answer can one give to that question, so posed? Malcolm smiled and managed to say that, yes, he had done considerable work on radio. The Pope wished nothing further, smiled, and offered his hand to David Niven. To whom he said, "Yes. You were very close to my predecessor."

David's eyes widened, and he stammered out, "I had great admiration for him, Your Holiness." So much for David Niven, on whom he smiled, turning and extending his hand to me.

I had to act quickly, I thought, if there was any hope of rescuing our papal audience. Clearly the machinery in the Vatican had got tangled. One bureaucracy had authorized the private interview with the important gentlemen who had been given the Sistine Chapel for their work. One of his visitors, the bureaucracy might have informed the Holy Father, was perhaps the most eloquent English-speaking Christian alive. Another was a renowned and greatly loved actor and—together with Princess Grace of Monaco and another famous actor, both of whom had had to leave Rome—all were at work on an unprecedented documentary in the Sistine Chapel with the Catholic American journalist influential in conservative thought . . . It flashed through my mind that a second bureaucracy had probably briefed the Pope about an entirely different set of people, one of whom was "radio," another perhaps a biographer of Pope Paul VI.

I thought I might give the Pope a lifesaving lead, so after shaking hands, before he could speak, I said to him, smiling, "It's going to be *very* hard, Your Holiness, for me to get used to my own private chapel back home having spent so many hours in *yours!*"

Far from serving to alert the Holy Father to what was going on, my words clearly startled him, and he stepped back a pace, which motion signaled his attendants—who instantly escorted him to the conventional site, politely nudging my wife into the company. A photographer materialized, shot his picture, the Pope blessed us, smiled again, and left the chamber.

There can never have been such revelry in the Vatican elevator that took us down to our waiting car. At lunch Malcolm practiced "being radio," and David demanded attention so that he could proceed with the life story of Pope Paul VI. When in future days Malcolm's voice would come in over the long-distance line, he would always hear from me, "Is this Radio on the line?"

But when I visited him at his little country cottage in Sussex, there were here and there a few pictures of his family, and one of him and Pope John Paul II.

CHAPTER FOURTEEN

The Godfather. Church and State.

Sin, and the Question of a

National Culture

1. The Unmaking of the Godfather

In the summer of 1987 I was invited to address the annual Baptist
Convention in Washington, in September. The invitation was tendered
by Charles Colson, with whom I felt an instant affinity when our paths
crossed some time after he left the penitentiary for the sins of Watergate. It is here and there disputed who was the principal executive in
that episode, Colson or Howard Hunt. My friendship with Howard
Hunt has a little place in this book because of the random events that

resulted, almost overnight, in my being appointed the godfather of Howard and Dorothy Hunt's first three children.

The circumstances were unusual. In the few weeks between my graduation from Yale (June 1950) and my marriage I had applied for admission to Yale Law School and also to the graduate school and had been accepted by both, but the Korean situation threatened any future plan. Professor Willmoore Kendall, my close friend and tutor, told me he had had ties to the intelligence community and asked whether I really wanted to return to the army for another stint as a second lieutenant in the infantry. If not, I should resign my commission in the reserve and consider more interesting work. I agreed.

The initial overture from a youngish man whom I met at an off-campus restaurant in New Haven informed me that if I were accepted, the Central Intelligence Agency would want me as a deep-cover agent, which meant: no observable traces whatever to the CIA. I submitted to long and detailed interrogatories and observed (most of) the rules. Although it would be six months before my prospective induction, I was told to come up with a plausible reason for staying on in the Yale community without committing myself to law or graduate school.

This turned out to be easy, as I had begun to write a book on Yale that took up much of my day. And then after World War II Yale had been very short of Spanish-language teachers. Three undergraduates were recruited to help carry the teaching load. I was one, had taught for three years, and was welcome to stay on an additional year (my rank was Assistant in Instruction).

My wife and I rented a house in Hamden, a suburb of New Haven, and I started in on my book, taught Spanish five days a week, and enjoyed hugely the company of my talented brother-in-law, Brent Bozell who, married to a beloved sister, was beginning in Yale Law School. Three or four times during the fall and winter of 1950 I was interviewed or questioned at odd addresses—"safe houses," as now designated, usually in New York. It wasn't until I was formally enrolled in the CIA that I needed to devise a credible reason, to give friends and family, for leaving New Haven to go to Washington, en route to Mexico.

My dissimulations were plausible. I had finished my book, it had been accepted for publication, and the teaching semester had ended. Why an interval in Washington? Because I wished to pursue studies on the history of academic freedom under the tutelage of Willmoore Kendall, whose own schedule required him to be in Washington. Why was I then going on to Mexico? At the request of my father: He had lived twenty years in Mexico practicing law, had an illustrious career which, however, ended abruptly when he was expelled from Mexico by President Carranza, who accused my father (quite accurately) of backing a revolution against his government. My family knew that Father had scattered interests in Mexico and that the years having gone by, there were fair prospects of my retrieving, or at least identifying, stray royalties and properties here and there under the guidance of a Mexican businessman/accountant who had worked for my father for over forty years.

The schooling I had in Washington as a deep-cover trainee I detailed twenty-five years later in my novel *Saving the Queen*. When I left Washington, I didn't know the real identity of a single one of the dozen men who had trained me. When I arrived in Mexico, I was given the only name I would ever be given of a member of the Central Intelligence Agency. He was to be my boss, Howard Hunt.

He and his wife, Dorothy, became close friends of my wife and me. Dorothy had been married before and had been raised a Catholic. I was not aware that during those months in Mexico I was under rather formal observation by her. Was I a practicing Catholic? I don't remember that she brought up the subject of her own faith, which I would learn she had not lost, even though, by remarrying, she had defied Church law. They had a single child at the time we left Mexico (after nine months). Howard and I kept in touch and in the years ahead I would know about his second daughter and a son. It was after the birth of the third child that I had a letter from Dorothy (the Hunts were then in Japan, as I remember) telling me that the entire family was becoming Catholic. She asked if I would consent to be godfather to their three children. (A fourth child, another boy, was born later.)

There are responsibilities for being a godparent (one is supposed to see to it that the godchild receives religious training), but I know of no one who formally discharges such responsibilities. The reason is obvious: the godparent has no authority over the child. I have had a lot of godchildren, most of them nephews and nieces, but never a godchild who would be less than stupefied if ever I materialized at his/her house and asked when last he/she had confessed his/her sins (I promise not to do the gender-specific business any longer) and received the sacraments. The parents of two of my godchildren were divorced months after I was anointed; in another case the father committed suicide. My career as godfather consisted in sending little checks commemorating their birthdays, one dollar per year since birth, which is small potatoes, but then I remember a year in which six of my godchildren were twenty-one (at which age, to be sure, godparents are dismissed).

But with Howard Hunt the situation was extraordinary. I hadn't heard from Howard or Dorothy for about five years. The reason for their silence was indirectly personal: their children had become close friends of the children of my sister, Patricia Bozell. There was a car accident in which one of the Hunts' children (my godchild) was hurt, and there had been a lawsuit . . . It isn't easy to continue to send valentines to a godfather while suing his sister.

The years went by and then I saw Howard Hunt's name in print, in July 1972. He was identified as a suspect in a robbery that had taken place a few weeks before in Washington. He and several other participants (I noticed that they had Hispanic surnames) had been arraigned and would be questioned by prosecutors. It was the first ember of the great Watergate eruption.

But I heard nothing directly from Howard. A friend advised me that he and his family were living in a large house in the Maryland countryside. In the months ahead his name appeared more often in the papers. The public came to know that an organization called the Plumbers had been instituted under the direction of presidential assistant Charles Colson. What exactly their mandate was, and how high up the chain of command was it known about the Plumbers' operations, remained a mystery, though every day, it seemed, more details were published, and the cloud over the Nixon White House darkened.

On December 8, 1972, my wife and I, lying in bed, turned on the late television news. A fatal crash. United Airlines. Midway Airport, Chicago. Sixteen survivors. Among the dead: Mrs. Howard Hunt. The following day there were details. I learned on-screen that the executor in Dorothy Hunt's will was William F. Buckley, Jr.

A few weeks later, Howard came by with his second daughter (a godchild, whom I had never before laid eyes on) to my apartment in New York. In two hours he recounted the entire story of Watergate. In doing so, he put me about nine months ahead of the news as, day by day, it would develop—incidentally creating a professional problem (I was writing three columns every week and editing *National Review*) about which I have written elsewhere. But Howard knew that in a matter of months he would be in jail, leaving his orphaned children, aged twenty-three, twenty, sixteen, and seven, unchaperoned. His situation, to use just the right word, was tragic. To add to a mother killed and a father jailed, a large unsupervised country house giving out the sounds and smells of Woodstock drove home my helplessness as godfather.

As legal executor, I followed the advice of my own veteran attorney and turned the case against the airline, with Howard's consent, over to a Chicago attorney handling the complaint as a class action suit. In the twenty years since then I have stayed close to Lisa, the oldest daughter, who after an unhappy marriage embraced her Christian faith devotedly. Her talented sister, Kevan, is a happily married mother and practicing attorney in San Francisco.

It is disquieting, the role of the contemporary godparent. Though some appointments (Dorothy Hunt's, for instance) are seriously intended, most are merely honorific, gestures in social geniality. Catholics are not supposed to act as godparents for Protestants, but I think they do, and perhaps even the other way around. But no proposed reform of a convention routinely trivialized comes to mind. It struck me, during those years with the Hunt children, two of them still in their minority, that there was something wrong in the co-optative term "godchild"—something on the order of religious presumption. The depth of any godparent's concern tells us nothing. My parents raised ten children, nine of whom are, or were (three are dead), committed Catholics. The tenth, Carol, lost her faith: my godchild. The title trots along in creeping desuetude. A signpost of Christian slippage? Perhaps in the future the term will change. Honorary father?

2. Church and State

As everybody knows who cares, Howard Hunt's sometime collaborator, Charles Colson, came to the Christian faith at about the time he began to serve his jail sentence. His vocation was everywhere scorned as opportunistic. With justifiable skepticism—Colson had been proud of his utilitarian politics—he was widely thought a manipulator engaged in attempting to accelerate his release. It is, after twenty years, as believable that his faith is synthetic as that Hugh Hefner only pretends to be a libertine. Colson founded an organization (Prison Fellowship) oriented to two goals. The first, to expose prisoners to religion (as an alternative way of looking upon life and one's neighbor, potentially exhilarating); a second, to attempt to persuade penologists of the futility of prison sentences for those offenders who are not a menace to others (Colson advocates other forms of punishment).

Some time after we became friends, I asked Colson, on behalf of my elderly, retired music teacher who did voluntary service for prisoners, to address the prison population of a penitentiary in Katonah, New York. I had a keen curiosity to see him at work. After a few minutes it was manifest that the two hundred felons in his audience, ranging in age from eighteen to seventy were, many of them, curious to hear what a onetime intimate of an American President was now telling them. They were manifestly intrigued by his account of the universe of God. Probably most had heard it before, at home, or as children from a preacher. Their special attention now was owing to the combination: their plight, their seclusion, and the special skills of the exhorter, who had himself been jailed. At the end of the hour, Colson invited those who wished to do so to stand up, as a tentative expression of curiosity about—perhaps even faith in—a Creator whose Son was crucified and died in order to substantiate God's devotion to all men, including felons. Many stood; how many of them pursued the faith (Colson left material for those who wished it) I do not know. But no one could doubt that Charles Colson was living a life that defines the very idea of atonement.

He was twice on *Firing Line* to speak about his Prison Fellowship. He organizes his thought with the precision of a trained lawyer, and his imagination is active in adducing the apt quotation to highlight the critical importance of the spiritual dimension he seeks out. He reminded me, in his moving novel *Kingdoms in Conflict,* that John Adams had written that the United States Constitution "was made only for a moral and religious people. It is wholly inadequate for the government of any other." It was good, even if sad, to be reminded of the words of Lord Melbourne during the great debate in the 1830s on slavery. "Things have come to a pretty pass when religion is allowed to invade public life," was how his lordship proposed to handle the argument of William Wilberforce that, God having made men equal, slavery should be forbidden. The ultimate distillation of legal positivism was achieved by Sir Patrick Dean, legal adviser for the British Foreign Office under Prime Minister Attlee. When confronted in 1945 with the problems raised by the forcible repatriation of East Europeans and Russians to the Soviet Union, he summoned the majesty of the law to say, "This is purely a question for the Soviet authorities and does not concern His Majesty's government. In due course, all those with whom the Soviet authorities desire to deal must be handed over to them, and we are not concerned with the fact that they may be shot or otherwise more harshly dealt with than they might be under English law." The Gospel, according to St. Patrick, from a very new testament.

I had been seated a half hour before Colson introduced me to the convention of Baptists, and had been struck by the palpability of the faith and purpose of these ten thousand evangelical pilgrims. Their hymns were sung with a joie de vivre not easily coaxed out of a crowd in which there is indifference. I was reminded of a subterranean Mass at Lourdes, with thirty thousand communicants. The evangelical calling is horribly traduced by such as the cretin who went to jail a few years ago after swindling his followers and cheating on his wife, earning long tenure in the tabloids. It is such as they that we hear most about, as one would expect—the press is expected to report on the man who bites the dog. During that long evening at the convention in Washington—prayers, hymns, three speeches—the only disappointing feature was my own address. I lack whatever it is that gives to such as John Henry Newman, or Fulton Sheen, or Ronald Knox, or Martin Luther King, or Charles Colson, the power to move large congregations. It is sad that the skill of great orators so often recalls the evil ends to which such skills are put. Well, at least I didn't do that.

I thought it prudent to be unequivocal about my own religion, given that the listeners had never before heard from a Catholic American at their convention. I made explicit my feeling about America. I stressed what we had in common:

"You should know that I am a Roman Catholic, that I was raised in the faith, that I live comfortably in it however uneven my compliance with its higher demands, and that I hold my commitment to Christian truths to be the singular blessing in my life. You should know also that I am happiest as an American. I attempt to say this in such a way as to avoid what might otherwise sound as mere patriotic reaffirmation. Accordingly, I add that I could probably be happy as a Swiss, but only if I could learn to dominate one of the languages spoken there; I suppose I could have been happy in England or Ireland, though emigration would be difficult for all the obvious reasons, and for some less obvious, among them the irritating nature of other countries' eccentricities. Our own, we are accustomed to. I can hear the awful melody of our national anthem and still feel my heart pounding with pride; but I would find it most awfully difficult to curtsy to the Queen."

I spoke mostly about strong feelings I have on politically correct notions about the separation of church and state.

The theme, I have thought for years, is a thorn in the mind of reason. There is near unanimity on the inadequate performance of many public schools. The idea of a school voucher, to be used as educational tender by parents at schools of their choice, comes up. But of course the voucher question brushes up against constitutional inter-pretation, most conspicuously against the engulfing interpretation of the establishment clause as forbidding any grant-in-aid to religious schools. I have called the wide acceptance of this superstition a finger-print of a slothful press. Professor Eugene Genovese is a historian and political scientist of some distinction. He eased into just the right word for it when he designated as "monstrous" the rulings of the Supreme Court at the expense of the freedom of the community to specify the nature of religious instruction in the local public school. Ad hoc, we get away with it: in Brooklyn the schools close for Yom Kippur; here and there they close on Good Friday. But such freedoms are exercised in constant fear of judicial intervention.

The New York State Board of Regents and consulting bodies of ministers, priests, and rabbis of New York City combined thirty-five years ago to formulate a prayer which in their judgment was free of any denominational opportunism. That prayer—devised by religious leaders deputized to undertake that function by the men and women whose children attended and attend New York City's public schools— was struck down by the Court as constituting an encroachment on the separation of church and state. The Court was not quite willing, in *Engel v. Vitale* (1962), to opine that the mere recitation of that prayer constituted an amalgamation of church and state. Rather it relied, as most of the Court's votaries continue to do, on the slippery slope argument, that if you admit common prayer, or—as we would subse-quently see—the exposure of the Ten Commandments on a school wall, we are risking a loss of constitutional gravity, auguring free fall into the arms of theocracy.

My own preferences, perhaps for temperamental reasons, are for discreet celebrations of the faith. But of course there are, and should be, the occasions of great theatrical moment, when notes of triumphalism are in order, and one of these was the Baptist Convention I speak of. The placidity of so many Christians up against academic or judicial acts of aggression on their faith has astonished me ever since, as an undergraduate, I thought to remark the erosion of Christian belief, done under auspices traditionally Christian.

I have wondered why the courts' assault on self-government in the matter of religion and the schools is treated with such docility, and have concluded that it is so because antireligious sanctions appeal to secularist sensibilities. The counsel against establishing a single religion is well known and universally accepted. England has an established religion, and it is worth remarking that established religion in England has not, for 150 years, imposed privations on competing denominations. On an inconceivable assumption that the next Archbishop of Canterbury, backed by the sovereign, decided to ape the ways of a Muslim ayatollah, what could be predicted is an end not to religious freedom, but to the crown. At this writing, the British press deliberates whether the divorced Prince Charles can assume the mantle of Defender of the Faith. The question in America is, Why is it that what has evolved from the establishment clause in the First Amendment goes so much further than merely to affirm separation? We have a series of progressively aggressive decisions that go beyond separation and seem to argue an inchoate incompatibility between church and state. It was as recently as in 1952 that a fastidiously liberal Supreme Court justice, William O. Douglas, wrote in a Court opinion, "We are a religious people whose institutions presuppose a Supreme Being." If, forty years later, Robert Bork had given birth to such an ejaculation of fundamentalist imperialism, he would probably have been disbarred.

What is happening is the formal estrangement of religion. This has been done by a series of complicated, not to say incoherent, prohibitions. They include forbidding released time for religious studies, banning any display of simulacra of the scene at Bethlehem on public properties, the prohibition (already mentioned) of any display of the Ten Commandments, and forbidding public money even for secular textbooks in religious schools (though atlases are okay). Oh, there are the exceptions, but one suspects that the survival of Thanksgiving as a national holiday, and of chaplains in Congress, relies on the courts' conviction that, at Thanksgiving, few actually pause to give thanks to God; and their conviction that, at the opening of congressional sessions, no one really listens to—let alone is guided by—what the preachers preach.

3. The Evolution of an Ethos

I have to assume that there is a correlation, however loose, between the absence of all religious references in the schools and the ensuing practice of religion in adult life. The first religion editor at *National Review* was Will Herberg, the Jewish sociologist and philosopher. In one of his essays he argued that the prohibition against paying any classroom attention at all to God in the public schools has the effect of removing from the students' intellectual consciousness the entire supernatural dimension. The notion that this is a matter easily rectified at home ignores the question of status. Even when the mother and (in urban centers, increasingly rare) the father lead the child to church on Sundays and to Sunday school, the impression is inevitably left, Herberg argued, that religion is on the order of a pleasant, even useful, tribal convention. In the searing words of the eminent Protestant theologian Bernard Iddings Bell, ''a pastime preferred by a few to golf or canasta.''

What data, indicating a decline in religious practice, pass before our eyes? I have mentioned the decline in priestly vocations in the Catholic Church. Attendance at Sunday services is significantly reduced. Law enforcement officials who deal with juvenile offenders speak of the utter blankness of so many when any effort is made to speak about right and wrong in any ethical context, let alone a religious context. Do we risk an erosion of the ethical postulates of America, the very idea of which, to quote John Adams again—and

Justice Douglas—presupposes a Supreme Being (one nation, under God)?

For some years now, after contemplating the failure of our national drug-control programs, I have advocated alternatives. They would continue, with very heavy sanctions, the ban against drugs for minors. The reform would license drug sales to adults, to be done in tandem with a national educational effort to persuade potential drug users on purely utilitarian grounds that they would be better off preserving mind and body intact, rather than sacrifice them for quick nervous highs or dull, depressing lows. None of the reactions to my suggestion surprised me, with one exception.

It was the objection by Dr. Mitchell Rosenthal, writing in *Newsweek*. He is the head of Phoenix House, the splendid drug rehabilitation facility. He said that drugs should continue to be illegal pending the day when they were universally shunned, explaining that the only way to lick marijuana (he targeted that particular drug, merely as an example) was to engender "societal disapproval," and bring on "informal social sanctions" of a kind that would make the marijuana habit simply unacceptable. His objective is nothing less than, in his words, to "revive an ethos."

The nurturing of an ethos is something a society can attempt, and occasionally succeed in, as for instance the minority is prepared to accept the majority's vote when the time comes to organize Congress. I think of the consolidation of an ethos in my lifetime concerning two matters. I have on another occasion recalled the distinguished and scholarly Bostonian who told me one day at lunch that he would today get up and leave the room if he were to hear spoken in his presence any of the casual anti-Semitic remarks he routinely heard spoken as a boy in the dining room of his (eminent) father. Americans seventy years old or older have lived through a period in which lackadaisical anti-Semitism all but disappeared. It happened almost as suddenly as the anachronization of the word "Negro."

The second example of an evolutionized taboo has to do with

garbage on coastal waters. It isn't yet universal, but it has graduated, in my lifetime, from folkway to mores: one does not, in sight of land, throw the garbage off one's boat into the sea. You can take the most disorderly, self-indulgent twenty-one-year-old out sailing. He may smoke pot in his cabin while fornicating, but he will not throw his trash overboard. How come?

Deep moral wells of thought and feeling were affected by empirical observation and ethical analysis.

On the matter of anti-Semitism, one can hardly ask for a more melodramatic catalyst of racial tolerance than the Holocaust. Except in the Arab world (inflamed by irredentist and other passions), the lesson of anti-Semitism gone wild is vivid, burrowed into the sensibilities of the moral style-setters in our culture. On the ecological front, the idea of a vulnerable planet worked its way into the agenda of common concerns, especially among young college people. It was, to be sure, one part fad; but it was also one part dogma: an authoritative truth.

The moral theologians of yesteryear used the term *"ut in pluribus"* to tell us that moral preachments, if they hoped to grip the moral imagination, needed to be popularly plausible. That has happened: a fear (and loathing) of racial genocide, and a fear of, and a concern to prevent, a ravaged planet. These are correctly thought of as parts of the ethos.

The *capacity* to view an act as sinful continues to reside in us all. Professional philosophers (some of them) like to make the point that all conduct can be understood as the fruit of utilitarian calculation, conscious or unconscious. There is the religious analogy: That which is sinful is that which has been revealed as against the will of God. Inasmuch as the will of God is not comprehensively consulted, societies need to depend on mediating guides. Their teachers, their peers, their icons. All but the very few are influenced by extra-utilitarian considerations. The moral temper needs tempering. Although there are utilitarian arguments at the disposal of those who oppose mistreatment of ethnic minorities and highly plausible arguments for taking care of the planet, the sense of individual involvement in the enterprise invokes moral analysis.

How, then—to return to the question—to nurture an ethos? To encourage its evolution?

The three generic sanctions are of course social, legal, and divine. It isn't hard to define an act that offends one of the three sanctions but not the other two. You can arrive shirtless at a black-tie party without incurring political or, one supposes, divine displeasure. You can (illegally, i.e., by not paying the excise tax) transport a bottle of gin from Connecticut to New York without affronting one's neighbor or one's God. And you can take in vain the name of the Lord without incurring civil or (in most places) social disapproval.

On the other hand, the three sanctions here and there make common cause. Murder, rape, and theft are only the most obvious examples. But what about offenses one still defines as such—as *offenses*— even when social and legal sanctions against them fade or disappear? In most major cities in America you can (discreetly) smoke marijuana with de facto legal impunity. In most middle- and upper-class (''progressive'') households, when the weed is smoked it is done with scant social opprobrium. The use of marijuana is not specifically proscribed by Judeo-Christianity, but this is so, one supposes, only because no episcopal authority of note has got around to the particularization of the generic law against gluttony. It reasonably follows that to dope the mind is in the same category of excess as to overstuff the body, and is therefore a ''capital'' sin.

4. The Social Uses of Sin

What would happen if religious sanctions against the use of marijuana were made explicit? Would we notice any differences in conduct? When Dr. Rosenthal talks about vitalizing an ethos against the use of marijuana, he does not mean that our ministers, rabbis, and priests, by inveighing against drug-taking, will breathe life into a sanction hitherto mostly legal. I don't think he had in mind a clerical Rachel Carson who would transform the sensibilities of drug consum-

ers in the same way that sensibilities were generally aroused a generation ago in defense of nature. Yes, if the Pope, speaking through the
magisterium, were to denounce as sinful the use of marijuana, the use
of that drug by Catholics would diminish. But sin is by and large
ignored in progressive circles, where divine sanctions are simply im-
material; and this is an important social development. Whatever became of sin?

The highly touted Playboy/Woodstock philosophy (free and abundant sex), however dated it seems, is very much in point here. Some
years ago the then chaplain to Yale University, the Reverend William
Sloane Coffin, Jr., was asked to comment on the rampant sex associated with the Woodstock generation. I read about the exchange, but I
knew the second my eyes fell on the question posed to Mr. Coffin by
the inquiring student that he would not reply by saying that the Judeo-
Christian code specifies monogamy as the "code" by which one
judges acceptable sexual behavior. I.e., that promiscuous sex is
"wrong."

What Mr. Coffin told his audience was that anything—*anything*—
can be overdone. For instance (he explained), drinking a beer won't
hurt you, but you have got to guard against becoming an alcoholic.
The questioner was supposed to derive from this that a Yale student
should not have more than one affair at a time, because out there in
the murky psychological world of lust there is the equivalent of alcoholism of the libido. We can put it more suavely: take too many lovers
or mistresses and you deprive sex of its sublimer aspects, even as if
you were to chugalug a full bottle of Mouton-Rothschild 1959 you
would diminish its capacity to give extensive and acuter pleasure.

My old friend Bill Coffin had of course some very good points
here, psychological, sociological, and even biological: but his empirical approach struck me as exemplifying the lengths some moralists are
disposed to go, even if they are formal emissaries of the word of God,
to circumvent the concept of sin. Surely in doing so they are indirectly
subverting transcendent authority. I remember, about the same time,
reading a letter by a young self-designated groupie in *Rolling Stone*
magazine. "What I worry about," she asked in her letter to the

editor, "is—is semen fattening?" If so, the Reverend Coffin could presumably strengthen his case against promiscuous sexuality.

In his essay on sin in the *Great Books' Syntopicon,* Mortimer Adler gives us this conspectus:

> In the pagan and Judeo-Christian conceptions of sin, the fundamental meaning seems to depend upon the relation of man to the gods or to God, whether that itself be considered in terms of law or love. The vicious act may be conceived as one which is contrary to nature or reason. The criminal act may be conceived as a violation of the law of man, injurious to the welfare of the state or to its members. Both may involve the notions of responsibility and fault. Both may involve evil and wrongdoing. But unless the act transgresses the law of God, it is not sinful. The divine law which is transgressed may be the natural law that God instills in human reason, but the act is sinful if the person who commits the act turns away from God to the worship or love of other things.

So then: How is a society that strives for virtuous conduct going to encourage right-minded institutions and right-minded behavior without invoking the divine sanction? Those who believe that the secularization of our society is all but complete should pause over the word "sin": it survives, even as metaphor. It is a sign of latent life in a word that seeks to intone final gravity in the judgment of social conduct. Thus, "John's treatment of Jane was really . . . *sinful.*" Ancient ghosts. We are being told that even God was offended by John's treatment of Jane.

And of course expiation is not foreign to our culture. In formal religious circumstances, Catholics go to confession. There they enumerate their sins, plead contrition, and receive a "penance" and forgiveness. Judges in criminal law, under pressure to lighten the prison load and to mete out more imaginative punishments than time in jail, have recently cocked their ears to listen to the recommendations of Mr. Colson and others. Inventiveness is in the air. Instead of thirty days in jail, what about one hundred hours of community service? In New Jersey not long ago a judge sentenced a young miscreant, caught defacing a synagogue, to read *The Diary of Anne Frank.* That is the secular arm of the law reaching out to reinforce the dignity and influence of the divine arm. It is saying that graffiti on a synagogue is a graver offense than graffiti in a subway.

What has happened, in two generations, is the substantial alienation of the secular culture from the biblical culture. Irving Kristol has written that the most important *political* development of the nine-teenth century was the wholesale loss of religious faith. What happens is that man's natural idealism, struggling to assert itself and finding no congenial satisfaction in religious commandments about personal be-havior, turns to utopianism which inevitably—whenever formally ac-tualized—brings on the death of liberty. Enter the twentieth century. The impoverishment of religious sanctions imposes on the other sanc-tions a heavier weight than they are designed to handle. When that happens and society gets serious about something (e.g., drugs), gov-ernment has recourse only to force. Governor Nelson Rockefeller's solution to the drug problem was to apprehend the drug user, put him in jail, and throw away the keys. At this writing, the popular penologi-cal slogan is "three strikes and you're out"—three felonies, jail for life. The great totalitarian triumvirate (Hitler, Stalin, Mao) took the legal sanction further than Cotton Mather took hellfire: or, put an-other way, Hitler, Stalin, and Mao brought us Hell on earth. They had a vision.

Elsewhere, the imaginative Mr. Kristol came up with a celebrated piquancy, wonderfully—awesomely—grave in its inverted implica-tions. As far as he could figure out, he said, in New York City a man could have sexual intercourse with an eighteen-year-old girl on a public stage just as long as she was being paid the minimum wage. Social sanctions against offensive behavior dissipate. Offensive behav-ior! What's that? *"When one asks how a sense of guilt arises in anyone, one is told something one cannot dispute: people feel guilty—pious people call it 'sinful'—when they have done something they know to be 'bad' "*—Freud. Sanctions lose vigor as they go uncodified, and even then they lose vigor if the ethos that supports the laws is dissipated. Legal constraints crumble against the tidal waves of massive contumacy. As well, at this point in our culture, try to stop pornography (begin by rounding up 200 million X-rated cassettes) as prohibit the consumption of alcohol.

Sin sits in the back of the bus. But it is still there, an agent of conscience. Christians (and many non-Christians) believe that man harbors, within the limits of his perspective, the capacity to distinguish between right and wrong, and that he should be encouraged to feel something between an itch and a compulsion to exercise that capacity for virtuous conduct.

There is famine in the land and you harbor a supply of grain. And you know something no one else knows, which is that a caravan of supplies is on its way and will arrive within a few days.

Can you charge for your supply of grain a very high price, as if it alone stood between your client and starvation—concealing your knowledge that relief was around the corner?

Yes, you are at liberty to do this, Thomas Aquinas said: but it would be wrong.

Wrong?

Why?

Because it is *wrong,* sinful; *ipsa res loquitur!* And you shouldn't need Immanuel Kant to explain it to you. I said over the air a few years ago that I believed in metaphysical equality, that otherwise there was *no way* I could be made to believe that Mother Teresa and Sister Boom Boom were equal. A letter came in. He didn't understand; he couldn't find in any dictionary the use of the word "metaphysical" as apt in defining the word "equality." Why (I wrote him), the word means, as I used it, *equal in the eyes of God,* and that is all the explanation *I* need: equal beyond measurement. I'd find it sinful to reason otherwise, even about Sister Boom Boom.

It isn't only the Pope who speaks of the necessity of a spiritual revival in order to enhance civilized life. Years ago, the late Professor Richard Weaver pointed out what should be obvious, namely that Marxism and Communism are redemptive creeds, while liberalism has no eschatology, no ultimate sense of consummation. Free speech and private property are terrific, but they do not deal with the great ends of life. Lacking that, liberalism is at a grave disadvantage contending with secular religions that offer visions of comprehensive achievements. The rediscovery of sin as defined in the Bible would cause us to look up and note the infinite horizons that beckon us toward better conduct, better lives, nobler visions.

CHAPTER FIFTEEN

On the Uniqueness of Christ

One would expect that God, incarnate, would be a striking figure. In my random thoughts on the matter I have not reasoned from Christ/God to Christ/unique. Inasmuch as Christ was divine, how striking was His singularity? My mind turned, as most others I expect would, to reasoning in the other way: Is the uniqueness of Christ such as to tolerate?, encourage?, require? the conclusion that he was divine?

There is no explaining his miracles, if we suppose that they happened. The skeptic here will need to place his faith on false witness.

"Although Matthew thought he saw Jesus risen from the Tomb, in fact it was all illusion." "His messianic impact is undeniable, but that of Muhammad can be compared with it, while bearing in mind that Muhammad did not claim divinity for himself . . ."

There was the surrealistic beauty of the words He used. "Consider the lilies of the field, how they grow; they toil not, neither do they spin: And yet I say unto you, That even Solomon in all his glory was not arrayed like one of these. Wherefore, if God so clothe the grass of the field, which today is, and tomorrow is cast into the oven, shall he not much more clothe you, O ye of little faith?" Do we dismiss it as sublime poetry, pure and simple? An old, Judaic Shakespeare? But in doing that we augment implausibility. A Shakespeare, raised as a carpenter, under the reign of Tiberius Caesar? "It is easier for me to believe in God than to believe that Hamlet was deduced from the molecular structure of a mutton chop" is how someone once parsed the alternatives. The psalmists were great spiritual poets, but it is more credible that their words were inspired than that they were exnihilations. To object that the Sermon on the Mount is after all nothing more than a collection of ethical commonplaces does not readily account for their unique resonance. There is no reasonable explanation for the surrealistic ethical beauty of Christ's thought and expression. I had noticed the point when made by Louis Auchincloss (in *The Rector of Justin*) and it is made by Arnold Lunn in *Now I See*. I thought to try it out on my Forum. My question:

How much importance do you attach to the "uninventability" of Christ? (It was C. S. Lewis's contention that the life and in particular the preachings of Christ could not have issued from someone merely human.)

Fr. Neuhaus grants the uniqueness of Christ's words (and, of course, his deeds) but cautions against constructing a theological house on them. "It doesn't 'prove' anything, and is powerfully influenced by our dispositions," which are predisposed to Christian acceptance. "Just say no on any Christ-to-God deductions based on text," Fr. Neuhaus cautions, turning quickly to the deeds of Christ.

What one must reasonably judge to be uninventable is the account of Jesus and its historical consequences in producing "the Christian thing." Could "the preachings of Christ have issued from someone merely human"? Yes, His moral teachings, parables, and the such could have come from one "merely human." Could have. But His being raised from the dead indicates that He was, as He claimed, Son of God.

Once again, Fr. Neuhaus is insisting on viewing Christ wide-screen, from prophecy to Resurrection. This last deed is in and of itself conclusive he thinks (as St. Paul thought), but the tapestry arrests the imagination, urging and indeed fulfilling the whole, Christian view.

Father Rutler disagrees:

There is no possibility that someone "merely" human could have been so consistent in His purpose, so infallible in His parabolic examples, and so accurate in His assessment of the human condition. That is why Lewis says rightly that if He was not the "I Am" He was either mad or a demagogue. But He could not have been either, because of the facts attendant upon His life and the life of the Church.

Russell Kirk accepts the argument of divinity derived from words spoken but is quick to reach for confirmation in history. (1) Only someone with a divine mandate would have spoken the words Christ spoke; and (2), as Fr. Neuhaus observed, the historical circumstances clinch the point: " 'He speaks as one having authority.' " Of this the Pharisees accused Jesus.

Anyone desiring imposture on a grand scale would have told a neater tale, with the Gospels perfectly consistent one with another, any implausibilities deleted, or perhaps otherwise shored up with greater detail. The claim to be the truth, the way and the life; to be the only channel through which a soul might pass to the Father; to confer the keys to Heaven and Hell; to open the gate to paradise for the repentant thief—these and other passages, and especially the Sermon on the Mount, are too startling to have been invented by a mystagogue. The doctrine of the resurrection of the flesh and of the life everlasting was far more than any Orphic cult ever had suggested, and scarcely could have been accepted by Disciples and Apostles except for an overwhelming impression of wondrous knowledge and truth that those who had known Jesus of Nazareth had received from His presence and His words, and had communicated in turn to their auditors. Paul of Tarsus, and Peter the Fisherman, possessed intellects that would have detected imposture or fantasy.

Powerful sentences, these from Russell Kirk, arguing the congruity of faith and history.

Jeffrey Hart faces directly the question of Christ as poet and handles it as follows:

Shakespeare and Dante, along with Homer, are probably the best writers generally known to the educated West. They have moments superior to any other writer, and more of them. But they do not widely change lives. The statements of Jesus do change lives. Not long ago, some scholars made the argument that more than one ancient prophet was responsible for what we call the statements of "Jesus." On the face of it, that represents a dizzying leap of faith— that there were two, three, or even more people wandering around Judaea speaking in an overwhelming way.

In his book *Now I See,* Arnold Lunn makes the point often cited, as it is here cited by Fr. Rutler. It is that Christ was never ambiguous on the point, even if he only once initiated the question Who *was* He? No mere man would have said, "Whosoever therefore shall confess me before men, him will I confess also before my Father which is in heaven'' (Matthew 10:32). Or, ''No man knoweth who the Son is, but the Father; and who the Father is, but the Son'' (Luke 10:22). Let alone, ''All power is given unto me in heaven and in earth. . . . I am with you always, even unto the end of the world'' (Matthew 28:18, 20).

It is forever disconsoling, at first thought, that God does not now reveal Himself, even on the Internet. Yet the Gospels tell us that faith is a necessary instrument of communion between men and God. Christ gave us the most vivid demonstration of this, or parable suggesting this, in his encounter with the doubting Thomas. He needed, in order to believe that he was once again in the company of Christ crucified, to probe the wounds on the body, absolutely to confirm by empirical means that this was Christ. And when Thomas did see, and then adore, Christ spoke the words that presaged his eternal impalpability: Blessed are they who do not see, yet believe.

It is, once again, one of those divine arrangements one grits one's teeth over. The alternative, as mentioned before, would be *so* simple, say worldwide thunder at three in the afternoon (local time) on Good Fridays, or a very bright star at midnight on Christmas. But the struggle to believe has got to have been intended as exactly that, an achievement of the will and the spirit, seeking concordance with divine purpose. It is vexing that Christian teaching is to the effect that no human being can achieve belief without the grace of God Himself. But this can only mean, if I penetrate it, that all good fortune must be supposed to have been a blessing of God, or at least tolerated by God. What we need, then, to tell ourselves is that *the inclination* to believe will be satisfied. The rationalist will find abundant reasons to support his conclusion that there is no acceptable explanation for it all than that a divine intelligence is there as the prime mover. The poet will deduce the sweetness of life, and his taste for marvel will heighten. And the lonely, and the sad, will know that they in fact have company, which is divine.

CHAPTER SIXTEEN

On the Special Blessings, and Problems,

of Catholics

I turned to strengths that sustain, and problems that beset, the little circle of converts I brought together to give me their thoughts.

I grew up, as reported, in a large family of Catholics without even a decent ration of tentativeness among the lot of us about our religious faith. Protestants were a majority everywhere we lived and studied, except for the few months I spent at St. John's in England. Our sense of it was that ours was the truly serious exercise of Christianity; an underinformed judgment, obviously, but then that can be held always to be the case. Catholic Christianity was beleaguered in the sense that American traditional culture is Protestant. In this sense, in the thirties and forties, the U.S. Catholic had some sense of it that his culture was alien. But direct anti-Catholicism was rarely expressed in doctrinal terms. Such criticisms as I heard—or thought I had heard, as a boy and teenager—weren't orderly indictments of the anti-Catholic faith. When the subject arose—What are the special disqualifications of American Catholics?—it was usually the political point that was being pursued, the question of divided loyalties.

We all knew that in 1928 many voters who would normally have gone with the Democratic Party did not do so because the party's candidate was Al Smith. Much of Protestant America didn't like the idea of a Catholic in the White House, even feared the idea. When Paul Blanshard's famous book came out *(American Freedom and Catholic Power)*, about which I have made mention, the case was crystallized: American Catholics were burdened with a divided loyalty and for that reason incapacitated from being at once dutiful Catholics and dutiful Democrats. It struck me, when as a freshman I first heard the argument put with some force, that the Blanshard objection was entirely valid. It highlighted, however indirectly, the doctrine that crystallized during my sophomore year. It came to be known as the Nuremberg Defense: The only reason, your honor, I helped to slaughter six million Jews was that Hitler told me to do so, and Hitler was my superior.

The argument hadn't worked in Nuremberg for Göring et al., nor should it have. In the inconceivable event that a majority of Americans decided to end liberty—specifically, religious liberty—a Catholic sheriff would certainly have a problem requiring a synagogue—or a church—to close down after duly authorized instructions to do so had been handed down to him through proper, democratic channels. In such a situation one likes to think that non-Catholics would join the resistance; but there is no question that, in such a situation, a Catholic official true to his faith would heed the authority of Rome, not Washington. If critics then chose to accuse him of divided loyalty, they'd be only half right. *All* loyalty to Washington would have been forfeited.

Most critics were focusing on Christianity at large. The special exposures of the Catholic—divided loyalty, the authority of the magisterium—were surely counterbalanced, I thought, by Catholicism's strengths. What were they? What was it about my faith that especially attracted to it the men who constitute what I have called my Forum, all of them born and raised as Protestants?

For a Catholic to read about another Catholic's journey to Damascus is an exhilarating experience, reminding us of satisfactions that may have become jaded. I wanted to hear about what especially engaged the mind and heart of my Forum. And wanted also—an adjacent question—to know what it was that kept some of them, for so long, at the gates. My inquiry was wonderfully rewarding for me and, I devoutly hope, others. The question exactly as I posed it:

Was there one feature of the Catholic Church, distinguishing it from other Christian sects, that in particular drew you toward the Church? If so which was it (or them)?

> Permit me to suggest that it is not accurate (nor is it nice) to speak of "other Christian sects." For one, it suggests that the Catholic Church is one sect among others. The Catholic Church is not a sect. [*American Heritage Dictionary:* "A group of people forming a distinct unit within a larger group by virtue of certain refinements or distinctions of belief or practice."] The reason I became a Catholic is, entirely and alone, because of the ecclesial claims of the Catholic Church, which I have for many years held to be true.

There was no personal narrative in Fr. Neuhaus's account. Later, he would be more revealing.

And then Fr. Rutler, formerly a High Church Episcopalian priest:

> I was drawn by three things. First the papacy (which, as a High Anglican, I had considered the principal error of Rome). The utter consistency of the papal magisterium over against all teleological extremes of every age, combined with the evidently supernatural ap-

pearance of a Slav Pope at this tumultuous period in world affairs, made the Petrine office seem essential to Church and culture. Second, I came to appreciate the uniqueness of Catholic "systematic thought," which has no parallel in any philosophical structure and which proved itself by working coherently in our antinomian and highly subjective age.

What you have read is not the complete passage given me by Fr. Rutler. I didn't want to relay the sentences that follow without first making this point, namely that I am not a bit certain that I myself fully understand them. I don't mean to say that I don't understand why Fr. Rutler is taking the position he takes. I mean something else, that I am not confident I understand what exactly he is *saying*. He is using theological concepts that my mind does not fully fathom——maybe can't fathom? I know that I could pick up the telephone and call——how many? three?——friends who would endeavor to explain them to me. But such spelunking for hidden treasure is for explorers and specialists.

I thought also, on deciding whether to reproduce the abstruse sentences, that I shouldn't resist the temptation to expose the reader to far reaches of theological language and speculation. The typical modern academic is quite simply ignorant of theology. Mostly this is because scholars proceed happily on the assumption that theological studies are voodoo, deserving ignorance, condescension, or contempt. But even if God did not exist, were not real, theology would remain a profound philosophical science. Even if trees do make noise when they fall down in a forest out of human earshot, David Hume and George Berkeley are engrossing epistemologists. Fr. Rutler's words, whatever they mean, bring to mind the refinements of the theological mind at work. He is not merely "spinning wheels" (Professor Kendall's term for student papers in which nothing really was being said or thought, merely pages being filled). There are those who scorn the very idea of extra-worldly phenomena, and deem all language devoted to the study of them a philosophical conceit. You will hear it said that it is not surprising that less than the most talented graduate students go on to divinity schools. That last may be so, but it is not a matter of brain-power, but of calling. Just to begin with, it requires a profound ignorance of the achievements of the human mind to ignore all the work of the primary thinkers in the Christian tradition between Augustine and Kierkegaard. Herewith the balance of Fr. Rutler's reply:

> This [the uniqueness of Catholic systematic thought] made clear the "scrutability" of paradox, and provided an economy in which natural law and revelation were compatible and effectively defined the use and limits of reason. By the *via negativa* I had to observe that nothing else "worked" and this did. Third, I was converted by the fact of the saints. There is no isolated psychological phenomenology of the saints—the utterly natural supernaturalness of grace *(gratis non tollit naturam sed perficit)* [Grace does not destroy nature, rather, perfects it] in the lives of the saints of heroic virtue is proof positive that there is grace and that it is available. Léon Bloy's line (the only tragedy is *not* to be a saint) seemed to sum up the reason for Christ and the whole meaning of existence. As we enter a "postmodern" age we may consider the neglect of the lives of the saints to have been the single most curious lacuna in modern intellectual life.

What I take away from that is (1) that which was thought impene-trable as a paradox is, by Catholic reasoning, in fact discernible; (2) only by exposure to the incomplete road (presumably to religious thought finally rejected as incomplete—Anglicanism, in this instance) was it possible for Fr. Rutler to acknowledge the true road; (3) the mere existence of the saints, never mind that the exact properties of saintliness have never been absolutely defined, establishes that divine favor is there, and available to us. The striking failure of humankind is to have eschewed a (sufficient) study of saintliness, and aspiration to saintliness; and it is above all strange, given the perspectives we have in postmodern thought, that that failure itself fails sufficiently to engage the attention of modern intellectuals.

There it is. It can be parsed, as here done. But do you fully understand it? I don't. Not fully.

Russell Kirk, by contrast, was plainspoken, and exemplary in dramatizing the necessary end of his temperamental resistance to relativism. He adds a fine paragraph about the lateness of his baptism, the result of a very long series of inferences that finally—but only then—made up his Holy Grail.

What I found in the Church was Authority. Catholicism is governed by Authority; Protestants, by Private Judgment. I had become painfully aware of the insufficiency of Private Judgment in the twentieth century—every man creating his own morals. In my search, over the years, for a sound apprehension of the human condition, I came at last to recognize in the Roman Church the elements of Truth, as sustained by two thousand years of continuity; by the wealth of wisdom in the Church's pronouncements; by the lives and words of St. Augustine of Hippo and St. Gregory the Great, particularly, among the Church Fathers; by Acton's observation, if you will, that no institution purely human could have survived, over the centuries, so many blunders.

I was not "converted" to the Church, but made my way into it through what Newman calls *illation*—fragments of truth collecting in my mind through personal experience, conversations, knowledge of exemplars, and much reading and meditating. (I was not baptized in any church until 1964, when I attained the age of forty-five years.) Mine was the god of the philosophers, Pascal notwithstanding (though I read Pascal, too), rather than the god of Abraham, Isaac, and Jacob. Father Hugh O'Neill, S.J., at the University of Detroit, who gave me some instruction during 1953–54, replied in answer to an inquiry of mine that most people seeking knowledge of Church doctrines came to him out of some psychological distress or want. It was not so with me: rather, I still was seeking the source of wisdom.

Kirk left the impression that people who contemplate conversion and consult priests are driven by psychological disorders. Yes; but psychological distress (or "want") can be the symptom of spiritual hunger. Even if I thought I could competently handle the psychoanalytical vocabulary, I would let it alone, and say simply this: that I know human beings who are unhappier than they would be if they believed that God could give solace, and that He cared.

Jeffrey Hart answered in a single sentence:

The answer here is in the plural: (a) continuous distinguished intellectual tradition stretching back over two millennia; (b) doctrinal coherence; (c) institutional stability, produced by its theory of church
government, which is monarchical; (d) universality; (e) liturgical stability, even now.

Wick Allison, a generation younger than the rest of us, gave his
own itinerary with simple and, I think, effectively solemn conviction.

Five things attracted me in stages to the Catholic Church:

1. Its understanding of human nature and of human society. I was
a student in the sixties when theories about the perfectibility of man
and schemes for new utopias were the intellectual air one breathed. I
thought they were all rubbish. But I didn't have a clear sense of why I
thought that, and as I looked for intellectual support I stumbled across
the Church Fathers, or writings about the Fathers: their clarity, their
appeal to the evidence of the senses and, most of all, to common
sense, their insistence on the unchanging nature of creation, all these
were to me like drinking from a freshwater spring. I became interested in the religion that seemed to foster such clear thinking.

2. Its antiquity. I became impressed that such views were held and
argued with a consistent vigor over the centuries by all sorts of
different people who were Catholic. I became interested in such
subjects as the apostolic succession and the Church's claim that it is
the original Church founded by Jesus. Just as any thinking person in
the West sooner or later has to confront the claims of Jesus, sooner or
later he has to confront this claim of the Catholic Church.

3. Its universality. I found it interesting, when I read them, that
St. Augustine and Cardinal Newman both came to the conclusion that
the Catholic faith was the true Christianity by this fact of its ubiquity.
I was raised in a denomination (Methodist) where one felt uncomfort-
able attending a church service in another part of town, much less

another part of the country (in another part of the world was inconceivable). When I started getting interested in the Catholic faith I began to attend Mass. I was only an observer, and I really didn't understand the significance of what I was observing, but I liked to go, and it was with a start one Sunday that I realized I was going to Mass in a city I was visiting, that I had been to Masses in lots of different places and that nothing much seemed different about any of them. This probably never occurs to a born Catholic but it comes as a shock to the rest of us.

Part of the universalism is the diversity. In Protestantism a particular church, like a particular magazine or particular retail store, is geared to a demographic segment. It's where like-minded people gather together to worship, so there's no surprise that everyone looks, acts, and thinks the same. The first time I attended a Mass a Mexican gardener in his work clothes knelt down beside me.

At first I was put off; I was raised among people who associated bad smell with unwashed Mexican gardeners. Here was one sitting next to me in church. Then I was dazzled. Of *course* it had to be this way! In the original Christian church the strictures of St. Paul are still followed: "Here you are neither Greek nor Jew. . . ." Of all the things about the Catholic Church I love, this is the thing I love the best.

4. Mary. How does one talk to God? How does one relate to Christ the Savior? For me it was difficult. And so I turned to Mary. To this day I am not at all sure about the theological underpinnings of Mariology, and I suspect I'll never investigate them. I took the concept of Mary as my Mother to heart from the beginning and, as Dante chose Virgil, made her my own personal guide to the Catholic faith. She has been wonderful.

5. The Eucharist. This took a little longer. When my brother lived outside London he took me to see the oldest standing church in England, a squat Saxon building made out of stone. We went inside. The building was still set up as a church, with old wooden pews and altar fixtures. But what struck me immediately was how empty the place felt. And then I realized what was missing: the Eucharist. A

church is warm; this place was cold. A church is somehow made alive by the Life inside it; this place was dead. It was sad. The chain of worship that should have united me with the sturdy, sixth-century yeomen who built the church had been broken.

It was that experience that made me understand how important the Real Presence had become for me and what my forefathers had given up when they discarded it.

The thought that the Real Presence should give off emanations is widely dismissed as psychological autohypnosis. If such phenomena are analyzed by strict scientific standards, then the skeptic cannot lose the argument. By scientific rules, all sensations related to special presences are self-induced; what you feel while waiting, the heartbeat a little faster, to enter the Oval Office; in the presence of the Pope; in the hotel lounge when the girl—your girl—comes in. But the rules are abundantly violated. They don't seem, to me, to make it. And anyway, how do they account for the sensory perceptions in homing pigeons, let alone in some who think they feel—do feel?—something in the company of the Real Presence?

The next question followed naturally. I put it this way:

Was there one feature, or more, of the Catholic Church that kept you from joining it sooner than you did? If so, please say which, and (a) explain why they antagonized you; and (b) how you overcame that antagonism, if indeed you did.

Fr. Neuhaus spoke of the journey from Lutheranism and its "Augustinian Christianity," the devotion to a God of all-encompassing love, who gave the world the Incarnation (the emphasis is otherwise on man's effort to qualify for God's love), and of the three dogmatic pronouncements of the Catholic Church, made after the Reformation: the Immaculate Conception, that Mary was born without sin (1854); that the Pope cannot mislead in matters of faith and morals when speaking ex cathedra (1870); and that when Mary departed the earth, she ascended into Heaven (1950).

> The key discovery is that I was a Lutheran because I was an Augustin-ian, notably on the question of God's utterly gratuitous justifying grace in Christ. It was for me a providential coincidence that at the time I was wrestling with these questions, the chief guardian of Cath-olic orthodoxy was Josef Ratzinger, a thorough Augustinian. For me it is of great importance to emphasize that to be an orthodox Catholic today is to be an ecumenical Catholic. Catholics can afford to be very generous in acknowledging the grace and truth of God in other com-munions. That is the case at least if the teachings of the Second Vatican Council are right. Those who deny the teachings of the Coun-cil have a very hard time making the case that they are orthodox Catholics. (That applies to the Lefebvres on the right, as well as those on the left such as Fr. Richard McBrien, who defy the magisterium in the name of "the Church of John XXIII.")

Fr. Neuhaus grew to accept the three post-Reformation dogmas— Immaculate Conception, infallibility, Assumption—as "all of them understandable in a thoroughly evangelical and Christocentric way." He admits that the question of papal infallibility was difficult:

> At the same time, had I been around then, I expect I would have been, with Newman and many others, an "inopportunist" with re-spect to infallibility. Its magisterial interpretation, however, makes clear that it is derived from the "indefectibility of the Church" and reflects the Petrine ministry (firmly grounded in the New Testament) and therefore poses no problems. [Might it, sometime in the future?] Conceivably, yes. A Pope could not, for example, "infallibly" define that there are four persons in the Godhead. Such a definition would be invalid on the face of it and would be clear evidence of the incom-petence of the Pope who attempted it. To ask about some aberrant exercise of infallibility is like asking what you would think of your

wife if you knew she was planning to poison you. It is contrary to fact, and I trust will always remain so.

That is heady stuff. I found most striking the reminder that the Vatican Council acknowledged, if not the legitimacy of the heretical churches, at least the common ground we have with them, from which we deduce that ecumenism is the necessary objective. And Fr. Neuhaus reminds us that it is now as it was always, and throughout history has been. Although the Church is convincingly united, there are, in the current context, both left and right inclinations to heterodoxy. The Lefebvrites—led by Archbishop Marcel Lefebvre (1905–91)—protest the liturgical reforms and the new Mass of Vatican II. But it was only when Lefebvre undertook to ordain another bishop (this only the Pope can authorize) that indocility spilled over to schism. Fr. McBrien, who has been head of the department of theology at Notre Dame, is here mentioned as contumacious because of his continuing advocacy of women's ordination, a noncelibate priesthood, and birth control. It is helpful to remember that many priests considered deviant at this or another point in Church history are in due course restored. The distinction has surely to be between defective disciplinary compliance and the teaching of subversive doctrine. The structure of the papacy, as observed early on, requires final doctrinal authority; the institution of the Church, effective administrative authority. I was beyond measure happier with the old than with the new liturgy, I am relieved that the advocacy of birth control is less than an excommunicable offense, and I am serene, as a matter of faith, that the Church is not materially misguided. I like what Fr. Neuhaus says about the promulgation of infallibility in 1870. He has to admit that back then he'd have opposed it, but he has to admit now that it was there all the time.

Fr. Rutler remains difficult exactly to understand. Better put, he uses language both poetic and provocative, inviting us to parse his thoughts to the end of the night. He gives me a compelling view of the pilgrim seeking utter authenticity, going to Catholic Christianity to find it, but weighed down with sorrow by so much of what he finds in the modern Church, however irrelevant to its singularity.

The chief obstacle was the failure of the Catholic Church to be herself in practice. I do not mean being "holy" enough because she is always that and most conspicuously so, in a chiaroscuro way, when most corrupt in the material order. I do mean that Church's tendency to compromise with the most dismal conceits of progressivism just when they were proving to be philosophical and aesthetic phantoms.

The Catholic Church had ceased being properly universal and had in the West become bourgeois. This hit me as particularly evident in her liturgical life. Used as I was to the aesthetic "form without substance" of Anglican externals I did not enjoy the prospect of substance without form. English in "ghastly bad taste" had its drawbacks but that "gaudy meretriciousness" [the designation of a seventeenth-century Anglican theologian] of the post–Vatican II Church seemed revolting. Worse, this symbolized a loss of the sacramental vision and a petit-bourgeois surrender on the part of the Church which is properly the shared communion of kings and peasants, knaves and saints. I would be happy with both the Sainte-Chapelle of Louis IX and the hovel of the Curé d'Ars but not with a suburban church glorifying the shopping mall.

I overcame that, I daresay, by the grace which makes conversion possible. This was aided in the natural order by the realization that Anglicanism was over and done for having always been an illicit compromise between a truth and a lie, and the sheer desperation of realizing that the crises of our times are crises of saints and saints are the products of the Catholic fact.

For the most part, Russell Kirk resisted the confessional requirement of the Church, though he acknowledges that the institution was more offensive to his nature than to others'.

Although nothing in doctrine or dogma in any way repelled me, I was not attracted by the rite of confession—not that in my unchurched years I was much given to committing deadly sins, mine being the sins of omission, chiefly. (One thinks of a line from an Edwardian comedy: "I'm afraid I was a very *good* young man; but I'm not sorry; for that has enabled me to be a very wicked old one.") Shy and self-sufficient, I resented being expected to open my smug heart to anybody. My wife remarks that I do not let anyone into my secret garden.

My attitude toward confession has not much improved since my baptism in the Church, although requirements for frequency of confession have diminished since then. But more repugnant than the old sort of confession in some antique carven confessional is the latter-day notion—popular with "advanced" priests, especially those who rejoice in what they call the Jesus-centered liturgy (actually the priest-centered liturgy)—of the public, or open, or collective confession, reducing the sacrament to absurdity and hypocrisy.

I recognize now that confession fulfills a most important psychological function, as did the ritual ablutions of the ancient Greeks in some sacred river, washing away the haunting consciousness of grim guilt. But I refrain from confessing the outrageous sin of wandering thoughts at Mass; that failing of mine is incurable.

The public confessional formula (every member of the congregation recites to himself his sins, summons up contrition, and the priest grants corporate absolution) was one of those excesses of the Vatican II sixties, and after a little while was all but discontinued (penance services are still performed twice a year, in preparation for Christmas and Easter). In some dioceses the practice was never permitted.

Jeffrey Hart had no specific problem, Ernest van den Haag the problem of ignorant clergy, Wick Allison the problem of the "priest":

While most of the priests I've known have been warm and affable types, the priesthood itself is an intimidating institution to the outsider. I can't say that it is antagonizing; just intimidating.

Yes, the priesthood is intimidating, and so are individual priests. On that subject I thought Fr. Andrew Greeley said exactly the right thing in an essay* I stumbled upon during my research:

> The reader can make up his own litany of injuries the Catholic Church has done to him. I do not care how horrendous that litany may be, it does not provide a valid excuse for disengaging from the Catholic Christian heritage. Indeed, it is irrelevant. I attempt no justification and offer no excuse for what the Church may have done to you: I simply assert that the failures of Christians and the failures of Christian leadership have nothing to do with the validity of the Catholic Christian heritage. If you use those failures as an excuse for not facing the essential religious demands of the Catholic Christian heritage, you are engaged in an intellectually dishonest cop-out. The question is not whether the Catholic leadership is enlightened but whether Catholicism is true. A whole College of Cardinals filled with psychopathic tyrants provides no answer one way or another to that question.
>
> [And then a killer of a closing line.] Search for the perfect church if you will; when you find it, join it, and realize that on that day it becomes something less than perfect.

* *Why Catholic?* (Doubleday, 1980).

CHAPTER SEVENTEEN

―――――――

The Ordination of Michael Bozell

A half century after Beaumont, where I was every day in the company of priests, I would see it for myself, the transfigurative rite I had in my boyhood imagined, with my teacher/priests as young men and central figures. I had observed at St. John's the role of the two masters who were not yet priests (we addressed them as "Mr."). They wore the same habit as the ordained Jesuits, but they had not yet completed their training (thirteen years, the Jesuits put in, as mentioned above). I wondered, at age thirteen, about the event that made them into priests. It was, of course, ordination, the sacrament of holy orders.

Fifty-one relatives and friends traveled to Solesmes, 175 miles west of Paris, for the ceremony. A succession of memoranda had gone out from my sister Trish, the mother of the monk who would be ordained a priest in the reclusive Benedictine order. I remember the one memo whose detail brought home the force of the occasion. It was a reference to "the party"—the big party, hosted by the father and mother of Brother Michael—scheduled for the night before the great event. The memo from Trish was to the effect that Michael would not himself be present at the party.

That was hard to take. Yet the instant Trish explained it to us, in her distinctive way—calm, resolute, graceful—it became understandable, and we quickly understood: we were face-to-face with the singularity of Michael's vocation.

He would be required to forgo even the once-in-a-lifetime pleasure of a party in his honor attended by his parents, brothers, sisters, aunts, uncles, and lifetime friends, assembled from mainland America, from Hawaii, from Munich, from Strasbourg, and from Paris. When you are ordained a priest in the strictly contemplative division of the Benedictine order you are variously reminded what it is you have elected to do with your life; reminded, in this case, by getting the word that social engagements sponsored other than by your abbot are not appropriate. (The Benedictines would act as most agreeable hosts at a high tea in the afternoon at a guesthouse at the monastery after the ordination.) In search of a retailable explanation for the benefit of guests who wanted to know why Michael would not be present at his own party, I played once or twice with the idea of the fast that precedes the banquet (that is, being ordained a priest); but there aren't, really, any satisfactory secular analogues. The presence of the bride is essential to the wedding party, the guest of honor is necessarily there at any dinner given in his honor. But this party, given on Halloween Eve in the little town of St. Denys for Michael Bozell *without* Brother Michael Bozell, served as a kind of manifesto of the honoree's august decision formally and irrevocably to pursue a life so detached from the other life—our lives—that, in a paradoxical way, his absence from the party became, however inexpressly, the sustaining high moment of the evening.

As expected, it was a boisterous gathering. This was so even as we are unsurprised when we find ourselves participating in, or reading about, an exuberant wake. Many in the company are people you see infrequently, and so you are generating, or at least emitting, greater ergs than usual of social energy, designed—as in the case of the Christian wake—to make agitated obeisance to the dogma that the deceased has gone on to a better life, thereby mitigating melancholy.

It was so at the eleventh-century Roi René restaurant, as the guests filed into the large reception hall and waiters passed by with trays of table wine. I tasted it. It was so awful, I sought out the eyes of my sister Priscilla. Working intimately together in the same office for thirty-five years, we knew each other's body language. She nodded her head in the hubbub, acknowledging that if only on our own account, we simply had to do something about it, but we'd need for diplomacy's sake to circumvent our hosts; besides, neither Trish nor her late husband, Brent, drink. We could hardly protest publicly—my siblings and I are tactful almost to the point of impotence, so I walked discreetly to the maître d'hôtel and whispered my sister's and my desire for a different wine.

"What kind?" he asked.

"Any kind," I smiled.

He poured for Priscilla and me wine from another bottle. It was only a shade less awful. I reflected on a disastrous canal trip fifteen years earlier: the two worst wines I ever drank were served to me in France.

We went into the dining room, in which we had been carefully pre-seated by Trish. The master of ceremonies was Christopher Bozell, the oldest of Michael's siblings. He is, like his nine brothers and sisters, like his mother and his father, redheaded. Christopher is a businessman. He took immediate charge, launching gracefully and robustly the postprandial proceedings. He introduced his father.

Big Brent, as we had sometimes to designate him, Little Brent

Bozell having become something of a journalistic omnipresence, with his columns and broadsides at Hollywood and the wayward press, rose from his wheelchair, his lameness temporary but another in a series of afflictions from which he suffered up until his death in May, 1997. Brent was a manic-depressive, and in one serious bout several years earlier was hit by a car, his powers of sustained concentration irreversibly affected. He had most painstakingly written out a "letter" to his son, which he rose to read with solemn affection.

I first met Brent at Yale. He arrived on campus after service in the navy. His father had died a year or so earlier at an early age, having launched in Omaha a business (Bozell & Jacobs) that would become enormously successful. As bad luck would have it, his estate was modest, Mr. Bozell having died so young. At age twenty, Brent was an enthusiast for world federalism and was soon elected president of the Student World Federalist Association, huge at Yale in the early postwar years. We were drawn together politically by our adamant commitment to the anti-Communist cause. And he became my closest friend.

He was a formidable orator. His tuition at Yale was paid by the G.I. Bill of Rights but also with the substantial prize money awarded him as winner of the national American Legion prize as the foremost high school orator in the nation in 1943.

This skill had proved useful when, in our sophomore year, he attended a meeting of the Progressive Citizens of America to listen to a visiting speaker plead the cause of Henry Wallace for President. During the question period, Brent had held his hand high, seeking recognition by the chairman, the head of Students for Wallace, who had invited the speaker. The persistent refusal to recognize Brent's tall figure and his upraised hand had become provocatively obvious by the end of the question period, students with hands up having been recognized on his right, on his left, immediately behind and in front of him. When the chairman announced an end to the evening, Brent rose and said in a solemn, arresting voice that the chairman was exhibiting the manners of the movement he and the speaker were furthering, namely the cause of the Communist Party. The effect was electric on the two or three hundred students in the auditorium.

That period—it was the early spring of 1948—was the high-water mark of the American Communist movement in the United States. By the end of summer, most of the leadership of American liberals had renounced the Wallace movement, designating it, however painfully, for what it was: a Communist-run enterprise. Spokesmen for the Progressive Citizens of America, which with the launching of the presidential campaign had become the Progressive Party, had predicted 5 million votes for candidate Wallace. He ended with just over 1 million.

After Brent made his challenge, he was roundly denounced by the presiding chairman, the head of the Yale Law School branch of the Progressive Citizens of America, and booed by the young Progressives. A public debate was presently negotiated on the question whether the Progressive movement was de facto a Communist enterprise.

A few weeks earlier, Stalin had effected his coup in Czechoslovakia, extending the Iron Curtain around the forlorn country ten years after the Nazis had done the equivalent. President Truman and Secretary of State Dean Acheson denounced the Soviet move but the Wallaceites dug in. Political tensions at political Yale (a distinguished law school professor would run for governor of Connecticut on the Wallace ticket) were high, and an overflowing house turned out to hear a debate at which Brent's forensic eloquence and his mastery of the relevant data overwhelmed his opponent, deeply disturbing those among the young Progressives who had joined the Wallace movement in the beguiled pursuit of peace, and presumably also those who, however few in number, were following the Communist Party line because they were Communists or Communist sympathizers (Brent's challenger, a dozen years later, was revealed to have been a member of the party). The anti-Communists were elated. It was the highest political moment of our four years together at Yale and it was about that time that I discovered that Brent was a Catholic convert.

It has here and there been said and written that I converted him, which isn't the case. Late in the war, Brent's naval ship put in at San Francisco for one night and Brent's father was there to visit with his son. In a hotel room, Leo Bozell confided to Brent that he intended to become a Catholic. Brent surprised his father by telling him that that also was his own intention. His father said that he would postpone joining the Church until he could persuade the entire family—his wife, his other son, and a daughter—to join with him. His sudden death interrupted whatever strategy Mr. Bozell had designed, but Brent moved quietly into the Church. He had been a student at a Catholic preparatory school in Omaha and was much influenced by the Jesuit priest who, three years later, would marry Brent and my sister Trish. We did not talk very much, in college years, about the Church or about its special characteristics. But our common faith strengthened a bond which, many years later, would be tested very nearly to the breaking point, when Brent went further than I would do in pressing the demands of our Church in the secular realm.

During law school days Brent and Trish lived in Hamden, Connecticut, a suburb of New Haven. My wife Pat and I lived close by. I was writing my book on Yale and teaching Spanish to undergraduates. Toward the end of that year the Korean War was raging and I had accepted the job with the CIA. When my wife and I returned from my CIA stint in Mexico, Brent was beginning his third year in law school. We resolved to write jointly a study of Senator Joseph McCarthy, a long article for general circulation. We effected an introduction to him and before the end of the summer, having done extensive research, decided that the material we had accumulated was book-length.

McCarthy and His Enemies was published in February 1954, only a few weeks before the beginning of the Army-McCarthy hearings. Brent and his family had moved to San Francisco but came to New York for a week of book promotion. At the book party/press conference, Joe McCarthy appeared as he had promised to do. He was besieged by what seemed the whole press world, the lethal Senate hearings imminent. He greatly amused Brent and me with the careful words he spoke, the television cameras whirring, when asked directly for his opinion of the Buckley-Bozell book, which, although it defended the senator and his movement, criticized him on a number of points. "It is the first book about McCarthy not written by an enemy or by McCarthy."

Five months later, Edward Bennett Williams undertook the defense of McCarthy against censure by the Senate. Williams studied closely our book and, on learning that Brent had done the primary research on the hearings that would figure prominently in the Senate proceedings (the Tydings hearings), persuaded Brent to take a long leave of absence from his law firm to help in the defense of McCarthy. The defense failed, but McCarthy had taken a strong liking to Brent, greatly admiring his prose style. He talked him into leaving California. Brent would work a substantial part of the week for McCarthy, writing all his speeches. In the time left over, Brent would complete a book of his own, something he had started several years before, an inquiry into the judicial philosophy of the Warren Court.

By then there were four Bozells, all of whom stayed with Joe and Jean McCarthy in their house near the Capitol until they got lodgings of their own. Clarence Manion, sometime dean of the law school at Notre Dame, was a conservative activist. He recommended Brent to Senator Barry Goldwater and a profoundly important liaison was effected. Admiring McCarthy's speeches, Goldwater asked Brent for help with a speech or two of his own and as McCarthy's health declined and his activities lessened, Goldwater leaned more and more heavily on Brent. Manion conceived the idea of a book-length statement by Goldwater and suggested Brent as aide in this enterprise. What grew out of it was a small book, *The Conscience of a Conservative.* It became a historic best-seller, significantly responsible for the nomination of Goldwater as presidential candidate of the Republican Party in 1964.

We were in the sixties and it wasn't only antinomian flower children who were attracted to formulations *à outrance.* Brent took his family to Spain and by the late sixties found himself attracted to a movement in the triumphalist tradition of the Catholic Church. He would found *Triumph* magazine. He was not a merely sedentary critic: at one point he tried to bar entry into an abortion clinic in Washington; and Trish, the mother now of ten Bozells and the sweetest-tempered woman alive when her fiery temper is not aroused, would one day slap feminist Ti-Grace Atkinson on the face in rebuke for her ribald attack on the Mother of Jesus at a lecture at Catholic University.

With the gradual stabilization after the turn of the decade, *Triumph* ceased publication. Brent's disability would loom larger and larger in life, while Trish fought alcoholism, finally defeating it. Brent was now substantially incapacitated, and every few years suffered another seizure, devoting what weeks and months he successfully commandeered—from time to time the mania took over—to doing church work for nearby monasteries. He had profoundly attached himself to Catholic Christianity, written brilliantly on the subject, but had now to live a life largely passive. Trish continued to work as a freelance editor, and serves as chief editor for Regnery-Gateway publishers.

Brent could still compose, but only a sentence or two at a time. He had worked for many days on his "letter" to Michael, which he read out now in a room completely still.

His father spoke of Michael's new "way of life," which would now be "extended into eternity." ". . . this short letter is to be collected by you along with the other souvenirs of this triumphant occasion and studied for the love for you they carry."

It was brief, a few hundred words: "I know a side of Michael Bozell that covers him all over. He is a fool for suffering, of which he has had much, and which he has managed—for his suffering and that of others—to transform into joy. For himself, Michael has never acknowledged that the joy of helping Christ is his way of dealing with suffering. But I know it is."

He spoke very briefly about Michael's future as a priest. And then closed: "You will note, my son, that I have had difficulty in this letter in distinguishing words to you and about you. That is because you are the largest public glory of my life."

That close made it less than easy for speakers who followed. I was not able to conclude whatever it was that I was feeling my way to saying. My brother James succeeded me. He had been (1971–76) the "sainted junior senator from New York," as I persistently and matter-of-factly referred to him from time to time in my column, and now was a judge on the court of appeals. He had similar, if less pronounced difficulties. At the close of the evening I told Jim it was a lucky thing he had never been elected Pope, as I'd have had a hell of a time controlling my sentiments at his installation.

In the year 2010 the monastery at Solesmes will celebrate its one thousandth anniversary. The monastery, along with all other monasteries and nunneries, was closed down during the French Revolution. Following fifteen years of persecution beginning in 1790, there had been a vigorous renewal of religious life. Yet many antireligious measures are still technically in force. French law, for instance, "recognizes" only the secular clergy, pronouncing monks and nuns "useless"—a bizarre animadversion on people who, many of them, give over their lives to teaching, caring for the poor, and ministering to the sick.

In 1833 a young priest felt an afflatus. Dom Prosper Guéranger spotted a notice in the paper announcing that an ancient Benedictine property, only three miles from Sablé where he was raised, would be auctioned as a stone quarry. He went to the Vatican (the Benedictine order reports directly to the Vatican, skirting the bishop), asked for and received permission to reestablish the Order of St. Benedict on the ancient site.

Solesmes is now internationally recognized as the inspired and scholarly center of the repristination of the Gregorian chant (it had been dreadfully mauled by time and inattention), but that was not the immediate concern of Dom Guéranger. He sought primarily to bring to life the "pure traditions" of the Church, notably the centrality of the Holy See; of the Pope. He was an ultra-Montanist, defender of the doctrine that absolute authority rests, in the Church, with the Pope. Dom Guéranger had a personal hand in the formulation of the doctrine of infallibility (1870) and before that of the Immaculate Conception (1854). Three times, after Napoleon, the government of France sought to close the monastery down; but the Benedictines survived, and now nearly a hundred of us were kneeling in the long old stone chapel where the monks convene to chant and pray several times every day, and where we would be present at the ordination of Michael Bozell.

There was an unmistakable feel and aroma of age and piety and indomitability. The nave is very long, I'd guess 150 feet. The windows are of stained glass and in the choir the monks and priests sit facing each other—as in the little chapel at St. John's, Beaumont—on long pews, fenced off from the pews available to parishioners by an ornate baroque iron chancel rail. I had recently acquired a camcorder, intending to record at least the crowning moments of the ceremony, to which end I had sent off a letter to Brother Michael asking for his cooperation.

I had known him, so to speak, forever, a shy boy with large inquisitive eyes framed in red hair, shrewd, a little sleepy, maybe self-indulgent. He was an indifferent student (he went to Providence College), though in languages and in writing he excelled. After college he performed tasks of various kinds, working here and there, sometimes at home helping out his mother and younger sisters and brothers. He had an unmistakable flair for language. Much of his boyhood he had spent in Spain, speaking in English only to his parents, at home. At Solesmes, during the years before his ordination, he flourished in his academic work. At the monastery the languages are French and Latin. I cannot judge his Latin, but occasionally, as now when I wrote to ask if I'd be permitted to tape any part of the ceremony, I would experience his French. He wrote, ''J'ai fait tout ce que je pouvais à propos de ton projet pour filmer; c'était dur, même très dur, mais voilà le peu que j'ai pu obtenir. . . ." (He had done all that he could apropos my desire to record. *It would be hard, even very hard, but here was the little he was able to accomplish.*)

The rules, he wrote, are firm against photography, still or cinematic. Perhaps I might bury myself in the organ loft, up high at the narthex of the church. That would be one approach, effective if my camera was equipped with a telescopic lens. But, Michael continued, perched in the organ loft I'd find myself "about twenty kilometers, if my guess is correct," from the action at the altar. Never mind. Michael would arrange to conscript the cooperation of Iain Simcock, the renowned young organist from Westminster Cathedral, who had volunteered to play at his friend Michael's ordination. Maybe from there I might shoot "quelques instants *avant la messe* pour prendre quelques seconds de prise de la haut—de l'église elle-même." (From there maybe *before the Mass begins* I could from up high get a few seconds of useful shots of the church itself.) And, closing, "That's as much as I was able to do, to repeat myself, and you must really do everything you can to keep the monks—and, for that matter, the congregation—from seeing what you are up to. You'll have to satisfy yourself with a minute or two of the ceremony."

It was understandable to be thus deferential. I have never experienced such preliminary awe as one felt—as I felt—on entering the church, fifteen minutes before the ceremony was to begin. I suppose it must be that way fifteen minutes before a coronation, whether of a King or a Pope. But in those ceremonies there inheres in the principal—one must suppose—the climactic sense of glory achieved while the spectator experiences, empathically, the thrill of exaltation. Here and there are Kings who have abdicated their thrones, but not many—on the whole they seem to find it a fulfilling life. But it is a life incandescently the opposite of the life of a man stepping forward to bind himself forever to the anonymity of life in a reclusive order. Granted, Michael was already a monk and had already taken vows in perpetuity. To become now a priest was an elevation of sorts; yet the ceremony, as we would soon see, reinforced every contrast between the life he would lead and the life of the high and the mighty, for whom the crowds roar and the bands play, courtiers and servants surrounding them to gratify the least velleity, historians on their toes to record their wispiest thought. Michael was rather on the scale of Thoreau, who prided himself that every day he set out to make do with less than he had the day before. All that Fr. Michael would have was God.

The service lasted almost two hours. Before it began, Michael's friend Fr. Gregory opened with his key the door that led up the tower staircase to the organ loft. Fr. Gregory followed me up, sat down at the organ, and began to play some intricate Bach church music. Iain Simcock would arrive any minute now.

I turned to look down at the altar. It seemed impossibly remote. The little Sharp camcorder fitted easily in one hand, yet when I zoomed out as far as the lens would transport me, I had a startlingly clear view of the altar, much clearer than when using the naked eye. I wouldn't know until later whether there was light enough to impress the image on tape. Surely not, inasmuch as the inside of the long church was lit only by candles and here and there by the little shafts of daylight that darted their way through the stained-glass windows. In fact the tape proved marvelous and I filmed on, following the text in the manual that had been given out at the church door.

The ceremony began with an Introit *(Salve sancta parens),* Hail, O Holy Mother. It was followed by "Terce" (we did not know until much later that the little booklets telling of the ceremony had been translated from the French by Michael)—the office of Terce. The Romans computed the hour of the day by their distance from sunrise; thus "tertia" was the third hour of daylight. It is one of the seven offices of the day during which the monks gather at the church to sing the praises of God. Here (i.e., in that day's ceremony) it was reduced to an absolute minimum, with three Psalms preceded and followed by an antiphon sung in honor of Our Lady.

The Psalm sung was 122, which closes, "Pray for the peace of

Jerusalem: May those who love you be secure. . . . For the sake of the house of the Lord our God, I will seek your prosperity."

And then the Kyrie Eleison (Lord, Have Mercy), the Gloria, the Collect, the Epistle (Letter to the Hebrews 5:1–10), and the Gospel.

The Gospel passage (Luke 22:14–20, 24–30) was the account of the Last Supper, exquisitely appropriate for someone ending his life, to begin another:

> When the hour came, Jesus and his apostles reclined at the table. And he said to them, "I have eagerly desired to eat this Passover with you before I suffer. For I tell you, I will not eat it again until it finds fulfillment in the kingdom of God."
>
> After taking the cup, he gave thanks and said, "Take this and divide it among you. For I tell you I will not drink again of the fruit of the vine until the kingdom of God comes."
>
> And he took bread, gave thanks and broke it, and gave it to them, saying, "This is my body given for you; do this in remembrance of me."
>
> In the same way, after the supper he took the cup, saying, "This cup is the new covenant in my blood, which is poured out for you. . . ."
>
> Also a dispute arose among them as to which of them was considered to be greatest. Jesus said to them, ". . . the greatest among you should be like the youngest, and the one who rules like the one who serves. For who is greater, the one who is at the table or the one who serves? Is it not the one who is at the table? But I am among you as one who serves. You are those who have stood by me in my trials. And I confer on you a kingdom, just as my Father conferred one on me, so that you may eat and drink at my table in my kingdom and sit on thrones, judging the twelve tribes of Israel."*

The passage, I thought, gave Michael everything he would wish to hear stressed at this moment. That he would in moments be one with God and, moments later, embark on a lifetime's service of God as a priest.

The sequence, exactly as it appeared in English in the leaflet I have spoken of:

---

* The Holy Bible: New International Version © 1973, 1974, 1984 by International Bible Society.

The candidate is called by the deacon, "Let Brother Michael Bozell, who is to be ordained a priest, come forward."

The candidate answers, "Present." *He advances towards the bishop before whom he makes a sign of reverence.*

When the candidate is in his place before the bishop, the abbot says, "Most Reverend Father, Holy Mother Church asks you to ordain this man, our brother, for service as a priest."

The bishop says, "Do you judge him to be worthy?"

The abbot answers, "After inquiry among the people of God and upon recommendation of those concerned with their training, I testify that he has been found worthy."

The bishop proceeds, "We rely on the help of the Lord God and our Savior Jesus Christ, and we choose this man, our brother, for priesthood in the presbyteral order."

All present say, "Thanks be to God."

A brief homily was then given, after which the bishop turned again to the candidate:

"My son, before you proceed to the order of the presbyterate, declare before the people your intentions to undertake this priestly office. Are you resolved, with the help of the Holy Spirit, to discharge without fail the office of priesthood in the presbyteral order as a conscientious fellow worker with the bishops in caring for the Lord's flock?"

The candidate answers, "I am."

The bishop continues, "Are you resolved to exercise the ministry of the word worthily and wisely, preaching the Gospel and explaining the Catholic faith?"

The candidate, "I am."

The candidate kneels before the bishop and places his joined hands between those of the bishop. The bishop asks, "Do you promise respect and obedience to me and to your legitimate superior?"

The candidate, "I do."

The bishop says, "May God who has begun this good work in you bring it to fulfillment."

A litany follows, after which the monks join in chanting, "Deliver us, O Lord!'' *(Libera nos Domine).* The cantors sing, ''Be favorable. From all evil. From every sin. From eternal damnation. By your incarnation. By your death and resurrection. By the gift of the Holy Spirit.'' The monks repeat the phrase, ''We beg you, listen to us!'' *(Te rogamus, audi nos),* and the cantors sing, ''We who are sinners. Govern and keep our holy Church. Keep the pope, the bishops, priests, and deacons holy in your service. Bless and sanctify and consecrate those whom you have called. Give peace and true concord to all peoples. Pour forth your mercy on those steeped in tribulation. Comfort and keep those who are consecrated to your holy service. Jesus, Son of the living God. Christ, hear us. Christ, listen to our prayers.''

At the end the bishop alone stands and sings, ''Hear us, Lord our God, and pour out from these servants of yours both the blessing of the Holy Spirit and the grace and power of the priesthood. In your sight we offer this man for ordination; support him with your unfailing love. We ask this through Christ our Lord.''

And the deacon sings, ''Let us stand.''

Theologians specify, the text explains, that each sacrament, at its core, consists of a certain gesture, and certain words which constitute the sacrament; these are the ''matter'' and the ''form'' by which a simple human act becomes the conveyer of a supernatural reality. For the sacrament of Holy Orders, the crucial gesture is the laying on of hands by the bishop, and the words—those which are given below in small capital letters. As of that moment, the candidate has become a priest.

The bishop lays his hands on the candidate kneeling before him. Every priest in the congregation subsequently repeats the same act of laying on of hands.

The prayer of consecration concludes with the sacramental words: ''ALMIGHTY FATHER, GRANT TO THIS SERVANT OF YOURS THE DIGNITY OF THE PRIESTHOOD. RENEW WITHIN HIM THE SPIRIT OF HOLINESS.''

Michael was now a priest.

After the Eucharist, the ceremony is concluded. The priest and the monks file down the aisle and turn into the sacristy. Iain Simcock played Bach's demanding Passacaglia and Fugue in C Minor.

After the ceremony we dithered anxiously in the courtyard waiting for *Father* Michael to emerge. Everyone, it seemed, kissed and embraced the beaming parents. I poked anxiously the control buttons on my camcorder, and lo! the ceremony began to unfurl before my very eyes on the four-inch-by-four-inch screen, a perfect reproduction. Everyone crowded around to look. Suddenly the reverend bishop materialized, side by side with the abbot. Impulsively I thrust up the camcorder to his face so that he, too, could see our secular miracle! I could almost feel Trish wincing, Fr. Michael decomposing; but the bishop and the abbot both stared at themselves on tape and were visibly astonished and delighted. No doubt it was later that they focused on the formal infraction. Yes, and later—not that much later—everyone in the Bozell party had an edited videotape of a great event in our lives.

The male members of Michael's party had been invited to lunch in the refectory, from which women are excluded. During lunch, one monk read from the Bible (I falsely supposed—he read in rapid French [in *recto tonal,* I would be advised]) and nobody laughed. At the last half of the meal there was conversation. I remember making small talk in schoolboy French to a priest of great urbanity, and to a monk (I thought him a monk, but could not tell: there is no difference in the habits they wear). The meal was over in a half hour, after which we went to an old marble factory, recently donated to the monastery for conferences and large gatherings, where a reception had been prepared for Fr. Michael and his guests. Wine was served and cakes and biscuits and cheese and the conversation was animated. I saw Big Brent standing, but he could do so only for a few minutes, soon retreating to a chair. He looked pale but his eyes and the tremor in his voice relayed his feelings.

At night we went, still high from the event of that morning, to

tables set for five at the hotel dining room. My brother Jim, sisters
Priscilla and Carol, and Kevin Lynch sat together.

We had been wondering where Kevin was. He worked for many
years as articles editor at *National Review* before going to the foreign
service in Washington. He was soon detached to work for Radio Free
Europe, some time after brother Jim had served as its president. Kevin
kept close ties with the family and early the day before had set out
with his wife, Jo, to drive all the way from Munich to Sablé. But he
did not show up. We learned today that there are *two* Sablés in France,
one Sablé two hundred miles north of Paris, our Sablé about the same
distance west. He had marked out the first on his road map, unaware
of the other. When he arrived at Sablé-North he asked unsuccessfully
for directions to the monastery and finally came upon an elderly
Frenchman willing to give him instructions on how to get to the *other*
Sablé, about four hundred miles away. "A little mortification of the
flesh, Kevin," I said, raising my glass, and he laughed happily. He
always does. Kevin is a happy man, who makes others happy.

After dinner I went to my hotel room and wrote out a letter to
Michael. I would give it to him tomorrow, after his first Mass, which
we would all attend, after which I'd have to race to the airport. I
pressed the envelope into his hand, and one week later I had his
replies.

I had asked the most obvious question. Why?

He replied:

So why do monks remove themselves from the world at all? To use an
analogy, the Nobel Prize nuclear physicist who so greatly advances the
scientific knowledge of mankind, and who in so doing benefits his
fellow men, must nevertheless remove himself from the company of
those same men in order to bring his work to fruition. Men submit to
the monastic discipline—one important element of which is this rude
separation from the world—in order to liberate their hearts from

attachments and possessions which shrink their capacity for universal solicitude and compassion. To transcend the boundaries of their loves and loyalties they must physically remove themselves from the objects of those very loves and loyalties.

Next I wanted to know, "Who composes the Council that decides that a monk is qualified to be ordained as a priest?"

The abbot chooses whom he will have ordained as priest. He discusses the matter, as with all important decisions, with his counselors (three monks chosen by him, four elected by the community).

I asked further: "Are there many (some?) monks who are deemed qualified, but who elect to continue as monks, as distinguished from priests? If so, what reasons do they usually give for that decision?"

Yes, it happens that sometimes a monk will choose not to be ordained (humility, or simply a feeling that his specific monastic vocation is not meant to be wedded to the priestly state and function). Even before Vatican II, it was fashionable in certain monasteries to belittle the priesthood. The reason often given was that a true monk is never a priest (true, to an extent), and that ordaining a large number of monks in a monastery deforms the monastic charisma and ends up devaluing the monastic vocation. This is simplistic reasoning, and is fired in part by egalitarian impulses and disguised scorn for the priesthood. If indeed past experience has shown that the differences between simple monks and monk-priests can translate into a virtual caste system, then there would be the concomitant tensions, injustices and envies. It is nevertheless true that the priesthood, when limited to its essential expression—the sacrifice of the Eucharist, the ministry of reconciliation—blends well among monks and those who come to the monastery seeking the graces of pardon. Priests harmonize most wonderfully with the monastic vocation, giving it depths and dimensions that aren't there without the priests.

I asked, "Is it accepted that once settled in a particular monastery, a Benedictine priest will remain there? Or is it your obligation to be entirely docile in respect of where you are sent? Can you turn down pastoral duty, or is it in the nature of your order that such duties are never assigned to you?"

The classic monastic vows are: poverty, chastity, obedience. St. Benedict's vows: the transformation of one's life (chastity and poverty are implied here), obedience, and stability. Benedict had nothing but scorn for monks who might have "TGV'd" [traveled by a Train à Grande Vitesse, the super-rapid French train] their way from monastery to lovely monastery. We make [our] profession for a particular community, promising to abide in it for good. Still, the abbot can send a monk here, a monk there, for different reasons (a chaplain for a community of nuns; a monk or priest to a smaller monastery in need of reinforcements; to a new Benedictine foundation).

This leads to another important point. There is a basic divide in Benedictine monasticism. There are those establishments that are wholly contemplative, having no other activity than their lives of liturgical prayer, study and work, and there are others (the English Benedictine Congregation for instance) that have important schools attached to them, at which many of the monks teach, and who service parishes round about the monastery. Solesmes resembles Cistercians and even Carthusians (much more strict, semi-hermetical orders) more than, say, Ampleforth in England. I personally would not have dreamed of entering anything but a contemplative establishment, where the "quest for God" (St. Benedict's Rule) is conceived in terms of overwhelming silence and solitude. The irony here is that given specific personal talents [Michael is trilingual] and aptitudes [op. cit.] I have now been appointed to the guest house where I am in the daily business of receiving and speaking with people from literally all over the world who descend on our little hill above the river seeking solace, moorings, peace, guidance, beauty and spiritual refreshment.

Was there a point, I wanted to know, a particular day, moment, "when it struck you that you had found what you were looking for?"

The day I arrived at the monastery with the intention never to leave again, I discovered welling up within me a happiness I had searched for throughout my years as an adolescent and a young man. That unalloyed joy is always there, a spring refusing to dry, even when those long periods of acedia descend, or during the rare moments when things are frankly going very badly.

I wanted to hear from him something about the manifest tedious-ness of some of the monk's duties. "Do you in fact every three hours go to the chapel to worship? Is this duty something the human body comes quickly to accommodate, even as shipboard crew accommodate to watch duty? Or is it a perpetual reminder of the need to mortify the flesh?"

Our stints in choir occur, if my computing is right, at a rate of less than once every three (waking) hours. The hardship here is not so much corporal as psychological and spiritual. It is amazing how one becomes accustomed to sitting in wooden choir stalls for so many hours a day (or, for that matter, eating at table on benches without backs, when we are allowed to sit—breakfast is taken standing up). What is difficult about choir and its frequency is that with time you become very close to insensibility to the beauty and the mystery, and all you are likely to notice is your neighbor chanting ever so slightly off-key. It is to die. And then more deeply, a monk will be hit by periods during which the entire project seems so self-evidently wasted time. These are moments when his faith (in God, in his way of life, in himself) must wage war on creeping despair.

And, finally, "Is the sacrifice of contending ways of life once-and-for-all transcended, or are you warned, and do you expect it, that temptations of a secular nature will always be there: seductive, to be resisted at the cost of great spiritual agony? Is the saint singularly spared such agonies, or is it that he/she experiences them but over-comes them by a vivid mobilization of spiritual energy?"

Agonia means "combat" in Greek. The man whose monastic experi-ence has ceased to be a daily combat is greatly to be pitied. And why a combat? Why a fight? Because we experience ourselves to be torn between two often opposite longings: the natural (and to a certain extent healthy) pining of our appetites, and the spiritual imperative to transcend everything from legitimate impulses of natural self-fulfill-ment to the vile designs and egotistic desires which ceaselessly worm themselves into our hearts, however disguised they may be. Men who are drawn to be monks are radicals by temperament; there are other ways to "put on Christ." The monk feels a huge tug to go it the whole way, to climb to the very summit, and to dedicate his life to that and that alone. It is not for all Christians, and most of those who do take their call to sanctity seriously (we are all called to be saints) do so in less drastic modes. The monastic mode carries with it certain inbuilt demands and goals which make it easier to ascend to the summit, and more dangerous. One of the dangers is that in denying yourself even legitimate pleasures, pastimes, fulfillments, etc., you open yourself up to strange forms of revenge. Another is that in the most unobtrusive and surreptitious ways, a man can capitulate to the thousand little desires he thought he'd banished from his heart so as to leave room for the Lord God and without even knowing what has happened to him, find himself altogether off his proposed track.

I like to think of the metaphor of a road winding its way up a mountain, encircling it as it rises. The man on that road is conscious mostly of a never-ending series of obstacles and difficulties, which change but little in nature. Yet from time to time he can gaze out on the expanse below him and judge, with the thrill that comes only from sustaining long austerity in view of a reward, the distance he has traveled. The monk's life is a continuous striving, a daily battle, and the prize, the summit of the mountain, is Christ. Christ experienced from the inside, Christ fully known and possessed and imitated and loved. It is the highest realization of self, because it is perfect love.

At dinner I had remarked something a little different in the timbre of talk and laughter. More like what one might expect after a wake than after, say, a wedding; in part, I suppose, because we are no longer quite certain that wedding vows are final, irreparable. Yes, there are priests who are laicized, priests also who apostasize. But that is rare, and when it happens—whomever it happened to, or whenever—he is always spoken of, when the slightest suggestion of a biographical fix is called for, as "the ex-priest." People do not think of a divorced person as an ex-husband. And then, too, wakes are absolutely conclusive: that night everyone in our company knew Michael, whether as parent, sibling, nephew, friend; and knowing him, we knew that the vow he had taken would be everlasting. For that reason and because of the profound implications of life in a monastery, the solemnity of the occasion was with us, and that night in my snuggery in the hotel I thought of Michael in his cell, rising at midnight to sing his orisons, and I reflected that almost certainly he was the happiest of us all, and that only God can dispense such a needle as that.

CHAPTER EIGHTEEN

Aloïse Steiner Buckley:

An Epilogue

We have seen the triumphs of Huxley at Oxford, the seat of his enemies. Let us take leave of this somewhat ungrateful theme by calling up another scene at the same university. In 1864, there was a Diocesan Conference at Oxford. There chanced at this time to be in the neighborhood a man who was neither priest nor scientist, a man given to absurd freaks of intellectual charlatanry, yet showing at times also such marvelous and sudden penetration into the heart of things as comes only to genius. It was Disraeli. "He lounged into the assembly," so the scene is described by Froude, in a black velvet shooting-coat and a wide-awake hat, as if he had been accidentally passing through the town. He began in his usual affected manner, slowly and rather pompously, as if he had nothing to say beyond perfunctory platitudes. And then, turning to the presiding officer, the same Bishop Wilberforce whom four years earlier Huxley had so crushingly rebuked, he uttered one of his enigmatic and unforgettable epigrams: "What is the question now placed before society with a glibness the most astounding? The question is this: Is man an ape or an angel? I, my Lord, am on the side of the angels." The audience, not kindly disposed to the speaker, applauded the words as a jest; they were carried the next day over the whole land by the newspapers; they have often been repeated as an example of Disraeli's brilliant but empty wit. I suspect that beneath their surface glitter, and hidden within their metaphor, pointed to suit an Oriental taste, these words contain a truth that shall some day break to pieces the new philosophy which Huxley spent his life so devotedly to establish.*

Somewhere in my reading I came upon a warning: No Christian, however bent on conversion, should uninvited approach a nonbeliever. Perhaps an exception is if one happened to stray, as Disraeli did at Oxford, into providential theaters. I remember hearing about the telephone that rang in the apartment of Heywood Broun (1888–1939), the renowned journalist, member of the Algonquin Round Table, Socialist congressional candidate, founder of the American Newspaper Guild, witty, combative, impious in language and manners. He picked up the receiver and heard the caller say, "This is Fulton Sheen."

Monsignor Sheen in those days presided over *The Catholic Hour* on radio. He was perhaps the best-known prelate in the United States. Broun had never met him, and asked now, "What are you calling about?"

Answer: "Your immortal soul."

The exchange had a fairy-tale ending. Broun spent time with Monsignor Sheen and, some time later, was received into the Church.

Anyone willing to take the initiative in evangelization had better be armed with the mysterious properties of a Fulton Sheen. I have re-

* Paul Elmer More's concluding paragraph in his essay on Thomas Henry Huxley.

counted that I sat for one hour and viewed Charles Colson address prisoners in a penitentiary with quite mesmerizing effect. But that was different—one hundred men seated to hear a speaker who was there to talk about the faith. And then, too, how much—of whatever effect he had—traced to the straitened circumstances of his audience? The prisoner is ex officio looking for consolation, for hope, and suddenly he is offered a glimpse of a transcendent view of life. But was Broun restive? One supposes so, never mind the uproarious lifestyle. We all are constantly made aware that, in the cosmopolitan set, many are laughing only on the outside.

I have never sought to console in explicitly Christian terms anyone who wasn't, so to speak, already a communicant. This is so, I'd readily admit, in part a matter of temperament. It is widely assumed, I have gathered from public references, that I am a dogged evangelist of my political and economic views. It's true, but only when I write and speak publicly. Those who spend time with me know that I don't . . . *ever* . . . bring up my political faith unless specifically questioned about it, and this happens, among intimates, only when accidental turns of conversation lurch us onto a path that requires ideological exploration.

And so I wonder how the Apostles felt when they received *their* mandate. It is pretty startling stuff, to be told to leave your family and your trade as a fisherman, or a shepherd, to take on the entire world with your message. It is unimaginable to me that such a thing could happen except under such extraordinary auspices as moved Peter and his fellow Apostles. It was a very cruel age and they knew with the blinding force of their own eyes what had been the fate of their leader. He told them first that He loved them, and then that they must love Him, and love their neighbors as themselves. He gave them to see a few miracles and the gift of tongues. They surely knew that they had now let down their fishing nets and ploughs in order to spread the word, and that they would be tortured and killed for doing so. But it is reported of many martyrs that they died palpably happy men, happy women, transported by their faith and purpose.

In our day it is not as it then was, though there are always martyrs.

Many thousands, in this century, have been tortured or killed explicitly because they were Christians who wore formal dress, priests and nuns seeking to do the work of the Lord. David Niven, asked about any good samaritans in his own experience, gave an example of a quite unorthodox martyr, unthreatened by anything more than his own sense of ultimate sacrifice. This fraternal love prompted him to keep the company of soldiers, consigned to drown in the hold of a sinking ship. He could not do this without dying with them. He was blamelessly free to stay on deck with the survivors. Instead he descended through the one-way funnel into what would be a charnel house. We cannot know, but are free to speculate, whether that act itself, in the half hour or hour, until the Channel water pouring into their trapped quarters overwhelmed them, brought critical consolation. We can assume that at least to some of the young men it brought a transforming comfort, seeing with their own eyes a man surrendering his own life in order to bring a few minutes' consolation to the doomed, in the name of Christ. It surely crossed the minds of some of them, who knew something about the Christian faith, that perhaps that same very terrible day, they would meet their Maker and know paradise.

Yet there is something about the modern disposition (the social protocol absolutely rules over me) that compels even those who believe in Him to keep all such matters tidily secluded in their own tent. I am one of many millions who attend church on Sundays, receive the sacraments, say every day a prayer, particularly when a friend is ailing or gone; and yet I shrink from any religious communication that could possibly be thought intrusive. I cannot imagine circumstances that would bring me to pick up the telephone and call to anyone's attention the Christian vision. Professor John Murray Cuddihy remarks the phenomenon. In an essay on the subject he observed that ''public intensity is embarrassing unless it is turned into art. People have to sublate, to sublimate it. We live in a world we choose to call modernity and modernity means differentiation; it is signaled by coolness and control. [Religious talk] is unseemly and bids fair to destroy the fragile solidarity of the surface we call civility.'' Cuddihy then quoted a sentence of mine, in a television exchange with Malcolm Muggeridge, the question having been asked, Why don't we bring up the subject of God? "Because of the sense of the social situation," Cuddihy quotes me as saying, and writes that that is the exact, complete answer—even though he is uneasy about it. "How can we discuss ethical questions if we cannot bring up God?"

It is of course obvious that it is mostly features of *this* world from which we take our satisfactions. The love of our family, the company of our friends, the feel of the wind on the face, the excitement of the printed page, the delights of color and form and sound; food, wine, sex. But there is that other life that only human beings experience, and in that life, and from that life, other pulsations are felt. They press upon us, in the Christian vision, one thing again and again, which is that God loves us. The best way to put it is that God would give His life for us and, in Christ, did.

Thought given to that other world reminds us of our blessing and reproves us for our dumb failure to share it with others. There is very little one can hope to do, this side of praying for God's intercession, except to hang on, as with our fingernails, to the lifelines, but they can be electric in what they tell us. The President's hand on the Bible, swearing allegiance before God. The grace said before a meal; the bowed head during invocation. It is odd to think of God as someone whose foot you hope to see in the door, a presence in the room. But the protocols of secular life do not permit much more and, increasingly, they discourage even that.

I don't remember the exact language Albert Jay Nock used, and would rather not look it up—one part sloth, one part a fear that I don't remember it exactly. What I remember is that he always thought it appropriate (he had been an ordained minister and—so far as one knows—died an apostate) to address God man-to-man. I really do understand what I think Nock was saying and do not think it blasphemous. God is all those mighty things St. Augustine proclaimed, maker of Heaven and earth, etc., etc., etc. But He is also a companion. I have always acted on the assumption that God has no problem at all in idiomatic exchanges with His creatures.

Giovanni Guareschi made great sport of the whole idea a generation ago, in his books on Don Camillo, the young, bombastic priest in postwar Italy, waging daily war against Peppone, the Communist mayor of their little village. Christ hangs on the Cross in the little church of Don Camillo and acts somewhat like Hazel, the busybody maid in the cartoon who is always butting in with her advice.

One day Don Camillo, perched high on a ladder, was busily polishing St. Joseph's halo. Unexpectedly a man and two women, one of them Peppone's wife, came into the church. Don Camillo turned around to ask what they wanted.

"There is something here to be baptized," replied the man, and one of the women held up a bundle containing a baby.

"Whose is it?" inquired Don Camillo, coming down from his ladder.

"Mine," replied Peppone's wife.

"And your husband's?" persisted Don Camillo.

"Well, naturally! Who else would be the father? You, maybe?" retorted Peppone's wife indignantly.

"No need to be offended," observed Don Camillo on his way to the sacristy. "I've been told often enough that your party approves of free love."

As he passed before the high altar, Don Camillo knelt down and gave a discreet wink in the direction of Christ. "Did you hear that one?" he murmured with a happy grin. "One in the eye for the Godless ones!"

"Don't talk rubbish, Don Camillo," replied Christ irritably. "If they had no God why would they come here to get their child baptized? If Peppone's wife had boxed your ears it would have served you right. Don Camillo, watch your step," Christ said sternly.

Duly vested, Don Camillo approached the baptismal font. "What do you wish to name this child?" he asked Peppone's wife.

"Lenin Libero Antonio," she replied.

"Then go and get him baptized in Russia!" said Don Camillo, replacing the cover on the font.

The priest's hands were as big as shovels and so the three left the church without protest. But as Don Camillo tried to slip into the sacristy he was stopped by the voice of Christ. "Don Camillo, you have done a very wicked thing. Go at once and bring those people back and baptize their child."

"But, Lord," protested Don Camillo, "you really must bear in mind that baptism is a very sacred matter. Baptism is . . ."

"Don Camillo," Christ interrupted him, "are you trying to teach Me the nature of baptism? Didn't I invent it?"*

My mother, to whose memory I dedicate this book, dealt in exactly that way with God. Her worship of Him was as intense as that of the saint transfixed. And His companionship was as that of an old and very dear friend. Perhaps somewhere else one woman has walked through so many years charming so many people by her warmth and diffidence and humor and faith. If so, I wish I might have known her.

The great house where my mother brought us up in Connecticut still stands, condominiums now. But the call of the South, where she and my father were born, was strong, and in the mid-thirties they restored an antebellum house in South Carolina. There she was wonderfully content, making others happy by her vivacity, her delicate beauty, her habit of seeing the best in everyone, the humorous spark in her eye. She never lost a Southern innocence.

Her cosmopolitanism was unmistakably Made-in-America. She spoke fluent French and Spanish with unswerving inaccuracy. My father, who loved her more even than he loved to tease her, and whose knowledge of Spanish was flawless, once remarked that in forty years she had never once placed a masculine article in front of a masculine noun, or a feminine article in front of a feminine noun; except on one occasion when she accidentally stumbled on the correct sequence— whereupon she stopped (unheard-of in her case, so unstoppably did she aggress against the language) and corrected herself by changing the article: the result being that she now spoke, in Spanish, of the latest

---

* Quoted by permission. *The Little World of Don Camillo* by Giovanni Guareschi. Published by Amereon.

encyclical of Pius XII, the Potato of Rome ("Pius XII, la Papa de Roma"). She would smile, and laugh compassionately, as though the joke had been at someone else's expense, and perhaps play a little with her pearls, just above the piece of lace she always wore in the V of the soft dresses that covered her diminutive frame.

Her anxiety to do the will of God was more than ritual. I wrote her once early in 1963. Much of our youth had been spent in South Carolina, and the cultural coordinates of our household were Southern. But the times required that we look Southern conventions like Jim Crow hard in the face, and so I asked her how she could reconcile Christian fraternity with the separation of the races, a convention as natural in the South for a hundred years after the Civil War as women's suffrage became natural after their emancipation, and she wrote, "My darling Bill: This is not an answer to your letter, for I cannot answer it too quickly. It came this morning, and, of course, I went as soon as possible to the Blessed Sacrament in our quiet beautiful little church here. And, dear Bill, I prayed *so* hard for humility and for wisdom and for guidance from the Holy Spirit. I know He will help me to answer your questions as He thinks they should be answered. I must pray longer before I do this."

There were rules she lived by, chief among them those she understood God to have specified. And although Father was the unchallenged source of authority at home, she was unchallengeably in charge of arrangements in a house crowded with ten children and as many tutors, servants, and assistants. In the very late thirties her children ranged in age from one to twenty-one, and an inbuilt sense of appropriate parietal arrangements governed the hour at which each of us should be back from wherever we were—away at the movies, at a dance, hearing Frank Sinatra sing in Pawling. The convention was inflexible. On returning, each of us would push, on one of the house's intercoms, the button that said, "ASB." The exchange, whether at ten when she was still awake, or at two when she had been two hours asleep, was always the same. "It's me, Mother." "Good night, darling." If—as hardly ever happened—it became truly late, and her mind had not recorded the repatriation of all ten of us, she would wake, rise, and walk to the room of the missing child. If there, she would return to sleep, and remonstrate the next day on the neglected intercom call. If not there, she would wait up, and demand an explanation. I doubt she'd have noticed, half-asleep, if the person on the other end of the line had been God Himself, her most reliable friend, and lover.

A few years earlier she had raised her glass on my father's seventy-fifth birthday to say, "Darling, here's to fifteen more years together, and then we'll both go." But my father died not fifteen but three years later. Her grief was profound, and she emerged from it through the solvent of prayer, her belief in submission to a divine order, and her irrepressible delight in her family and friends. A few years later her daughter Maureen died at age thirty-one and she struggled to fight her desolation though not with complete success. Her oldest daughter, Aloïse, died three years later.

And then, three months before her own death, her son John. She was by then in a retirement home, totally absentminded; she knew us all, but was vague about when last she had seen us, or where, and was given to making references every now and then to my father ("Will") and the trip they planned next week to Paris, or Mexico. But she sensed what had happened, and instructed her nurse (she was endearingly under the impression that she owned the establishment in which she had quarters) to drive her to the cemetery and there, unknown to us until later that afternoon, she witnessed from inside her car, at the edge of an assembly of cars, her oldest son lowered into the earth. He had been visiting her every day, often taking her to a local restaurant for lunch, and her grief was, by her standards, convulsive; but she did not break her rule—she never broke it—which was never, ever to complain; because, she explained, she could never repay God the favors He had done her, no matter what tribulations she might be made to suffer.

Ten years before she died, my wife and I arrived in Sharon from New York much later than we had expected, and Mother had given up waiting for us, so we went directly to the guest room. There was a little slip of blue paper on the bed lamp, another on the door to the bathroom, a third on the mirror. They were love notes, on her three-by-five notepaper. Little valentines of welcome, as though we were back from circling the globe. There was no sensation to match the timbre of her pleasure on hearing from you when you called her on the telephone, or the vibration of her embrace when she laid eyes on you. Some things truly are unique.

Five days before she died, one week having gone by without her having said anything—though she clutched the hands of her children and grandchildren as they came to visit, came to say good-bye—the nurse brought her from the bathroom to the armchair and—inflexible rule—she put on her lipstick, and the touch of rouge, and the pearls. Suddenly, and for the first time since the terminal descent had begun a fortnight earlier, she reached out for her mirror. With effort she raised it in front of her face, and then said, a teasing smile on her face as she turned to the nurse, "Isn't it amazing that anyone so old can be so beautiful?"

The answer was, Yes, it was amazing that anyone could be so beautiful.

God's creature. Well done, Lord. My Lord. Our Lord.

APPENDIX A

—————

Further Commentary on the Millbrook

Christmas Celebration

I was sent, along with the candlelight program, a copy of the "Report by the Spiritual Life Committee to the Board of Education Committee of the Millbrook School Board of Trustees."

The Spiritual Life Committee disclosed its "mission statement," which "involves honoring and nurturing the development of the inner life, in whatever individual and communal ways that inner life is expressed."

One is required to observe that either that statement means nothing at all or else it is indefensible. Some inner lives, like some *Weltanschauungen*, simply oughtn't to be encouraged whatever the inner glow they generate. H. G. Wells wrote about his own inner life that it left him with "no compelling arguments to convince the reader that he should not be mean or cowardly." The Spiritual Committee's report goes on:

"Adolescent years are characterized by a spirit of inquiry about moral conduct, personal values, and awareness of a greater power. Since this is a crucial time in which young people form lasting belief systems, we feel that the community as a whole has a responsibility to provide a practical, educational, and reflective way for all to explore and express their growing spiritual and moral development in both a substantial and respectful manner." That is cant; it tells no one anything, furnishing only a semantical emollient for those who like to feel nice thoughts about growing moral developments. It is to be contrasted with, for example, a hypothetical: "Since young people form lasting belief systems, the time is opportune to teach the Ten Commandments and the ethical and historical reasons for abiding by them."

We move on. ". . . in so doing, we strengthen our understanding of ourselves and the spirit of our community." Why? Who says? It would be instructive to investigate the very question. A disabling problem in doing so is that we are without normative standards to measure progress, or the lack of it.

The Committee's "goals"?

"1. To educate the community as to our religious and spiritual diversity by a) providing programs to honor major religious holidays; b) considering course work in comparative religions in the curriculum and providing at least one major event of a spiritual nature through our endowed lecture series." How about Easter?

"2. To create a group that would a) discuss issues of spirituality, b) engage in inter-religious dialogue, and c) provide a vehicle for reflection as an essential component of a healthy community life." Why not describe that vehicle? And while at it, explain why the Bible, which in the Christian world has more or less officially served that purpose since Constantine (d. A.D. 337), is no longer adequate to serve such purposes?

Among the specific programs recommended by the committee:

"1. We surveyed the community concerning its views on the role and form of communal worship at Millbrook." The boys and girls were divided on such questions as whether there should be compulsory chapel services. As also, we must suppose, on others of the Ten Commandments.

"2. We organized and conducted required Thanksgiving and Candlelight Services." The Spiritual Life Committee treats the word "Christmas" as Victorians treated the word "syphilis," though more Victorians contracted syphilis, one supposes, than, at this rate, Millbrook students contract Christianity.

"3. In conjunction with the dean of students and a Student Committee, we developed a program celebrating Martin Luther King Day.

"4. We formally educated the community about Chinese New Year, Ramadan, and Bodhi Day.*

"5. We conduct voluntary Sunday Evening Prayer Service for people of all faiths, offering inter-religious reading, music, and opportunity for reflection." What *is* inter-religious reading, etc.? Or did the committee intend the word *multi*religious? As in ten minutes Buddhism, ten Islam, ten Jewish, that sort of thing? But if so, given that the exercise is designated as a "prayer" service, why would devout Christians or Jews wish to attend such a service, inasmuch as to do so as a participant would be to violate the commandment in both faiths which forbids the worship of false gods?

"6. We facilitate rides to places of worship."

The recommendations of the Spiritual Life Committee would not have needed altering by a single syllable if the Bible had never been written. The school could with perfect accuracy advertise itself as the Millbrook School for Pagan Boys and Girls.

---

* A celebration of the enlightenment of the Buddha.

APPENDIX B

A Listing of Religious Activities

at Various Schools

Here are quick profiles of prominent U.S. private schools' treatment of Christianity and, glancingly, other religious studies and celebrations.

GROTON SCHOOL

Groton, founded in 1884, is still a forthrightly Protestant school, Episcopalian in character. Students must attend chapel five times every week and always on Sunday. The prayers said during the week are not specific to any religious tradition, but there is a Eucharist service on

Sunday that, in the words of one official, is "very Episcopalian." Jewish and Catholic students are required to attend their own services. An official recounts with some pride the answer given to the father of an incoming Catholic student who asked whether his young son would be encouraged by Groton to attend Mass. The reply: "No, he won't be encouraged to. He'll be required to." In the curriculum, two terms of Bible studies and one term of ethics are taught, attendance required. The completion of Bible studies is a diploma requirement. From the academic guidebook: "Taking as a basic text the English Bible, both the Jewish Scripture and the Christian writings, the student is introduced to the history and stories which have influenced world civilization for thousands of years and which appear as basic material for much of the literature and art of the West."

BROOKS SCHOOL

Brooks is in North Andover, Massachusetts. It was founded in 1926 and affiliated with the Episcopal Church. Its chapel is still Episcopal. Students are required to attend four days every week. Sunday service of Holy Communion is, of course, voluntary. Prayers from other religious traditions are introduced into the weekly prayer service. Jewish prayers are said during the High Holy Days of the Jewish year, Islamic prayers during the Islamic holy month of Ramadan. Catholic Mass is held in the school chapel once every month, and there are special services during Holy Week. On Good Friday, the service is presided over by clergy of the Roman Catholic, Baptist, and Episcopal faiths. Hymns are regularly sung: religious clubs include a Chapel Fellowship, the Jewish Students' Organization, and the Koinonia Society, a group with a Baptist flavor, devoted to Bible study. An embryonic (four members) Islamic Society has been started. Religious/academic courses include The Bible, Introduction to Theology, Ethics and Moral Reasoning.

Deerfield Academy

Years ago the "Brick Church," a Unitarian church on the edge of campus, was Deerfield Academy's (the school was founded in 1797) own chapel. Daily chapel attendance was required, as also attendance at Sunday chapel. These requirements were eliminated in 1972. The Brick Church still has Sunday services, but fewer than 10 (of the 580 Deerfield students) attend. The church has been ceded to the town of Deerfield.

Attendance was also required at "The Sing." Every Sunday, the students would gather in the lobby of the main building to sing Christian hymns from the Unitarian/Universalist Pilgrim Hymnal and to listen to a speaker, usually a clergyman. By the 1970s, reports G. Richard McElvy, a resident Episcopal priest on the faculty, "it had become a sham," and so the tradition was terminated.

The Reverend McElvy does however write prayers that are recited at the annual convocation, held at the beginning of the academic year, and at the baccalaureate and commencement ceremonies. The texts are "fairly generic, but definitely addressed to a Judeo-Christian God." Students who protest these ceremonies on the grounds that they are religiously chauvinist are excused from attendance. In recent years an effort was made to eliminate Christian hymns from the central annual ceremonies. It was agreed to discontinue "Lead On, O King Eternal" as too forthrightly Judeo-Christian and much too masculine in imagery. In its place, "Morning Has Broken" was selected.

At meals, curiously, a grace is said, usually conducted by the Episcopal minister, who attempts formulations as unprovocative as possible, giving thanks for the food about to be shared, and for the friendship. Care is taken to avoid careless talk about a divine Provider. There was something of a problem in recent years. The director of the dining hall was an absentminded Catholic who sometimes followed the "thoughts" given as grace with a Christian prayer. Sometimes he even made announcements about the relevant dietary abstinences required of Catholic students (they are reduced to fast and abstinence on Ash

Wednesday and Good Friday). But he is retired now, the embarrassment ended. There are three religion courses: Judeo-Christian Tradition, Religions of the World, and Philosophy and Religion electives.

ROSEMARY CHOATE

"Choate" is, formally, Choate Rosemary Hall (founded in 1890). It was founded one hundred years ago as an Episcopalian school for New England sons of affluent Protestant families, though John F. Kennedy got in and, since then, many other Catholics and Jews. Its first headmaster, George St. John, was an Anglican priest who reigned for forty years. The school was privately owned by the St. John family but, in the sixties, was institutionalized. The role of religion declined. In the seventies, compulsory attendance at chapel was discontinued.

Choate still has a matriculation ceremony held in the chapel. At the one-hour service, the headmaster reads a statement on the traditions of the school and conscripts new students into Choate's Honor Principle. On the second Thursday of each month, students and faculty attend chapel, where they are addressed by the headmaster or by a chaplain on "some aspect of religion, spirituality, ethics, human behavior, or general good times."* Any prayer spoken at these Thursday gatherings is interdenominational and intercredal, taken from different religious traditions. Fr. Joseph Devlin, a Catholic priest who is director of Campus Ministry, began the last academic year by reading a poem of Emily Dickinson, "Some Keep the Sabbath Going to Church."†

---

* The quotations, if not otherwise attributed, are paraphrases done by Mr. Marcello (see p. 37).
† The text:

> Some keep the Sabbath going to Church—
> I keep it, staying at Home—
>
> With a Bobolink for a Chorister—
> And an Orchard, for a Dome—
>
> Some keep the Sabbath in Surplice
> I just wear my Wings—
>
> And instead of tolling the Bell, for Church,
> Our little Sexton—Sings.
> God preaches, a noted Clergyman—

Before liberation, there were mandatory Sunday Eucharists in the Episcopal tradition, at which conventional Protestant hymns were sung. Today hymns are not sung in chapel. A few years ago an effort was made to reintroduce them. "It was an absolute bomb," an official of the school reported. The Campus Ministry at Choate has resolved to attempt to reintroduce hymn singing at some point in the future.

Choate's chapel was never formally consecrated—just why, no one appears to know. The result is that the Campus Ministry has no problem in explaining to nervous students, fearful of involuntary spiritual service, that the chapel is "just like any other building on campus." There are no outward indications that the chapel is a church, other than that its superstructure is a steeple. The interior is devoid of religious art or symbol. In the bad old days, a cross hung in the chapel, but during the sixties the headmaster, evidently sympathizing with complaints, formal or inchoate, agreed that the cross was provocative and instructed the school's maintenance man to remove it. As it happened, the deputized embalmer turned out to be a devout Mexican Catholic. He informed the headmaster that he could not, would not, "remove God from his House." Someone else was got to perform the exorcism, and the cross now lies in storage in the chapel's basement.

For the Catholic students, Fr. Devlin instituted a candlelit Mass ("Candle-lit Liturgy," in the Choate guidebook). At first, only three students attended. Now, a few years later, 175 students turn up.

Choate offers its students five courses in religion, one of them New Testament Studies, one in Hinduism, another in Buddhism, still another in Taoism.

PHILLIPS EXETER

Phillips Exeter, of Exeter, New Hampshire, founded in 1781, has a full-time chaplain ("Bobby") who helps students of all religious faiths when they approach him for counsel. The academy has its own church

---

And the sermon is never long,
So instead of getting to Heaven, at last—
I'm going, all alone.

and its pastor is the school's minister. Attendance at chapel was required, as at so many other schools, with attendance taken each Sunday. In 1968 the practice was ended. Abolition of compulsory attendance was done at the initiative of the school's chaplain, who reasoned that by limiting attendance to those who come voluntarily, worship would be more meaningful.

There is a weekly Catholic Mass, and there are Hindu puja, Muslim prayer, Buddhist meditation, Jewish Shabbat services, and a Quaker meeting. And there are two nondenominational, voluntary prayer services at Phillips Church each week. One of these is the Tuesday Evening Prayer, a half-hour candlelit service in which the students hear readings from various religious texts, usually non-Christian, and hear performances by student musicians. The other, the Thursday morning Meditation, is framed by music and includes reading of a statement prepared by students and faculty members on any subject that, for the speaker, has had a special meaning through his life.

Exeter provides a wide variety of courses in religion and requires two term credits in religion. The courses are extraordinarily abundant. They include The Hebrew Bible/Old Testament: The Beginning of the Story; The Hebrew Bible/Old Testament: Monarchy and Prophecy; Religious Traditions in America: Jewish, Catholic, and Protestant; New Testament: Gospels; New Testament: The Mission and Expansion of Christianity; The Experience of Religion; Judaism; Islam; Social Ethics: Values in a Changing World; Religion as Literature; Religions of the East: Hinduism and Buddhism; Personhood and Belief; Existentialism; Greek Views of Life; The Holocaust: The Human Capacity for Good and Evil; and Zen Buddhism.

HOTCHKISS

Hotchkiss School, in Lakeville, Connecticut, founded in 1891, has a chaplain who was born and raised Jewish, converted to Christianity, worships as an Episcopalian, and is married to a Catholic. Hotchkiss was never church-related but has always had a chapel. In days gone by, chapel attendance was required. There survives one weekly mandatory chapel service at which, however, prayers are not given, and the Gospels seldom read, on the grounds that to do either might offend non-Christian students. Basically the chapel service has become a place where several different kinds of things happen: religious, spiritual, and ethical issues that arise in Hotchkiss life are openly brought forth for common reflection and students are invited to ponder questions put to them by people from various traditions, Buddhist, Muslim, Christian, even nonreligious. Hymns are rarely sung, and when they are, care is taken not to include any specifically Christian hymns. A Catholic church is within walking distance of the school and a voluntary Christian community worship service is held each Sunday. It is attended by approximately 30 of the school's 500 boarders.

There is no religious requirement at Hotchkiss, but students must take one semester of either philosophy or religion. The mandatory course, The Bible and Ethics, taught by the headmaster during the fifties and sixties, is gone. But there are current religious academic offerings which include The Hebrew Bible: Yesterday and Today, and The New Testament and Its Legacy: One Jesus, Many Christs. There are no school-wide celebrations of religious holidays, but there is a (voluntary) program of Advent Lessons and Carols, in Protestant tradition. In 1995 some Jewish students objected to campus decorations during the Christmas season on the grounds that they gave the impression that the entire community was engaged in celebrating Christmas. The objections are under consideration.

KENT SCHOOL

Kent (founded in 1906), in Kent, Connecticut, has a female Episcopal priest ("Anna") who serves as chaplain. The school was founded by an Anglican monk and is still affiliated with the Episcopal Church. Chapel attendance is mandatory. Students must attend prayer meetings on Tuesdays, Evening Prayer on Thursdays, and Sunday Eucharist services, unless excused to go to a neighboring church of their own faith. By current standards the requirements are strict, even if much less so than the eight-times-per-week attendance in years gone by. On Good Friday there is mandatory chapel service, at which the reading of the Passion of Christ is done. Grace is said before the seated meals, twice every week. Hymns sung during chapel services are from the 1982 Episcopal hymnal. Kent requires a minor term-contained course and a major term-contained course in theology for graduation and offers a half dozen courses on religious subjects.

MILTON ACADEMY

Milton had no religious affiliation at its founding (1798), but chapel attendance was always mandatory and remains substantially so, including Sunday service. But one thing is excluded during these prayer services, namely any reference to Jesus Christ, whether in prayer or in a hymn. The word "amen" is not permitted. The prayers are composed by an Episcopal priest who serves as Milton's chaplain. He reports that notwithstanding the ban on Jesus, the prayers are truly God-oriented, that the exclusion took place during the past six years during which an effort was made to make the chapel service more inclusive and multicultural.

An integral component of the chapel service is the "chapel talk." These talks may not touch on religion or on any aspect of the Bible, but nevertheless, in the judgment of one official, they "feel very churchy." Some recent chapel talks have touched on general spirituality, rape, homosexuality, the need to follow one's heart, and the need to remember one's community. There are readings, but from works of secular literature. In recent days these have included Thoreau's *Walden,* the poetry of Maya Angelou, and literature from Amnesty International. The religion department at Milton consists of two courses, one (noncredit) titled Ethics, the second, History of Religion.

ST. GEORGE'S

St. George's (founded in 1896), with its spectacular chapel, is in Newport, Rhode Island, its chaplain an Episcopalian priest. As at so many other schools, there was for many years required chapel attendance. During the sixties, this was reduced to two mandatory and two voluntary chapel services per week. Students who attend services of their own faith on Sundays are excused from Sunday services at St. George's. In anticipation of Christmas there is "a medieval candlelit service which features Bible readings, hymns, and a procession of the Three Kings." In order to graduate from St. George's, students must take two semesters in the Bible and theology department. A very wide range of courses is offered including The Human Condition: Religious Themes in Modern Western Literature, and Twentieth Century Religious Thinkers.

St. Paul's

St. Paul's (founded in 1856), in Concord, New Hampshire, has a stunning chapel, its choir portion bigger than that in many churches. The school is still affiliated with the Episcopal Church and all students are required to attend a daily chapel service, which has hymns and prayers (and sometimes litanies and liturgies) four days every week and on the first Sunday of the academic term. The Eucharist service is voluntary and about 100 of the 500 students attend it. In order to graduate, a student must take four years of a humanities requirement, and in these classes the Bible is either studied or observed and theology taught in a historical and literary context. Contemporary theologians are introduced, including Paul Tillich and C. S. Lewis, and work is done in the traditions of Islam, Judaism, and Buddhism. The entire school observes certain religious holidays, such as Good Friday, when all students are present in chapel for the reading of the Passion of Christ.

Taft

The Taft School, in Watertown, Connecticut (founded in 1890), no longer has a chaplain. It was never affiliated with any religious denomination and continues almost deliberately to lack religious identity. Students were formerly required to attend church services at local churches on Sundays (there is no chapel at Taft), but this was discontinued in the 1940s, well before this was done in other secondary schools. Prayers and hymns were still being done through the 1960s, but no longer. Now, on such occasions, the setting and tone are, in the words of one official, "completely nonreligious." There is, however, a voluntary Advent service of Lessons and Carols in the Anglican tradition, generally presided over by an Episcopal priest. Two courses that touch on religion are listed: Race, Class, and Gender in American Society, and Introduction to Jewish Oral Tradition.

LAWRENCEVILLE

Lawrenceville, in Lawrenceville, New Jersey, was founded in 1810 without formal affiliation to any Christian denomination, but roughly allied to the Presbyterian Church. An official spoke of the religious attitude at Lawrenceville as "schizophrenic" because the school affirms that religion and spirituality are important but does nothing officially to encourage religion. In the seventies, compulsory attendance at chapel ended, even as a chaplain was hired and a huge pipe organ was installed in the emptying chapel. Boarding students in all forms are required to attend two on-campus religious services per term. There are weekly services available: Protestant, Catholic, Muslim, and Jewish. Prayer is said at central school events, but these are nonreligion-specific and the name of Jesus is forbidden. The hymns sung at these functions are likewise nonreligion-specific and do not mention a Christian God. The school spokesman said that there is a Lawrenceville school hymn, but that inasmuch as it is "Christocentric in nature," it is no longer sung.

There are voluntary Jewish services on Friday evenings, nondenominational Protestant services on Sundays, a weekly Quaker meeting, and a Catholic Mass. These services are not held in the chapel, which is reserved for convocations, concerts, a Good Friday ecumenical service, and a voluntary Christmas service, at which Bible readings and Christian hymns are sung. The chapel was built "as more of a meditation center than a chapel per se, and was never consecrated as a chapel or as a special place set aside for the worship of God." The hymnal in the chapel is edited to conform with gender sensibilities. "All Creatures of Our God and King" continues to appear as such, but the refrain that used to read, "O Praise Him . . . Alleluia," now reads, "O Praise Ye . . . Alleluia."

For many years, Lawrenceville required two courses in religion, one from the Judeo-Christian tradition, the other from any other course offering. Policy now requires one of the courses to be a world religions survey course, the other to be from any of the department's other offerings.

The curriculum, like that of Exeter, offers numerous courses. Introduction to the Bible; Myth and Ritual; Great Jewish Books; Buddhism; The Family; Ethics; Christianity; Prophets; Judaism; Roman Catholic Vision; Literature and the Bible; Introduction to Philosophy; Comparative Religion; Islam; Godspell and the Gospel According to Matthew; The Mystical Experience; Creation to Liberation in the Hebrew Bible; Chinese Philosophy; New Testament Account of Jesus; and Bach and Luther.

INDEX